ON
REPENTANCE
AND
REPAIR

ON REPENTANCE AND REPAIR

MAKING AMENDS IN AN UNAPOLOGETIC WORLD

DANYA RUTTENBERG

BEACON PRESS, BOSTON

BEACON PRESS
Boston, Massachusetts
www.beacon.org

Beacon Press books
are published under the auspices of
the Unitarian Universalist Association of Congregations.

24 23 22   8 7 6 5 4 3 2 1

This book is printed on acid-free paper that meets the uncoated paper
ANSI/NISO specifications for permanence as revised in 1992.

Text design and composition by Kim Arney

Library of Congress Cataloging-in-Publication Data is available for this title.
Library of Congress Control Number: 2022012997
Hardcover ISBN: 978-08070-1051-8
Ebook ISBN: 978-08070-1059-4

For everyone engaged in the hard,
painstaking work described in these pages.

For Nir, as ever.

CONTENTS

AUTHOR'S NOTE

This book discusses many kinds of harm, caused by many different types of perpetrators, both individual and collective. I'm not sure what kind of single trigger warning or content warning I could put on a book that would address sexual abuse and assault, intimate partner violence, slavery, racism, white supremacy, police brutality, ableism, homophobia, transphobia, gun violence, colonialism, mass incarceration, genocide, and the other painful topics that are discussed at various points. So suffice it to say that there are difficult stories in here. Please take care of yourself as you read, as you take breaks, as you skip the stories you need to skip, as you engage with the book in the ways that make sense to you.

This book also tells many stories and cites the insights of many people. There are times when particular aspects of a person's lived experiences are especially relevant to a conversation at hand, and it is disingenuous to pretend otherwise. So, for example, when race is at stake in the conversation, I try to center race by naming whether a scholar or journalist is Black, white, and so forth, to situate their comments in the context of their own lives. I am inconsistent about this, both because not every story discussed here requires that kind of additional context and because not everyone's identity is known to me. And, of course, people have other aspects of their identity that are not necessarily mentioned that may inform their perspective as well. I cannot say that I have done this perfectly, but the attempt is there—to offer transparency and to highlight the ways in which our lived experiences can be, in themselves, a source of authority. These choices are, of course, filtered through my own identities and experiences—as, among other things, someone who is white, Jewish, feminist, queer, has experienced a mobility disability, and a myriad of other things— and others may have made wildly different choices as a result of theirs.

Translations of Jewish texts are a mix of the translations offered on Sefaria.org (notably Rabbi Adin Steinsaltz for Talmud, and both Rabbi Simon Glazer and the Sefaria Community Translation for the *Mishneh Torah*) and my own original or adapted translation. Whenever possible, I tried to translate cases involving a generic person with the pronouns "they" and "them." That classical Jewish texts use the third-person masculine singular ("he" and "him") to describe a person doing a thing may be understandable, given the vicissitudes of both the Hebrew language and the patriarchy. But in places where the text clearly intends to describe "one who . . . ," I use the singular "they" to create a more open reading from a gendered perspective.

INTRODUCTION; OR, WHAT'S MISSING WHEN WE SEEK TO REPAIR HARM

Kelly's sister Susan was often angry as a kid, and her parents did little to contain or check her behavior as she was growing up. During their childhood and early adulthood, Susan often abused Kelly verbally and emotionally, and once, when they were in high school, she physically assaulted Kelly. As a result, Kelly distanced herself from Susan, and they have been semi-estranged for years. Since Susan's divorce, however, Kelly's parents have increasingly pressured Kelly to forgive her sister, to be more understanding about Susan's current challenges as a single mother of small children, and to show up as a support during this difficult time. Should Kelly forgive her sister? Should she reenter her life? Does it matter whether or not Susan has apologized for her past actions? What are Susan's obligations, here? What about their parents' obligations? What, if anything, is owed to Kelly, and from whom?

Isabella I of Castile and Ferdinand II of Aragon, rulers of Spain, expelled all the Jews from the country in 1492, a devastating blow to a robust community that had been on the Iberian Peninsula for over seventeen hundred years. In 2015, the Spanish Parliament sought to offer redress, inviting descendants of those who had been expelled to apply for Spanish citizenship. But despite the law's declaration that Spain welcomed these people to "reencounter their origins, opening forever the doors of their homeland of old," the process for doing so seemed astonishingly demanding. In fact, as the provisions of the law were being discussed, several members of parliament noted how onerous these requirements appeared to be. The window for sumitting applications was open for only four years, and those seeking citizenship had to supply proof of lineage, pass a four-hour Spanish-language test, and complete a citizenship test covering various topics in Spanish culture and society. To even be considered, applicants had to travel to Spain to finalize their file with a Spanish notary. And in the end, Spain approved only about 20 percent of the applicants and retroactively implemented additional requirements, claiming that they were concerned some applications might be fraudulent.[1] Should this law be considered appropriate amends to the descendants of the Jewish community? If more allowances had been made—a greater window of time or less red tape—would the gesture be adequate? What else, if anything, might Spain be obligated to do with regard to the descendants of the Jews banished for the "crime" of being Jewish? Does twenty-first-century Spain even owe these descendants anything at all?

The woman who created and popularized the "gender reveal" party— writing up a gathering she held during her first pregnancy in what would become a viral blog post—shared, eleven years later, that she regretted having done so. Part of her regret was because of the immediate, material harm that was sometimes caused as a result of increasingly outrageous "reveals"—wildfires, accidental deaths. But mostly she felt bad about placing even more cultural emphasis on the sex assigned a baby at birth. She now understands, as she has shared on Facebook and elsewhere, that this emphasis can damage trans and nonbinary kids, as well as limit the gender expression of cisgender kids. What, if anything, should she do now? What could or should her repentance work look like? Are her obligations tempered if, at the time, she was ignorant of the potential harm of her blog post? If she had no idea that her party idea would create such a significant cultural impact?

The challenges surrounding apologies and forgiveness, repentance and reconciliation, amends and atonement invite a lot of questions, and they're neither simple nor theoretical. They impact the very structure of our criminal justice system. They are ever-present in our rapidly shifting conversation on sexual abuse. These questions haunt the legacies of every country touched by colonialism and white supremacy, and they hang painfully over our intimate bonds, our family and professional relationships, and our communities.

And in the United States, most of the time, we've gotten them very, very wrong.

To put it bluntly, American society isn't very good at doing the work of repentance or repair.

And though we've seen a recent increase in public attempts to hold harmdoers to task, there's still a lot of confusion in the cultural conversation about what that might entail. What are we asking of the person who has done wrong? What work must they take on in order to repair, to whatever extent possible, the harm that was done? How should we regard them if they have caused harm and tried to fix it? If they have not done any amends work? What does justice look like, what does healing look like, and what are the roles of the victim and the perpetrator in this process? And what, if any, is the role of those who were neither harmed nor perpetrated harm in all of this? There's still a lot of uncertainty in our social discourse on these matters—even more so when we're not talking about individuals perpetrating harm, but rather institutions, other organizations, or even nations.

However, there does not need to be. There is a model for meaningfully addressing harm—from the daily intimate sorts of harm that manifest in personal relationships to larger wrongs perpetrated at the level of a community or a culture, right up to genocide.

Of course, not every atrocity can be magically fixed, as though it never happened. But in the Jewish tradition—rooted, specifically, in the work of the twelfth-century philosopher Maimonides—there is a robust and sophisticated system that can help us grapple with everything from embarrassing missteps to horrific evils and do the work in our power to repair and transform. And, I believe, it can be useful for all of us—regardless of background, culture, religion or lack thereof—here, now, today.

We all cause harm sometimes. Maybe it's intentional, a result of a calculated attempt to gain power, or from a place of anger or spite. Maybe it's out of carelessness, or ignorance, a reaction to fear, or because we were overwhelmed and dropped some balls. Maybe it's because we were acting out of our own broken places or trauma, or because, in our attempt to protect some interests, we ran roughshod over others. Maybe it's because our smaller role in a larger system puts us in the position of perpetrating hurt or injustice. Maybe it's for one of a myriad of other reasons, or a combination of them.

We have all been harmed. We all nurse stories about the tender places where we have been bumped, cut, battered by others—by people, institutions, or systems. Sometimes, maybe, we have managed to heal completely; sometimes a scar is left behind. Other places still ache now and again. Some injuries may hinder us from being able to do things that we once could, or even cause immeasurable, even irreparable damage—to ourselves, our families, our communities, or our heritage.

We also are all bystanders to harm. We read about it in the news, debate it on social media, decide when to speak up about it at work or to a family member, and witness social structures that do not deliver on ideals of equity, respect, and justice.

And we occupy all of these roles on the small scale—in personal relationships, for example—and on larger ones, as members of society, as stakeholders in institutions, as citizens or inhabitants of nations. So it's critical for all of us to think through the work of repentance, accountability, and transformation, for a lot of different reasons.

In Judaism, the concepts of repentance, forgiveness, and atonement are very separate categories, and the tradition places the highest emphasis on the work of repentance. Maimonides, in his landmark work *Mishneh Torah*, codified and developed earlier traditional thinking, itemizing very specific steps to this process—including public confession of harm, a particular approach to making amends, and deep transformational work that culminates in changed actions. A sincere, victim-centric apology—potentially with others present to help ensure that everything goes as it should—is certainly part of it, but that's neither the beginning or the end of the process. And regardless, the focus is not on whether forgiveness is granted but on whether the person who has done harm engages deeply in the steps of repentance and repair. (Forgiveness is, in fact, a whole other conversation—we'll get there.) And when this lens is applied to some of the most significant and painful issues of our day, it just might illuminate the path forward in new ways.

Before we talk about what that path forward might look like, it might be helpful to pause and untangle some of why we are where we are now.

There are a number of reasons why our society is so lacking in the tools to engage deeply in the work of repentance and repairing harm. Maybe none of them will surprise you. Needless to say, each of these topics merits its own broader study, but we have to get on with the book at hand in a moment, so I hope you'll indulge me in making this the briefest of overviews.

One factor in our cultural resistance to the work of repentance has to do with the post-Enlightenment move toward individualism and how this took shape in the United States. The French diplomat Alexis de Tocqueville warned, in his 1835 tome *Democracy in America*, that our country's extreme form of individualism would cause people to feel that they "owe no man anything and hardly expect anything from anybody. They form the habit of thinking of themselves in isolation and imagine their whole destiny is in their own hands."[2] And indeed, our society, as the influential international law scholar Louis Henkin has noted, focuses on *rights* afforded to the individual, rather than on our *obligations* to one another, and on limitations to what the government can do to the individual, rather than what the government is required to offer its constituents.[3]

This, then, impacts how we interact with one another, particularly when there is a violation of trust or safety. When a harm is perpetrated, the "rugged individualism" of American culture (as Herbert Hoover famously put it)[4] has the potential to leave people alone, nursing their wounds in solitude, without support. We lack a sense of collective responsibility, a communal ethos or process that might help hold victims' pain and urge perpetrators to hold themselves accountable. "Just let it go," can become an adaptive strategy in a culture that doesn't have other meaningful mechanisms to offer after a rupture of relationship or care. In the public sphere, bad or incomplete apologies from public figures are so notorious that there is even a blog, SorryWatch, dedicated to chronicling the missteps, narcissisms, and the many variations on "I'm sorry that you feel hurt by this perfectly reasonable thing that I did."

In fact, a recent study of empathy across cultures found that cultures with a greater tendency toward collectivism score higher in terms of empathy than those with more of an individualistic bent. The United States scored well behind countries in the Middle East, South and Central America, Scandinavia, and East Asia.[5] There is, of course, a strong correlation between empathy—the ability to understand and share the feelings of another—and the impulse to address harm caused to another. If it matters to you that someone has been hurt, you're more likely to try to do what's needed to make things right.

So, OK, individualism. That's one thread in our national attitude toward repentance work. Another has to do with its hyper-capitalist ethos. Certainly, our culture's thirst for instant gratification feeds the desire to resolve challenges quickly, to privilege immediate catharsis over the hard, painstaking work of process and transformation.

Perhaps even more to the point is the perspective of many who laud unfettered free enterprise, fancying themselves the heirs of the eighteenth-century "father of capitalism," Adam Smith, who observed that we are all ultimately motivated by our own self-interest rather than altruism. This self-interest, in practice, has often looked like the pursuit of ends without concern for harm or exploitation caused in the process. Examples of this self-interest abound. To cite just one example, America's billionaires added a trillion dollars to their net worth in 2020, during the darkest months of the COVID-19 pandemic, as people worldwide plunged into layoffs, poverty, and food insecurity. Jeff Bezos, the CEO of Amazon, himself made $70 billion during this time, boosting his overall net worth to $186 billion.[6] This happened not only in the shadow of longtime documented[7] abuses[8] of Amazon's workers, but also amid issues about safety of workers during the COVID pandemic and the company's union-busting efforts.[9] But this is not just about Amazon; the majority of corporations and most industries would track neatly onto the patterns shown here. The point to note here is that "self-interest" is for those with power, and it disincentivizes the work of repentance.

How might it be in the self-interest of those profiting from the current system to do a moral accounting—let alone amends, repair, and transformation work—with regard to the exploitation of workers, the for-profit prison industrial complex, privatized medicine? Periodically we do see change, but it often comes in response to immense public pressure and is often the result of decades of tireless organizing. Such efforts may persuade owners of a sports team that it is now financially prudent to change its racist mascot or brand managers that it could be useful to make a commercial featuring a family with same-sex parents. That's not the same thing as fostering an ethos of repentance, repair, or care for those who have been harmed. Rather the opposite—it's simply an extension of, once again, that self-interest.

Another salient thread long woven into our national fabric of thinking about repentance is a watered-down, secularized distortion of Protestant thinking that has infused American culture. Some of this approach to faith dates back to the sixteenth-century reformer Martin Luther's notion of *sola fide*, the conviction that God's mercy and forgiveness are available to all those who believe, and that belief alone is sufficient for divine salvation, without "works"—that is to say, external actions or deeds. This idea was a response to the Catholic Church's selling of indulgences, or monetary payments that ostensibly absolved people of past sins in this life and after death released them from purgatory. Indulgences were forgiveness with a price tag. Luther's stance moved the real action of a person's spiritual life into the internal realm. And though Luther asserted that Jesus "willed the entire life of believers to be one of repentance,"[10] and that good actions were part of a necessary Christian life, in the following centuries, the notion that "you just need to feel sorry for your sins" (as the Lutheran pastor and religious studies scholar Cory Driver put it) began to emerge. This, coupled with Jesus' teachings about turning the other cheek to those who harm you and forgiving "seventy times seven," made interpersonal forgiveness an emergent focus of Protestant life. None of this is the issue.

This focus on forgiveness has, however, had results that its originators likely did not intend. It was originally almost certainly not meant to elide questions of accountability, disincentivize perpetrators from taking responsibility, or put the onus of forgiveness on victims without meaningful redress. This goes against the Gospels themselves, where the verses about forgiving "seventy times seven" are situated in the larger context of a discussion on accountability, and where Jesus modeled community accountability in relationships with Peter and others. And yet, a dismissive attitude toward repentance nevertheless became so widespread in Protestantism that the Lutheran theologian Dietrich Bonhoeffer famously lambasted preaching forgiveness without simultaneously demanding repentance as "cheap grace."[11]

Additionally, the Methodist minister and author Rev. Bromleigh McCleneghan has suggested that this emphasis on salvation by faith alone, and the resulting emphasis on one's inner state over one's outward actions, may have had a cultural consequence of privileging intent over impact when considering our actions and their outcomes.[12] That is, if a person's truest internal self is the reference point, it becomes easy to focus on "what I meant," and to assume that meaning well is enough to be let off the hook, even if one's actions unwittingly harm others. This may be why it's so common, when someone suggests that a public figure has said or done something racist, to hear a chorus of defenders quickly and loudly deny that this person is a racist. Whether they have *done* something racist and whether they *are* racist—"not a racist bone in their body!" we hear—are conflated. Inner state and outer action become the same thing—if a person meant well, there could not possibly have been any harm. But we all know that sometimes people mean well but cause harm nonetheless—out of ignorance, out of carelessness, out of deeply ingrained ways of thinking they haven't examined, out of an emotional reaction that got the better of their lofty intentions, or . . . well, the list goes on. This, of course, is not to say that some people are not in fact racist, or sexist, or transphobic, and so forth; just that a cultural bias that tends to privilege intent over impact may have deep, complex roots.

Even if there is no real theological basis for these cultural attitudes, they line up perfectly with any basic power analysis. That is to say, if harm is perpetrated by a person—or an industry, or a state—that possesses more power than the individual or communities harmed, denying ill intent can serve the interests of the more powerful party, allowing it to evade accountability and maintain the status quo. Admitting culpability opens the possibility that change might be needed; claiming "those bones aren't racist at all" is a way of saying that no change is necessary. This resistance to facing harm head on is a form of gaslighting—a manipulative way of denying reality—which piles more harm on top of the original offense. As soon as we get to debating the inner state or intention of a perpetrator, the focus of the conversation moves away from any actual injury or injustice and the question of how to set things right. When this happens, the needs of victims are rarely met in meaningful ways.

Another thread in the American privileging of forgiveness over repentance has to do with how theology was used in the service of power in the wake of the Civil War. Shortly after the conflict ended, northern white clergy began preaching forgiveness, reconciliation, and unity with white southerners, at the expense of justice, or even safety, for Black Americans, whether newly emancipated or already free. One of the main proponents of this viewpoint was the white Congregationalist minister Henry Ward Beecher, long known for his support of abolition alongside other progressive issues like Darwin's theory of evolution and women's suffrage. And yet, by 1865, he was preaching things like, "There are no antagonistic interests between the North and the South. Religion, blood, business are same, and if there are no social or political reasons for hatred, why should we not be the best of friends?"[13]

But more than that, Beecher encouraged white northerners to ignore reports of abuse committed by white southerners against Black Americans—writing, for example, in the *New York Independent*, "You must not be disappointed or startled because you see in the newspapers accounts of shocking barbarities committed upon"[14] newly liberated people.

One reason for this approach, as the white historian Dr. Hanne Blank puts it, is that

> forgiveness—and finding common ground—between white south-erners and northerners was part of the larger political project of thinking about the U.S. as a union that was "unbreakable." The stress that state-level autonomy placed on the federal identity of the U.S. as a whole was seen as something that had to be "managed," and one of the ways to manage it was to [approach it as] "Okay, we've had our fight and now we need to kiss and make up so we can be Americans again."[15]

But that reunification was predicated not only on white northern-ers ignoring white southerners' violence against Black people, but on the assumption that the "we" who had been fighting were white, that the "we" who would kiss and make up were white, and that "we" would not ask anything of those so attached to the institution of slavery that they were willing to wage the bloodiest war in American history over it. "We" were all fine now, went the logic. And perhaps "we," united in this way, could thus also exclude Black Americans from the equa-tion, making it easier to deny them the full rights of citizenship and belonging.

And it certainly wasn't just Beecher making this move. According to the white historian Edward J. Blum,

> throughout postwar Reconstruction, a coterie of white Protestant leaders joined together to authorize and sanctify the northern em-brace of southern whites . . . A growing majority of Protestants increasingly favored denominational and national reconciliation. Through a variety of media, including sermons, novels, short sto-ries, denominational meetings, and political cartoons, these apostles of forgiveness lobbied for national reunion at all costs . . . With more regularity, Protestant Yankees wished to forget and forgive southern whites for the war . . . Christian ideologies of forgiveness, sacrifice,

and atonement functioned as supposedly disinterested arguments for resolidifying American nationalism.[16]

Beecher's writings in the *Independent* included missives such as this:

> And if I say that I will forgive a man when he repents, and not before, I do not know what to do with the example of Christ . . . And when I see men that are doing things that are wrong and wicked, wickedness and wrong are hateful to me; but there is the feeling of benignity, compassion, tender sorrow for them. And I am sure that it is Christ's spirit . . . there is no form of wickedness so gross that in our individual capacity we are not bound to love the perpetrator of.[17]

Here, even those who commit horrific wrongs can be forgiven with no effort on their part. Accountability and waiting for, or demanding, the work of repentance fall by the wayside. This was a convenient way to reinscribe white supremacy at a moment when it was in grave jeopardy, and it wasn't only the white southerners who benefited. True Reconstruction—and repentance, and justice, and equality—would have put white northerners' superior social status at risk in ways that they were, one presumes, unwilling to entertain. Calling for forgiveness and unity, without looking too hard at the atrocities in the South and those who committed them, enabled the white leaders of the North to move forward after the war without disrupting the status quo and the role they enjoyed within it.[18]

Needless to say, those who wished to see deep systemic change after the Civil War weren't having it with this uncritical approach to forgiveness. Many who advocated for human and civil rights for all Americans—including Frederick Douglass, Frances E. W. Harper, and other thinkers, both Black and white—argued that Christianity demanded repentance from former Confederates as a condition of forgiveness.[19]

For example, Douglass—the Black abolitionist, preacher, and statesman—wrote in 1870 that the South "has been selling agony, trading in blood and in the souls of men. If her past has any lesson, it is one of repentance and thorough reformation."[20] The next year, he gave a Memorial Day speech at Arlington Cemetery in which he said,

> We are sometimes asked in the name of patriotism to forget the merits of this fearful struggle, and to remember with equal admiration those who struck at the nation's life, and those who struck to save it—those who fought for slavery, and those who fought for liberty and justice.
>
> I am no minister of malice. I would not strike the fallen. I would not repel the repentant, but may my right hand forget its cunning, and my tongue cleave to the roof of my mouth, if I forget the difference between the parties to that terrible, protracted and bloody conflict.[21]

He would not repel the repentant. Those who caused harm—indeed, those who went to war to defend the institution of slavery—could be allowed back into the conversation, were they to work toward reformation and accountability. But, Douglass was saying, he could not and would not abide the Beecher-esque attempt to ignore or gloss over harm, to forgive without demanding repentance. That unity (of those with privilege) could not be more important than justice (for those without). That the way forward for the country must be in asking the enslavers and their defenders to repent for the sins of slavery.

Needless to say, that's not what happened. And our country as a whole—Black and Indigenous people in particular, and Black people most of all—have had to live with the legacy of these late-nineteenth-century choices to prioritize unity over accountability, forgiveness over repentance, in ways that have caused untold suffering and oppression for generations.

Similar calls for unity without critical analysis have characterized other inflection points in the history of the United States, perhaps most recently around Donald Trump's defeat in the 2020 presidential election. Even before the election, white people were sharing memes online that said things like "Guess who will be your friend no matter who you vote for. Know why? Because that's called being an adult" and "We need to be able to disagree politically but love unconditionally."[22]

These rather glib positive statements were made by those least impacted by Trump's embracing of white supremacists as "very fine people," of his Muslim Ban, his tear-gassing of Black Lives Matter protesters and referring to them as "thugs" and "terrorists," his referring to COVID-19 as the "Chinese virus," his policy of separating migrant children from their parents, and his telling a far-right terrorist group, the Proud Boys, to "stand back and stand by."

After the election, Trump spent six weeks challenging Joe Biden's electoral victory in a series of losing court battles. He then, on January 6, 2021, incited a violent attempted coup to prevent the certification of Biden's win in the electoral college. The Democrats in Congress immediately began discussing the possibility of impeachment proceedings, to make Trump's role in this insurrection more public, for the sake of accountability, and to bar him from ever holding federal office again. In response, the white House minority leader Kevin McCarthy released a statement on January 8, calling for unity:

> Impeaching the President with just 12 days left in his term will only divide our country more. I have reached out to President-elect [Joe] Biden today and plan to speak to him about how we must work together to lower the temperature and unite the country to solve America's challenges ... As leaders, we must call on our better angels and refocus our efforts on working directly for the American people. United we can deliver the peace, strength, and prosperity our country needs. Divided, we will fail.[23]

The Cuban American Florida senator Marco Rubio—who a few months earlier had encouraging words for a mob of Trump supporters who had swarmed and boxed in a Biden campaign bus, forcing the cancellation of an event due to safety concerns—tweeted on January 10, "Biden has a historic opportunity to unify America behind the sentiment that our political divisions have gone too far. But instead he decided to promote the left's efforts to use this terrible national tragedy to try and crush conservatives or anyone not anti-Trump enough."[24] The white Representative Kevin Brady's call for unity darkly hinted at further mob action, saying, "Those calling for impeachment or invoking the 25th Amendment in response to President Trump's rhetoric this week are themselves engaging in intemperate and inflammatory language and calling for action that is equally irresponsible and could well incite further violence . . ."[25]

Though the language used by meme-makers and Republican politicians in 2021 didn't necessarily invoke forgiveness per se, it resembles the rhetoric used after the Civil War to push unity without accountability for the benefit of those who might otherwise be held accountable. Both these social media users and politicians are trying to say, as Dr. Blank Boyd put it, "Okay, we've had our fight and now we need to kiss and make up so we can be Americans again." And perhaps in this more recent episode, as in the nineteenth century, the "we" that is kissing and making up is once again intended to reinscribe white supremacy, to remind everyone who is, and isn't, truly seen as a real American. Needless to say, many people were not having it with these calls to move forward. Mekishana Pierre, a Black woman, wrote, "Why is it that the price of unity has always been at the cost of our freedom? Why is it the job of those who are constantly denied their humanity to compromise?"[26]

In the months following Trump's attempted coup, as in the post–Civil War era, we must ask who benefits when harm is swept under the rug and whose interests are even further marginalized when that happens. And the next time unity and forgiveness are used as keywords during a time of great national tension, we must again stop and ask: Unity at the expense of whose justice? Forgiveness without demanding what repentance?

This book started on Twitter. Well, it actually started when a journalist I know emailed me. They were working on a story about what repentance might look like for famous perpetrators of sexual abuse. This was probably about six months after #MeToo had hit, and we were all, as a culture, starting to ask a new set of questions. I replied with some thoughts, the piece came out, and, as these things go, only a snippet of what I had shared made it into the article. I thought maybe it'd be of interest to folks, so I decided to tweet out the rest of it. The thread started with "I want to distinguish between 'repentance,' 'forgiveness,' and 'atonement' . . ."

Honestly, I was surprised by the force of people's responses.

I realized that some of the things that seem obvious to me, as a Jew steeped in my tradition (OK, as a rabbi), are not obvious to everyone. I mean, I grew up in the United States and have unconsciously absorbed a lot of the thinking about individualism, self-interest, and forgiveness that permeates the conversation here, in probably more ways than I am yet aware of. But I was also raised with at least a nominal connection to another way of thinking. My tradition's teachings on repentance are so foundational that, even as someone who had a more casual acquaintance with Judaism—as I was until my twenties—it was always part of the water I was imbibing. After all, we didn't go to synagogue very often when I was growing up, but we did make it there for the High Holy Days, which is when sermons tend to go in that direction. And as I got more interested in Jewish practice and eventually made it to rabbinical school, I developed a soft spot for Maimonides, especially his work on the subject of repentance. What can I say? I think his approach powerfully illuminates the work of taking responsibility for harm.

In any case, the Twitter thread led to an op-ed, which led to a couple of NPR interviews. The thing that was most notable about all of this was the intensity of the energy that came at me every time I raised the topic. Everyone had questions—philosophical ones, personal ones, ethical ones, questions about things happening in the news that week or about a story they heard in college that had stuck with them ever since. Something about the conversation about repentance, repair, amends, and accountability kept landing in this place where people didn't seem to feel like they knew what to do. Since I've started writing and speaking about this, my email and direct messages have filled up with stories from people who have been hurt and were told by their teacher, parent, pastor, or partner that they should just forgive, that reconciliation is important, or even that they should return to an abusive situation with an open heart. These emotional letters drove home to me the extent to which American culture emphasizes letting go of grudges and redemption narratives instead of the specific obligations of a perpetrator of harm and the recompense that is due to one who has been harmed or even traumatized. I also discovered the degree to which people are seeking another model.

I believe that this other model can offer a new way to navigate personal relationships, to read the news, and to participate in the organizations, institutions, and society in which we play a part. I hope that you, after reading this book, will have more tools to use in demanding meaningful accountability from yourself and from those around you, and that you will be better equipped to help repair more kinds of harm and focus more meaningfully on the needs of those who have been hurt. I wrote this book because I'm convinced that this approach has the potential to bring real healing and transformation to individuals, to relationships, and to communities—and maybe it can ripple out even farther, into the wider cultural conversation and beyond.

This book is for everybody. It is based on Jewish thought, but I am, very intentionally, applying these concepts to secular life and relationships. It's for Jews and non-Jews; for atheists, agnostics, and theists; for secular people, spiritual people, religious people, and for everybody in between. We've all caused harm, we've all been harmed, we've all witnessed harm. We are all always growing in our messy, imperfect attempts to do right, to clean up, to repair, to make sense of what's happened, and to figure out where to go from here. This is, I hope, a way in to the work.

The orientation of this book holds some tensions and complexities. It necessarily focuses on perpetrators—the harm that they have caused, the work that they—that we—must do to find the way back. And I want, more than anything, to show you, to show everyone, that this work is not impossible to do, but it is work, and it can be done (though we must not be too generous with participation trophies or cookies for people doing the bare minimum).

Yet any attempt to address harm that does not put the victims of harm and their needs at the center will necessarily come up short. I truly believe that the approach taken in my tradition and by Maimonides is almost always profoundly victim-centric; where I think he missed the mark, I say so, and I try to chart another way forward. (At times in this book, I use the word "survivor" to describe a person who has been harmed, but the choice to use that label can be very personal and, for some, it reflects a process of recovery from trauma. Since this book addresses a wide range of situations, I will use the word "victim" in most cases. This is, of course, not intended to imply that one word is preferable or better than the other; those who have been harmed should use the language that resonates most for them.)

So I've tried to write a victim-centric book on the work of repentance. Whether or not I've succeeded—that's the work, that should be the work.

Chapter One lays out a broad overview of Maimonides' steps of repentance. Subsequent chapters will expand on various aspects of the work—how to do effective rebuke, the dangers of excessive formalism, the role of the community, and so forth—while looking at the ways in which these principles play out in personal, communal, institutional, and national spheres. In some chapters, Maimonides will feature prominently, as we explore particular dimensions of his, and others', teachings on the work of repentance. In other chapters, his presence will be implicit; you will by then have internalized his basic steps, and their application in different contexts will be the focus.

I use the word "harm" to describe a wide range of impacts, from fairly resolvable difficulties to great atrocities. The word is generally used to refer to hurt, injury, or damage of some sort, whether mental, emotional, or physical, which may be sustained for a brief amount of time or across generations. "Abuse," on the other hand, is generally defined as unfair, cruel, or violent treatment—it is a form of harm, but not all harm is abuse. While it's not an accident that many of the examples that you'll find in this book involve notable differentials of power or privilege, I do not believe that harm is only something that can be committed by someone with more power against someone with less power, or at different intersections of power. That would deny something of our essential humanity, the way we all, as messy people trying to do our best, can hurt one another, regardless of our identities, roles, and relationships to larger structural forces. However, power matters—a conflict between a parent and a child, a male dean and a female student, or a white police officer and an unarmed Black motorist is not neutral. What is said or done by the person with less power in that moment cannot be compared in any way to the responsibilities of the party with more power. It harms us all—it hurts, injures, damages us—as individuals and as a society when we pretend that it can. The work of repentance requires clear-sighted thinking about this.

I also want to name a fear that I have. I have no way of preventing this work from being weaponized, not really. That is to say, an abusive person might hand this book to their partner, their adult child, someone else—and say, "Here! See? You need to repent to me!" And yet I would hope that readers will share this book with those who have genuinely hurt them, as a vulnerable invitation to a conversation. My advice would be, if you think someone is demanding your repentance as part of an abusive move, please go learn more about abuse and seek out support, OK? You deserve all the care and tenderness in the world.

If you find that you are feeling defensive about being invited into accountability for harm you have caused and thus want to blame the person who is asking for your repentance for making you feel uncomfortable—well, there's some extra work you might need to do. We sometimes commit the greatest harm when we are busy convincing ourselves that we are the ones who have been hurt, and we use that hurt to rationalize our damaging behavior. (I might here refer you to the trauma psychologist Jennifer Freyd's concept of DARVO, a reaction perpetrators of wrongdoing may display in response to being held accountable for their behavior. DARVO stands for "Deny, Attack, and Reverse Victim and Offender.")[27]

Harm is of course not dualistic—we can sometimes both be hurt ourselves and hurt others—and sometimes our experiences of hurt may be related to deeper, older pain rather than only the immediate situation at hand. We may have an outsized reaction to what's happening now because of pain that we're carrying from before. Trickier still, people in abusive relationships might be prone to questioning who the true victim is, and those who have been in (or who grew up in) abusive relationships are more prone to assume that they're in the wrong. (And sometimes they actually are in the wrong, but maybe not always, so it's all trickier and trickier still.) Obviously there isn't one simple answer to all of these questions or issues, but they're relevant over the course of the book, the course of many of our lives, and to the stories of many, if not all, of the societies and nations that we inhabit.

In this book, I quote other thinkers quite a bit, and my use of their voices is intentional. My tradition is all about engaging with both the wisdom of the past and with the insights of our contemporaries, and we do so by carefully and thoughtfully citing sources. I am standing on the shoulders of giants; many brilliant people, of the past and the present, have much to contribute to the conversation. This includes, but is not limited to, people directly impacted by the structural issues discussed in various sections of the book, whose insights often drive the conversation—as they should.

I also periodically cite people who comment on social media; I mean, this is the place where people write, think, share, and say wise and true things here in the twenty-first century. Many of the most insightful folks around offer thoughts online in addition to, or instead of, publishing in conventional venues. This too—as the rabbis of the Talmud were wont to say about less traditional sources of wisdom— is Torah.

In any case, it's time to get started. The work of repentance demands curiosity, care, and a willingness to face hard things with bravery and honesty. While we can't undo the past, we can address the present with integrity and endeavor to create a future that is much more whole than anything we can imagine from here. So let us begin.

CHAPTER ONE

A REPENTANCE OVERVIEW; OR, WHAT MIGHT BE POSSIBLE

People hurt one another.

Sometimes the harm is unintentional, even born of goodwill and the desire to help. Sometimes it's the result of ignorance or lack of information. Sometimes it happens because of cowardice. Sometimes it reflects a self-protective impulse—a desire to preserve one's own self-image or concern about organizational public relations. Sometimes a long process of dehumanization makes atrocities possible.

But whatever the cause, people manage to inflict damage in a myriad of ways, from hurt feelings to lost livelihood, the infliction of trauma, the perpetration of hate against a vulnerable demographic, or the loss of life.

Sometimes harm can be repaired. Sometimes it can't.

Regardless, in a moral universe, there is work to be done whenever harm is inflicted.

Moses Maimonides was a twelfth-century philosopher and scholar of Jewish law. He offers a powerful, game-changing path to healing and repair, which can be useful for everyone, regardless of background or belief system. Yes, he wrote and codified Jewish law intended for Jews living within the religious framework of the Torah and the Talmud, but the stages of repentance that he lays out in his masterwork, the *Mishneh Torah*—and the nuances of each stage—are clear and specific, and can illuminate many situations that to our contemporary American eyes may seem messy and impenetrable. Applying his lens to the challenges of today—even in ways he might not have dreamed of, or that he might consider novel or unorthodox—can illuminate, quickly and profoundly, questions about what to do in the wake of harm: how to deal with it, who is responsible and what that responsibility looks like, how far it extends, and what its limits are. After years of working with Maimonides' stages of repentance, I have become convinced that they make sense not only in our individual lives—as we make mistakes with our coworkers, friends, family, and intimate partners—but also on the communal, cultural, and even national level.

Moses ben Maimon—commonly known as Maimonides—was born in Córdoba, in what's now Spain, around 1135 CE, under the Berber Muslim Almoravid Empire. When a different caliphate conquered the area in 1148, the Jews living there became vulnerable to forced conversion, death, or exile. His family escaped, and Maimonides eventually settled in Egypt. By the time he got there, in 1168, he had already gained some acclaim through his authoritative commentary on the Mishnah—an ancient collection of Jewish laws compiled around 200 CE, the cornerstone text of Rabbinic Judaism known to Jews as the "Oral Torah."

In Egypt, Maimonides first worked with his brother in an importing business and, after his brother's untimely death, returned to being a doctor, his former profession. Eventually he served as physician to the sultan Saladin. Around the same time, he began working on his magnum opus, the work that would define him and his legacy. The *Mishneh Torah* (along with his later philosophical treatise, *The Guide for the Perplexed*) came to be considered so important, his tombstone is engraved with the majestic epitaph: "From Moses [of the Bible] to Moses [ben Maimon], there was none like Moses."

Maimonides—also known as Rambam, an acronym for Rabbi Moses ben Maimon—set out to write the *Mishneh Torah* in order to make it easier for Jews to follow Jewish law without having to study

the Talmud—a complex, often winding, frequently unresolved discourse on the meaning of the Torah and the Mishnah. He assumed
that scholars would still go deep into the Talmudic debates, but most
people just needed the bottom line: what to do and how to do it.
This was a brilliant step forward in the evolution of Judaism: clear,
concise instructions, organized in a way entirely different from the
Mishnah and the Talmud, taken primarily from the Talmud and other
authoritative sources but also developed, in places, with Maimonides'
own innovations and flourishes. (So yes, many of the ideas and even
phrases I cite here with the opening "Maimonides says," are, in fact,
Maimonides' rephrasing or even quoting of the Talmud itself. For sim-
plicity's sake, I mostly stick with the text of the *Mishneh Torah*. Those
of you who care about chasing down sources—and you know who
you are—can certainly do so with greater ease now that we live in the
Great Golden Age of Sefaria.)[1]

Many extraordinary things make up the *Mishneh Torah*; Maimonides' Laws of Repentance are among them. Here, as elsewhere, he
takes ideas scattered all over the tradition and lays them out, sometimes with his own crucial additions, to give a clear, systematic guide
for not only repairing harm but for becoming the kind of person who
will not cause harm in the future.

The Laws of Repentance are about amends, but also about
transformation.

According to Maimonides, a person doesn't just get to mess up,
mumble, "Sorry," and get on with it. They're not entitled to forgiveness
if they haven't done the work of repair. (And they're not necessarily
entitled to forgiveness even if they have.) Another human being's suffering is not magically erased because the person who caused it says
that they didn't mean to do it. This is true in our personal lives, and it's
also true of politicians caught saying racist things, celebrities named as
sexual abusers, human resources departments that cover up employee
complaints, and governments perpetrating harm against individuals
or groups. Fixing damage involves taking specific steps; there's a process. We can't ever undo what happened, but we can transform the
situation and ourselves.

But you can't cut corners.

Of course, it's hard. Owning up to the hurt you have caused some-one else is difficult. And how much more so when an injury was not accidental, when you must admit that you knowingly lied to a loved one, let down someone in need, unfairly lashed out in anger, chose to be complicit in abuse, violated boundaries, or took other actions with real, painful implications.

Owning the fact that we've done wrong is challenging—even threatening or scary—but it is the work we are obligated to do. Mai-monides is very clear about what that work is meant to look like—and his clarity can help guide us.

OK, so, some context: Jewish thinking on repentance comes originally from legal writing about Yom Kippur, the Day of Atonement. A long time ago, Yom Kippur was the day on which the High Priest purged the ancient Temple in Jerusalem of ritual impurity and made expia-tion for himself, his family, and the Israelite people—a clearing out of sin, a spiritual purification.[2] When the Second Temple was destroyed by the Romans in 70 CE, the more personal, sin-clearing aspect of the day became even stronger. The Mishnah—the ancient oral tradition mentioned earlier—notes that the atonement for interpersonal sins offered on Yom Kippur will not work until the person who did harm "appeases their friend."[3] The holy atonement reset button doesn't work until we've cleaned up our own mess.

The Babylonian Talmud, which expounded on the Mishnah and was redacted around the fifth century CE, struggled to understand what it means to "appease" one's friend. What do you need to do? When? How? What are the limits to and obligations of this appeasement?

As mentioned earlier, Maimonides' Laws of Repentance took many of the questions and much of the thinking in the Mishnah, the Talmud, and elsewhere and synthesized them into distinct steps—a path to follow. In a moment, we'll get into the weeds of what those steps are, and in the chapters that follow, we'll apply them to a range of situations and types of harm, including those with deep histori-cal roots. Occasionally it will make sense to translate Maimonides' thinking into our twenty-first-century context. Things that we now know to be true will bump up against the limits of his medieval-era thinking, and we'll discuss them as needed. (Do I wish Maimonides could do repentance work for some of his writings about women, among other things? Sure. But that's outside the scope of this book.)

As noted in the introduction, Judaism doesn't emphasize forgiveness to the same degree that Christianity and secular American society do. Jewish law teaches that the person harmed is certainly not obligated to forgive a perpetrator who has not done the work of repentance. And even if repentance is wholehearted and demonstrable, if apologies have been offered and amends made, how and when forgiveness factors in is not always straightforward, as we'll see in Chapter Seven. Is forgiveness something the victim can choose to do at any point? Definitely. Can it sometimes be a useful part of the healing process? For sure. Is a victim *obligated* to forgive? Well, as we rabbis are fond of saying, that's a whole other conversation.

It's worth mentioning that forgiveness isn't the same as reconciliation—returning to some sort of relationship that will continue into the future. Regardless, I want to spell out that, in Judaism, a person can do real, profound, comprehensive repentance work and even get right with God—experience atonement—even if their victim never forgives them. Repentance and forgiveness are separate processes.

For the rabbis of the Mishnah and the Talmud, and for our guide Maimonides, forgiveness is much less important than the repair work that the person who caused harm is obligated to do. The Hebrew word that is often translated as "repentance" is *tshuvah*, which literally means "returning." In Modern Hebrew, a *tshuvah* is an answer to a question—you've gotten back to someone—but it also means "returning" in the sense of "I'll also need a return ticket for this bus ride." In a spiritual context, *tshuvah* is about coming back to where we are supposed to be, returning to the person we know we're capable of being—coming home, in humility and with intentionality, to behave as the person we'd like to believe we are.

In order to see how Maimonides' ideas about repentance can help transform our own lives and personal relationships, the institutions of which we are a part, and our culture and country as a whole, we need to have a solid grasp on what those steps are. As we look at some complex and seemingly intractable situations in the chapters to come, it will be crucial to understand the basics of Maimonides' thinking, so that we can apply it to today's challenges with flexibility and ease. For the rest of this chapter, we'll do a deep dive into his five steps of repentance and the ways they can potentially effect not only repair and healing for those who have been harmed, but also profound transformation for the person who—intentionally or unintentionally—caused that harm in the first place.

Step One: Naming and Owning Harm

Maimonides often likes to begin a new section of the *Mishneh Torah* with something of a philosophical investigation of a topic, but with the Laws of Repentance, he jumps right in; the philosophical stuff comes later. He launches the section immediately with an action step: confession. Before we even understand what repentance is, we're instructed[4] to name, out loud, the harm that we have caused. We're supposed to acknowledge that we feel ashamed by our actions and commit to not doing that thing again. Later, he notes that it is "praiseworthy" to make this confession of interpersonal harm in a public way.[5]

Notably, we're not even discussing apology or amends yet—those steps will come later. Here, what is demanded is a simple acknowledgment of what happened.

Of course, that may not be so simple. Starting the process with a confession of harm goes against many of our cultural and often individual instincts—to shift blame, to minimize the problem, to focus on our excellent and pure intentions, to put off an uncomfortable conversation to another day.

But those impulses are short-circuited here. There is no repentance process without the naming of harm, without owning it. Which means, of course, that the person doing this work has to actually comprehend the harm that they have caused. A person can't repent if they don't understand why the thing that happened is actually a big deal—why the person who has been hurt is actually hurt. This is true for the person who chronically picks up the phone while their partner is talking; the person who borrowed, without permission, something they didn't realize was an heirloom; the cis person whose curious question of their trans neighbor dehumanizes them; the organizational culture that habitually silences women's voices at meetings; the city whose zoning laws reinforce structural racism and decades of disenfranchisement.

So there is work to be done even before taking the first step in Maimonides' stages of repentance: understanding the harm caused. And to get there, there must be a willingness to face it—an engagement with the people trying to teach about the harm, or the introspection required to hear those little voices of discomfort deep within—the ones that were drowned out when the choice was made in the first place.

And then that harm must be named, owned, in as public a space as is warranted. Certainly, not every situation is appropriate for a declaration in front of an audience—intimate situations, for example. Maimonides is also clear that what we might call victimless crimes— sins against God, not other people—aren't meant to be spelled out explicitly to the world at large.[6]

But many interpersonal mistakes do have a public dimension to them, whether on the individual, social, or even national level. And naming that can feel personally threatening, sometimes, but it's important and it's entirely doable.

"It wasn't OK that I told that joke in the staff meeting. I didn't realize it at the time, but now I understand it was pretty transphobic."

"I, um, have a confession to make. I know everybody's been trying to figure out who ran over Simon's cat. I feel horrible—it was me."

"I need to admit that I overcharged customers and pocketed the difference. Four have come forward, but the truth is, there are more."

"I finally understand how my decision to hold a writer's retreat at a plantation sanitizes the horrors of slavery."

"I know I told you all I was sick last weekend and that's why I couldn't come help out. But actually I went away with my girlfriend."

"Our organization continued to solicit the donor even after we found out that his money was obtained through criminal means and, uh . . . the donor hasn't been held accountable for that."

"Our state has, for centuries, and is even now continuing to violate treaties with the Sioux Nation. Our possession of this land and our development of it constitute theft."

As I read Maimonides, I don't think we need to assume that each of these confessions needs to be equally public (though he may be right that it is indeed praiseworthy to make oneself vulnerable and accountable even in front of those not directly impacted). But we can assume that a public confession needs to be proportionate to the harm. The person who made a transphobic joke in a staff meeting would need to offer accountability in that same staff meeting the following week (assuming the harm is not noted and repaired immediately), or initiate a conversation on the team's Slack channel, or something of the sort. The person who owns up to accidentally hitting a beloved pet might need to do so in a neighborhood where people have been looking for the cat—at an in-person gathering, or on the group chat or listserv. A person who harasses another on a closed Facebook group should, at minimum, own their actions in that same digital space. A famous writer advertising widely for her plantation retreat would, however, need to address this choice in a broadly public way—online, or to a newspaper, or in some other channel that is commensurate to the mistake itself. Would an organization knowingly accepting dark money need to disclose this to everyone receiving their services? On their email list? To the wider public? Some details may need to be tailored to the specifics of the situation—which is why we will delve much deeper into more concrete examples in the chapters that follow.

Regardless, even just this first confession step can be incredibly hard and painful. For so many people, this work can trigger defensiveness—the desire to justify one's actions in order to stave off shame, guilt, humiliation, or loss of reputation or power. It tarnishes our cherished belief that we are always doing good, always helpful. And for many people, admitting error in this way may touch some very old, very deep pain from childhood. It might seem to confirm a message they often heard about being a screwup; it might feel threatening in light of a belief that they were always required to be perfect; or it might run head on into other kinds of stories about their value and worth that they have consciously or unconsciously absorbed. And, of course, acknowledging and taking responsibility for harm is not only ethically uncomfortable; there are sometimes significant legal and monetary consequences as well, as we'll discuss later.

Owning the harm caused means that it must actually be owned fully, entirely. Many of the public statements offered by famous men in the first year after #MeToo broke offer a master class in how to fail at this. Their slippery apologies offered to the press could, at best, be considered to be part of the first step of repentance, except that they didn't begin to take ownership of their actions—not Kevin Spacey's bet-hedging language ("If I did behave then as he describes"),[7] not Garrison Keillor's whining about how being named as an abuser has impacted his work,[8] not Matt Lauer's moaning about how the revelation that he assaulted women hurt his family,[9] not Mario Batali's focus on how his predatory behavior will be received by his fans,[10] not Charlie Rose's minimizing of the complaints against him,[11] not Bill O'Reilly's blaming of God,[12] and not Louis C.K.'s speculation about what the victims might have thought.[13] These perfunctory, narcissistic public statements didn't center their victims, didn't name comprehensively and clearly what the men had done, and didn't address their bad behavior without justifying it or making excuses.

There are other ways to do it.

In the realm of statements made by celebrities called out for misconduct during #MeToo, that of *Community* showrunner Dan Harmon offers a clear contrast. Speaking on his podcast, he discussed his sexual harassment of Megan Ganz, one of the writers on the show:

> I knew I wasn't doing anybody any favors by feeling these things and so I did the cowardly, easiest, laziest thing you can do with feelings like that and didn't deal with them and in not dealing with them I made everybody else deal with them, especially her . . . And so I let myself keep doing it and it's not as if this person didn't repeatedly

communicate to me the idea that what I was doing was divesting her of a recourse to integrity. I just didn't hear it because it didn't profit me to hear it, and this was, after all, happening to me, right?

He described what happened after she rebuffed his advances:

I was humiliated. So, I continued to do the cowardly thing. I continued to do the selfish thing. Now I wanted to teach her a lesson. I wanted to show her that if she didn't like being liked in that way then, oh boy, she should get over herself. After all, if you're just going to be a writer then this is how 'just writers' get treated . . . Just treated her cruelly, pointedly, things I would never, ever have done if she had been male and if I had never had those feelings for her . . . I've never done it before and I will never do it again, but I certainly wouldn't have been able to do it if I had any respect for women.[14]

Harmon's statements evince the real work of *cheshbon hanefesh*, the profound soul-searching that must precede repentance. The harm he caused was important enough to him to try to understand, really, what even happened. This demanded real inner work, and facing the uglier parts of himself—challenging his self-concept as someone heroic. On the podcast Harmon talked at length about the ways he lied to himself, the way he ignored feedback that "didn't profit" him, his vindictiveness, and the fact that, despite his avowed stance as a feminist, he could not have treated Ganz the way he did if he had really respected women. Difficult stuff to face—and it didn't happen overnight. Harmon's earlier public statements started with half-assed allusions to his harassment of Ganz and then vague apologies for being a bad boss. He finally got to the place—when Ganz herself pushed him to go there, in fact—where he was able to own his actions.[15] In fact, his legal team advised him not to admit to all the things that he did on the podcast because it might open him up to litigation. But, as the radio producer Nancy Updike put it, "By admitting them openly, he chose her wellbeing over his own comfort, maybe for the first time in their whole relationship."[16]

The podcast confession was significant for Ganz. As she noted,

The most important part of the apology was its specificity. He gave
a complete account of what he did. Not the salacious details that
people focus on—was it in a bar? what time? who was there?—but
the ugly little realities. He knew that I didn't welcome his advances.
He did it anyway. He treated me differently than he treated the male
writers. And when people confronted him about it, he lied. We both
know what happened, but these were the parts of the story that only
he could confirm for me. Whenever I talked to friends about it afterward, they would of course say, "It wasn't your fault. You didn't do
anything wrong." And I know that's true. But some small part of me
would always think, "You weren't there." The irony is, Dan was the
only person who could wipe those doubts from my head. That's why
I was able to accept his apology. Because I felt vindicated, to others
but more importantly to myself.[17]

Harmon's confession, among other things, validated for Ganz her
own experience, her own suffering. It helped her feel less alone and
grounded her in her own truth in a way that, she found, she needed
as part of her healing process. After hearing the podcast, she was first
moved to text Harmon her thanks and forgiveness, and then made the
decision to tweet publicly that she accepted his apology and forgave
him. For, she said, "People should see the good that can happen when
you aren't afraid to accept responsibility for your mistakes. He gave
me relief, and I hope I was able to give him some in return."[18]

A confession of harm is only regarded as part of the repentance
process when someone actually intends to do the work. Maimonides
says that someone who confesses their sins but "has not abandoned
sin in their heart" is like someone who becomes immersed in the ritual bath[19] while holding a lizard[20]—the living waters cannot purify
as intended if someone is clutching a non-kosher creepy-crawly that
will invalidate the whole process. Nothing is accomplished. It's a waste
of everyone's time and effort. If a person is not resolved, in the deep
places of their being, that they're done doing the harmful thing—or if,

even worse, they're *still doing it*—then the verbal confession isn't valid. It's not a step on the pathway to repentance.

Everyone has probably experienced this feeling of being pulled in two directions—part of us wants to move forward into the work of change and transformation, but part of us is secretly—or not so secretly—holding on to something that can sabotage our efforts.[21] Identifying those obstacles is critical. Sometimes they are personal—related to emotion or psychology. Sometimes they appear in the form of advisers or managers concerned with controlling an image or public perception. They may arise from fears, founded or unfounded, about the possible consequences of admitting to having done something wrong. In cases related to harm done at the collective level, obstacles to confession may appear as concerns about the bottom line, differences of opinion among powerful stakeholders, or structural barriers. But regardless of the nature of the lizard, it must be dropped to continue further. Truly being ready to change—to be different and to make different choices—is a critical, nonnegotiable part of the process.

Step Two: Starting to Change

After delving into the concrete, actionable matter of public confession in the first chapter of the *Laws of Repentance*, Maimonides begins the second chapter by looking at the big picture. "What is complete repentance? The [case of] one who had it in their power to repeat a transgression, but separated themselves from it and did not do it because they had repented."[22] That is, true repentance happens at the moment when a person comes into a situation similar to one in which they had previously committed harm, and this time, do it right. The second (or fifth, or twentieth) time around, when you finally behave in accordance with your values and ideals? That's *tshuvah*. But a person might reasonably ask: Why would you end up in the exact same situation as the one in which you had previously screwed up? Who gets an instant replay like that?

My own rabbi, Alan Lew, used to say something like, "Well, if you haven't done the work, you'll get back there." That is, a person who hasn't faced their problematic traits and unhealed wounds, or grappled deeply with harm caused in the past, or done the work to change processes and structures, will undoubtedly manage to find themselves in some variation of the same situation over and over—whether the harm in question is chronically sabotaging relationships, lashing out in anger, serially abusing those with less power, or using institutional or even governmental resources to quash dissent or preserve the status quo. The United States of America, for example, has never reckoned deeply with its enslavement of people of African descent, so the country continues to find opportunities to commit the same sins of white supremacy again and again and again: from slavery to lynchings, from Jim Crow to redlining, from mass incarceration to voter suppression. The precise nature of the harm may be different—just as the sabotage and lashing out in relationships may not look exactly the same each time—but the patterns are undeniable.

According to Maimonides, only when a person does the work needed to become a different person can they, naturally and organically, make a different choice. The person (or institution) that has done harm must become the kind of person (or institution) that doesn't do this thing anymore. They must engage in a profound process of transformation. Obviously this doesn't happen overnight, but it's a crucial process that must be undertaken—even if it takes years, decades, or a lifetime. Because step two may take a long time, it often runs concurrently with some of the subsequent steps, as we shall see.

In Maimonides' time, this work of transformation might have included "crying out in tearful supplication, giving charity according to one's means, distancing oneself exceedingly from the thing causing the sin," and/or making choices "to change one's identity and . . . conduct . . . and exiling oneself from the place of residence . . . because it leads them to submissiveness and to be meek and humble-spirited."[23] Translated to our own time, the work of transformation might include tearful grappling with one's behavior in prayer, meditation, and/or some other practice; making financial sacrifices that have meaningful impact both on one's own wallet and the world; changing one's self-conception and self-identity in appropriate ways; putting oneself in new situations both to consciously avoid the opportunity to cause harm and perhaps to experience what it's like to not have control or power—someplace where one might get some practice in the virtue of humility.

These days this process of change might also involve therapy, or rehab, or educating oneself rigorously on an issue about which one had been ignorant or held toxic opinions. It might mean actively seeking out fresh perspectives to help shape a new understanding of a complex situation. It might involve a request to spend time with the victim to better understand the nature of the impact and the problem it caused, or seeking out others not directly involved in the situation who can help unpack the issue. Maybe a concrete action plan for making different choices in the future is needed. Maybe it's about grappling with the root causes of the harm. Some of these things may be necessary even before the confession stage, some may be appropriate at this point in the process, and in many cases, the answer might be both.

Maimonides was a stickler for details, and it's not a minor point that his discussion about beginning this transformation precedes his discussion of amends/reparations and apologies. He doesn't spell out his thinking explicitly, but I think he was trying to tell us that apologies, and even amends and reparations, don't truly have the needed effect if the work to become different isn't already underway. And again, that work isn't just internal; it must manifest in external actions—different choices, even small ones, already being made. Even with the purest of intentions—the lizard has been dropped, the resolve to change is really there—without this crucial step of undertaking, even in a small way, what might be a lifelong project of becoming different, real repair may prove impossible. If a person apologizes sincerely and even offers restitution for the harm they've caused, but then, not long after that, commits the same kind of harm again, they have not repented—not really.

The goal here isn't merely making amends. It's transformation.

Here's one example of what it can look like when a country tries to jump from public confession to apology and reparations without interrogating the ways in which it needs to create profound internal change, so as not to continue perpetrating the same harm, again and again:

In 2011, Canada's prime minister, Stephen Harper, who is white, issued a formal apology to the country's Indigenous peoples for the government's role in a destructive residential school program—a network of boarding schools created to remove Indigenous children from their own communities for the purpose of assimilating them into the dominant Canadian settler culture, a form of cultural genocide. Indigenous children also frequently suffered horrific abuse at these schools. Thousands—perhaps many thousands—of children died at these sites and were buried in unmarked graves.[24] The residential schools operated for about 130 years and impacted over 150,000 children; the last one did not close until 1996.[25] Harper acknowledged that the residential schools' "objectives were based on the [erroneous] assumption that [Indigenous] cultures and spiritual beliefs were inferior and unequal" and that "the government recognizes that the absence of an apology has been an impediment to healing and reconciliation."[26] In 2008 he established the Truth and Reconciliation Commission, which, in 2015, published a list of ninety-four "Calls to Action" on things like health, education, and child welfare in order to improve Indigenous lives now and to adjudicate justice on harm perpetrated earlier.

During this same era, however, Harper pushed for the development of oil and gas pipeline projects on Indigenous treaty land—at one point, 94 of 105 projects under review were "located on reserve, within an historic treaty area, or in a settled or unsettled claims area," and leaked documents indicated that federal meetings on the subject had concluded that "we can no longer afford the investment uncertainty created by issues around Aboriginal participation,"[27] meaning that the government would simply ignore the lack of Indigenous consent. Presumably, Canada did not engage seriously with questions about how it might need to reconsider its energy sources and economic models in light of its aspirations toward "healing and reconciliation." This, of course, would not be a simple project, but how else could the country find a way to approach the same sin—the discounting of Indigenous needs, interests, and rights in favor of the colonialist national agenda—and make a different choice? Harper didn't help his country do the transformational work, and when the opportunity to behave differently arose, he wasn't ready or, perhaps, willing.

And it wasn't just Harper. Canada's next prime minister, Justin Trudeau, who is also white, made Indigenous rights a cornerstone of his election campaign but has also been criticized for the gap between his rhetoric[28] of reconciliation and his actions, pushing environmentally damaging pipeline projects through Indigenous territory,[29] appealing a ruling from the Canadian Human Rights Tribunal that the government owed possibly billions of dollars in compensation to up to fifty thousand Indigenous children who were "willfully and recklessly" harmed by discrimination in the welfare system,[30] and forcing Indigenous people to sign away land rights.[31]

Public apologies and statements of intent aren't meaningful if harm is still being perpetrated. Indigenous sovereignty is still being treated as "inferior and unequal" in many ways in Canada. Indeed, some Indigenous people have criticized the way in which Harper's apology and the Truth and Reconciliation Commission framed harm against Indigenous people as something that happened in the past, as though it has no bearing on ongoing relations between the Canadian government and Canada's Indigenous population.[32] The government is still committing harm, environmental injustice, colonialist land theft, and more. The work to become different didn't happen, so the government, in the end, did not make different choices. Without transformation, there's no repentance. There's only the same harm, again and again, perpetrated in different ways.

Step Three: Restitution and Accepting Consequences

Repair work isn't really repair if the only thing that's changed is the perpetrator. Despite the fact that Maimonides hasn't yet, deep as we are into his Laws of Repentance, explicitly mentioned the victim of harm, his approach to repentance is, I believe, profoundly victim-centric. Everything we've discussed up to this point has been largely about the accountability of the perpetrator. True repentance begins when the perpetrator confesses to a harmful action, perhaps publicly, and initiates the process of becoming someone who does not perpetrate this harm—thus investing in the prevention of future victims.

It behooves us to ask, at this juncture, if Maimonides made a mistake in not putting the victim's needs first in a more explicit way—after all, we're only getting to the person harmed and to making amends all the way down here in step three of the process. Why doesn't the *Mishneh Torah* start with caring for victims and repairing the harm done to them and only then move to accountability and repentance for harmdoers?[33]

I think the reason Maimonides doesn't say anything about the importance of taking care of victims' immediate needs first is because, frankly, it was so obvious to him that it didn't need to be stated. Jewish law is pretty clear about the fact that those in need of immediate care should be given immediate care, which may involve a financial component that could factor into the larger picture of restitution.

And I think there are also good reasons for ordering the steps of repentance in this way, that it's actually something of a gift to the victim. A person who caused harm (even unwittingly! even with the best of intentions!) will be better positioned to truly make amends after they have gone off to do some of the work described already—to own what they've done and to begin to become different. If we ask a perpetrator to engage too early with their victim—before they've confronted the seriousness of their actions and their impact, before they've begun working to change—the likelihood of their causing additional harm, rather than meaningful repair, is much higher. We don't want to expose someone who has been hurt to a penitent who is not ready to take responsibility in the ways that matter. And jumping to the larger work of making amends without a plan in place to make sure that the same misdeed is not committed again and again would miss a crucial part of the process. Focusing on the work of the penitent before coming back to the victim is a critical piece of caring for the victim.

Of course the victim is not sitting on the sidelines, wounded, while the perpetrator is having a heart-to-heart with themself about why, exactly, they threw that sucker punch. Depending on the nature of the harm, there may be other things happening to and with the victim at this time, with other supports, other community. But this book is on repentance, so our focus is on the work of the perpetrator—the inner and interpersonal labor they must perform in order to mend, as much as possible, the damage done, and to change in powerful and critical ways.

Which brings us back to amends. Of course, those who have suffered must receive redress. Once the work of repentance has been undertaken in earnest, restitution must be made, in whatever way might be possible. Maimonides writes, "For instance, [if] one injures another, or curses them or plunders them, or offends them in like matters, [it] is ever not absolved unless they make restitution of what is owed and beg the forgiveness of the other."[34]

Here, you see that both steps three and four—restitution and apology—are mentioned in the same sentence. We'll get to apology in a moment; for now, we will focus on the questions that restitution raises for us. Maimonides isn't explicit about the timing of these steps in the repentance process. How long has it been since the public confession was made? How deep into the work of becoming a different person must one be before arriving here? It's not clear. I think the reason for this is that the answer absolutely depends on context. In some cases, these things might happen over the course of an hour or a week; in others, they might require years.

In this way, the work of step two—transformation, which may be ongoing for a very, *very* long time—and steps three and four, amends and apology—may happen concurrently, may overlap, or may happen in a nonlinear way. But regardless, ultimately the party that has caused harm must make restitution for that harm, in whatever way possible. Just like the confession work, just like the transformation work, this demands truly comprehending the gravity of the harm caused and humbly seeking the appropriate redress—not throwing money at a problem to make it go away. And in many cases, it likely involves consultation with the person or people harmed about what would feel just, or what might be actually needed by the real, live human being in question. One does not offer amends *at* the person harmed, but *to* them.

Does this include paying any costs incurred as a result of the harm? Maimonides is clear, in fact, that one who injures another physically must pay damages on five fronts: for the injury itself, the pain suffered, the medical costs, the time away from work, and the humiliation.[35] (Elsewhere, he itemizes the restitution required for other kinds of harm, as well.) This payment can take different forms, based on the situation. If the damage affected a person's work life, might it involve connecting a victim to new professional opportunities? Or, for something else, donating time or money to an appropriate organization? (Remember that Maimonides considers this a part of the transformation process.) Speaking out as an advocate? Paying someone back for the flight they missed? Underwriting therapy and a professional coach? Providing free housing for a community that's been forced to endure criminal neglect and unsafe living conditions? Paying reparations for crimes against humanity committed at the national level?

Of course, identifying the work of amends is not the same as completing it. Three years after Canada's Truth and Reconciliation Commission published its ninety-four "Calls to Action," only ten had been completed, and twenty-one were in progress, with projects underway. Sixty-three of them—more than two-thirds—had either not been started at all or only gotten to the project proposal stage.[36] If Canada truly cares to repent for the harms committed against its Indigenous population, the country will need to stop harming Indigenous people now and complete all the work it publicly committed to in making amends for harmful behavior in the past and bringing about justice.

Sometimes it's impossible to make amends to the person or people harmed. Nonetheless, the work of repentance demands that reparations be made—perhaps not for the exact harm caused, but for some other appropriate need. For example, someone who worked as a driver reached out to me for advice. He had been paid to drive a man back from the hospital, but it turned out that he did not have housing, and that he was still injured. He asked the driver to leave him at a truck stop, and the driver did. The driver did as requested; technically speaking, he had discharged his professional duty. But he felt awful afterward because he felt that he should have found the man a safer place to heal or offered him the money he had been paid by the hospital for the fare.

The driver went back to the truck stop later to see if he could offer belated help, but the man wasn't there, and the driver had no idea where he had gone; there was no way to make amends directly to the person whom he had failed. His tweets to me, unlocked and findable online, were a form of public confession; he owned what he had done, acknowledged its probable impact, shared regret about his actions, and stated a clear intention to try to make it right. He didn't have much money to donate—he himself was struggling to make ends meet—but he concluded that he could offer time volunteering for an organization that supported unhoused and similarly at-risk people. It was a way of putting his feet and hands where his heart was, to at least endeavor to help others, even if he couldn't help the man he had dropped off. And the combination of the public confession and doing this work in a regular, ongoing way will, I think, have a profound impact on him and help him make different choices in the future—a critical component of repentance.

And though Maimonides doesn't say this explicitly, I think part of the amends process involves also humbly accepting the fact that actions have consequences. In the case of, say, revelations of significant abuses of power by a high-profile person, part of amends might include, in addition to direct redress to those harmed, making no attempt at a career comeback, even if it might be possible, given the public's short memory. In more mundane situations it might involve humbly receiving rebuke at work, accepting that one is no longer welcome at the weekly game night, agreeing that one deserved to be called out online, knowing that hard work may be required to earn back a spouse's trust, and so on. This accepting of consequences may be considered, for some victims, integral to the process—a proof of sincerity.

Barry Freundel was a rabbi arrested and convicted for secretly filming over fifty women as they undressed for the ritual bath—a gross violation in any context, all the more so given the trust involved in the rabbi-congregant relationship and the sacred space of the ritual bath. Because of the statute of limitations, he was tried for only a small proportion of his crimes; he recorded over a hundred additional women who would never see their day in court. He issued a public apology that was clearly informed by his knowledge of Maimonides and other Jewish authorities on repentance. But as one of his victims noted, his words were profoundly undermined by his actions, which included appeals for a lighter sentence based on the claim that he had committed a single crime—a lesser harm—rather than multiple crimes, despite his numerous victims.[37] As we will discuss later, many open questions remain about prison as a vehicle for making amends. But from the perspective of one of Freundel's victims, the fact that he was sentenced to a punishment that did not accurately reflect the extent of the harm that he caused and, on top of that, that he felt entitled to reduced time in jail, communicated to the women whom he violated that he still didn't fully understand what he did and that he wasn't really sorry.

Step Four: Apology

Making amends and accepting consequences open up the fourth step in this process, apologizing for the harm caused. I hope it will be clear by this point that a generic apology crafted by a publicist and posted on Instagram won't make the cut; rather, the focus here is on what the victim receives rather than what the perpetrator puts out. Even after a person has made "restitution of monetary debt, they are obliged to pacify [the person harmed] and to beg their forgiveness. Even if they only offended their fellow verbally, they must appease and implore until [the harmed party] forgives them."[38]

Notice the language being used here—to pacify, to appease. The focus is the mental and emotional state of the victim, not the boxes that a perpetrator needs to check in order to be let off the hook. Is the person who was hurt feeling better? Have they gotten what they need, emotionally, spiritually? If not, why not? Perhaps it's clear why amends happens first—what are you apologizing for, exactly, if the other person still hasn't been cared for, attended to? Action first. Words later.

An apology, here, does not consist of the words "I'm sorry," though that statement might be part of it. (It is certainly *not* "I'm sorry that you were hurt by this perfectly reasonable thing that I did.") And, as with making amends, a real apology is not aimed *at* the person who has been hurt, but rather is given in relationship with them. It requires vulnerability and empathetic listening; it demands a sincere offering of regret and sorrow for one's actions. It requires understanding when approaching a victim might harm them further and navigating that with sensitivity. The goal is not to do more harm, but to do work that is healing, repairing. This means that the victim's needs must be centered in the process, always. In subsequent chapters we'll explore some of the more complex questions around apologies and forgiveness—what to do if approaching the victim may in fact inflict trauma, what it means if the victim is dead and cannot forgive, what it means for the penitent if the victim is not willing or able to be appeased, and the nature and limits of forgiveness.

It is important to note again that, here, repentance and forgiveness are not as tightly intertwined as they are considered to be in contemporary culture. That is to say, from a Maimonidean perspective, repentance is about righting as much of the harm as can be done, and this involves knowing what parts of the process are out of one's hands.

The work of pacifying, appeasing, and begging forgiveness can feel fraught for some people. It may seem uncomfortable and scary, or embarrassing. It may feel guilt-inducing to own one's mistakes, selfishness, lack of impulse control, or cluelessness. And yet, the penitent person has already been on a profound journey by the time they arrive at this point. They have had to understand the harm caused, to acknowledge and seek to be accountable for it, to begin working toward deep transformation related to the issue in question, and to invest concretely in reparations. In this way, approaching the victim to try to appease and soothe the wounds one has inflicted may be a natural, organic next step. It may feel like the next obvious thing left to do. By now, the perpetrator's remorse might be so strong that the apology flows from an open heart seeking change. That is the hope.

Jacob Dunne was out drinking with friends when a fight broke out with another man, named James. Jacob got involved and threw a hard punch, and the resulting injury ultimately killed James. Jacob served time in jail. After he was released, his parole officer put him in touch with James's parents through a restorative justice program, and he began to understand what they had gone through. At first Jacob was "overwhelmed with guilt and shame," but he realized that he had an obligation to undertake the work of transformation. "I decided I had to move forward in a more positive way," he wrote.

The young man Jacob had been, the one who had punched James, had been expelled from two schools for skipping class and causing trouble and had assumed that he didn't have much of a future. After he began his process of repentance work, however, Jacob went back to school and, in his words, "succeeded far beyond what I believed I was capable of," becoming someone very different from the young man who had had no compunction about beating up a stranger. Two and a half years after the crime, Jacob met James's parents face-to-face. He wrote, "Opening the door into the room where both David and Joan were waiting was the hardest thing I've ever had to do in my life, but I knew how important it was that I looked them in the eye and told them how sorry I was."[39] Jacob's apology wasn't about checking off necessary boxes or seeking an outcome that would benefit him. It was a natural outgrowth of the repentance work he had been doing all along; he knew that sharing his genuine regret and sorrow was necessary for him and for James's parents, and it needed to be done.

Step Five: Making Different Choices

The work of repentance, all the way through, is the work of transformation. It's the work of facing down false stories and engaging with painful reality. It's the work of being open to seeing ourselves as we really are, of understanding that other people's needs and pain are at least as important—if not more so—than our own. It's about figuring out how to be the kind of person who sees others' suffering and takes responsibility for any role we might have in causing it. It's about ownership—owning who we have been and what we have done, and also owning the person that we are capable of becoming.

The critical fifth and last stage of this process is that the perpetrator must, when faced with the opportunity to cause similar harm in the future, make a better choice. This can happen only if they've done the deep work of understanding why the harm happened, stayed out of situations that would make the harm easy to perpetrate again, and reoriented themselves and their life in a totally different way. When these steps have been taken, the choice will happen naturally because the person making it is a changed person in the ways that matter.

Lindy West was used to being deluged by trolls on Twitter. She's a feminist writer, and much of her work has focused on embracing her body even if society didn't—on being unapologetically fat. And despite the frequency of abuse she received from men who did not like her or her articles, one day she logged on to find something extra hurtful—an abusive tweet from a troll masquerading as her recently deceased father. Someone had created an entire account based on him—a mocking variation of his name, a photograph of him, a mean bio, everything—apparently with the express purpose of upsetting West. The troll succeeded. She wrote a blog post about this particular troll and his impact, candidly sharing her feelings about seeing this while she was still grieving her father's death. But then she got an email:

> Hey Lindy, I don't know why or even when I started trolling you . . . I think my anger towards you stems from your happiness with your own being. It offended me because it served to highlight my unhappiness with my own self. I have emailed you through 2 other Gmail accounts just to send you idiotic insults. I apologize for that. I created the PaulWestDunzo@gmail.com account & Twitter account. (I have deleted both.)
>
> I can't say sorry enough. It was the lowest thing I had ever done. When you included it in your latest Jezebel article it finally hit me. There is a living, breathing human being who is reading this shit. I am attacking someone who never harmed me in any way. And for no reason whatsoever.
>
> I'm done being a troll. Again I apologize. I made a donation in memory to your dad. I wish you the best.[40]

So many elements of repentance can be found in this email: The confession of harm, including voluntary acknowledgment that he was behind more than one troll account and an introspective owning of why he made those choices. Beginning the process of change, by deleting the accounts and offering intentions to make different choices in the future. Amends, in the form of a $50 donation to the cancer center at which West's father was treated. An apology. And then, a year and a half later, there was reason to suspect that he was, in fact, making different choices.

West called him as part of an episode of *This American Life* on public radio.[41] They checked in on where he was then, and how he thought about the harm he had caused after some time had passed. In that conversation, he further acknowledged the misogyny that had motivated him—"You can't claim to be OK with women and then you go online and insult them. You know? Seek them out to harm them emotionally." He shared that the confession of harm had actually enabled him to free himself from the impulse that had led him to troll in the first place: "As a former troll, I never told a single living human being until now that I did this. So it's good, in a way, to get that off my chest. To get my secret life—my old life—I don't know. It just feels good to kind of exorcise these demons." He enrolled in graduate school and began teaching little kids. "Seeing how their feelings get hurt by their peers," he said, "on purpose or not, it derails them for the rest of the day. They'll have their head on their desk and refuse to talk. As I'm watching this happen, I can't help but think about the feelings that I hurt."[42] He told West that he no longer trolls, even when given the opportunity. She said that she believes him. He took step after step after step to become a person different from the one who made those original, toxic choices, and the result is an organic shift in perspective and action. He has, it seems, become different. He is no longer the person who stalked and harassed. He is still the same person in many respects—he is still, and always, himself—but he has changed, in profound and indelible ways. In ways that matter for him, and for everyone else he will ever encounter.

We can never undo what we have done. We can never go back in time. We write history with our decisions and our actions. But we also write history with our responses to those actions. We can leave the pain and the damage in our wake, unattended, or we can do the work of acknowledging and fixing, to whatever extent possible, the harm that we have caused. Repentance—*tshuvah*—is like the Japanese art of *kintsugi*, repairing broken pottery with gold. You can never unbreak what you have broken. But with the sincere and deep work of trans-formation, acts of repair have the potential to make something new.

We will look, in the chapters to come, at what this might look like, in concrete ways, when pain is caused in our personal relationships; in the public eye; in the institutions of which we are a part in our home, work, and recreational spheres; in our country; in the criminal justice system, and beyond. Whether the suffering is the result of a private domestic misunderstanding, a betrayal, a corporate decision, or even genocide, there are ways to face what's happened and to move forward along the path of repentance. As the early-nineteenth-century Hasidic teacher Rebbe Nahman of Breslov put it, "If you believe that you can damage, believe that you can fix. If you believe that you can harm, believe that you can heal."[43]

CHAPTER TWO

REPENTANCE IN PERSONAL RELATIONSHIPS; OR, WHY IS THIS SO HARD?

In theory, it all sounds simple enough: Own the pain you've caused, take steps to change, make amends, apologize, and don't do it again. But the reality is that each of these stages of repentance can be quite difficult, and each takes a great deal of inner work and personal resolve to do right—even with regard to some of the most everyday kinds of harm.

For example, not long ago, Christina served as the direct supervisor of Eva, who worked across the country; they'd meet in person a couple of times a year, but most of their work took place over the phone, in video chats, and on Google docs. Christina tended to make Google docs with a lot of color-coding; these spreadsheets would be shared among staff and strategic partners to help track project planning. One of the first times she used one of these documents at this organization, she was leading a video meeting and reviewing the plan with Eva and others.

About twenty minutes into the meeting, Christina had already gotten through most of the document when she made a comment about "the green versus the red parts," leading Eva to ask, "What do those refer to? I'm color-blind and can't tell those colors apart." Christina, focusing on keeping up the momentum of the meeting, said, "There is some color-coding, but it's not that important. Let's focus on next steps."

Years later, Christina still dwells on this moment—and similar infractions that followed in her work with Eva. She reflected to me:

> If anyone were to have suggested that I was mistreating, gaslighting, or disrespecting Eva, I would have convinced the observer that I was being as supportive as possible in the moment. Only now do I realize that I was publicly downplaying Eva's inability to scan and understand this group document. She was literally not seeing what everyone else saw—and, rather than my apologizing immediately or, at minimum offering to make it right in the future, I actually made it worse—in front of our entire team—by assuring her that the thing we could all literally see and she couldn't wasn't important. And, to be completely honest, this happened a few more times. I could never remember which colors she couldn't tell apart, and would get visibly annoyed when she reminded me.

From the perspective of now, she said, "I wish I could go back to that moment and apologize immediately. Now, almost three years later, it feels like too minor of an infraction to apologize about." We emailed back and forth about the incident. I asked why she felt that someone wouldn't want to hear an apology from a former boss who had mistreated them. (Assuming, of course, that this was part of the larger work of changed behavior—Christina herself was clear that she would be more careful to try to hear criticism in the future and to solicit regular feedback from people who reported to her.)

Christina first gave a few superficial excuses as to why she couldn't apologize—she had not maintained a relationship with Eva, Eva lived across the country, maybe if they ran into each other at a conference ... But as our discussion continued, we got deeper into what was really holding her back. She said, "I would also be concerned that she would see me as overemphasizing her color-blindness as an issue rather than the real issue, which is that I blew her off when she requested I change my behavior." And then, she said, "There is definitely some fear that if I were to tell her this, she would say, 'Well, yeah, that was annoying, but you know what *really* bothered me when you were my supervisor . . .'"

Owning the harm we have caused involves risk. And for many of us, it involves not a trivial amount of fear. It can be tempting to try to minimize the impact of our behavior or to justify it with *reasons* (there are always *reasons!*): "I was hurt." "I wasn't paying attention." "I didn't mean to." "I was told I had to." "I was being efficient." So many reasons. We all do this, at least some of the time. Or, as was the case with Christina—who, to her credit, owns the harm she caused and her choices and actions around that—it can be very tempting to come up with excuses to avoid undertaking the work, in whole or in part. But reasons don't address harm. And neither do excuses.

Addressing harm is possible only when we bravely face the gap between the story we tell about ourselves—the one in which we're the hero, fighting the good fight, doing our best, behaving responsibly and appropriately in every context—and the reality of our actions. We need to summon the courage to cross the bridge over that cognitively dissonant gulf and face who we are, who we have been—even if it threatens our story of ourselves. It's the only way we can even begin to undertake any possible repair of the harm we've done and become the kind of person who might do better next time. (And that, in my opinion, is what's truly heroic.)

As the psychotherapist Martha Crawford put it, "People don't want to lose anything. Mostly what people want is to go back, to put things back the way they were before as if they'd never broken anything, which is really different than finding your way forward, and allowing a failure to remake you and remodel you and reorganize how you see yourself."[1]

This work is challenging enough when facing the smaller failings in our lives—how much more difficult is it when our closest relationships or our professional reputation is at stake, or even the possibility of facing significant consequences? And yet this is the brave work we have to do. All of us. We are each, in a thousand different ways, both harmdoer and victim. Sometimes we are hurt. Sometimes we hurt others, whether intentionally or not. The path of repentance is one that can help us not only to repair what we have broken, to the fullest extent possible, but to grow in the process of doing so.

I won't, in this book, delve too deeply into the larger picture of Maimonides' philosophical thinking—where his writing on repentance fits into his vision of God, the cosmos, our purpose on earth, and so forth. Suffice to say that, on a basic level, his approach is about the things a person must do to become a better person—a *mensch*, as we would say in the Jewish world, a person of integrity and honor. In addition to their role in repairing harm, Maimonides regards the Laws of Repentance as a way to facilitate growth on a personal level, which also serves the larger culture—we all influence each other,[2] and we need more people who are good participants in the larger society so that it can become more healthy and whole.[3] Maimonides is adamant about this: We can all do the work of repentance and become better than we had been before we erred. A person who does harm is not irrevocably a sinner. Being someone who caused harm is not a fixed identity—or at least it does not have to be. We have free will, and we can always choose to clean up whatever mess we have made, to the fullest extent that we can, and change for the better.[4]

But that doesn't mean that it's not hard, painful work, or that the stakes of that work are not profoundly real. It's tempting to stay on the safe side of the bridge, where our self-conception, however incomplete, stays intact. It's easier to avoid risk. "Dear Prudence," the advice column in *Slate* magazine, featured a letter[5] by a man who was trying to decide how much information to disclose about his past as an abuser to his current boyfriend before they moved in together.

He wrote, "I was always kind of aware that I treated my boyfriends badly, but I didn't see it as a big deal. I'd just blame it on my violently abusive upbringing and act as though that excused everything I did." Even though he knew on some level that he was guilty of horrific behavior in his relationships, he spent years ignoring that awareness; he succeeded in justifying and minimizing his actions. We can have empathy for this—no doubt he had suffered greatly when he was young and, even as an adult, felt tremendous pain. We all hold the story of ourselves as the hero, and we can certainly imagine how important that story might have been to the letter writer, given his traumatic childhood. But we also can see how much damage he caused in his choice to stay on the comfortable side of the bridge.

One day, though, he was forced to face the damage he had been doing. He wrote, "I had a wakeup call last year when I got a message from an ex telling me he had been diagnosed with PTSD as a direct consequence of our relationship and asking me to help pay his therapy bills."

Sometimes people who do harmful things know that they're doing them while they're doing them, like the parent who loses their temper at their child, the employee who steals from the company, the nonprofit exec who hires a donor's grandchild instead of a more qualified candidate, the senator who votes against gun control in order to protect campaign donations from rifle industry lobbyists.

Sometimes the impetus to do repentance work can come from an accounting of the soul, as it's called in my tradition—the introspection that can help us face the ways in which we've missed the mark. Whether that introspection comes from beginning to sit meditation regularly or taking up another form of spiritual practice, hitting rock bottom with addiction, suffering hurt similar to the kind that we've caused, becoming more educated on issues when we had previously acted from places of harmful ignorance (as happened with Christina, whose respectful workplace training helped her understand what she had done to Eva), or from some other channel, sometimes we can begin to gain clarity, on our own or with help, about how our past actions have impacted others.

But sometimes—often, I'd suggest—understanding the full weight of our behavior doesn't happen until we have to face the harm we've caused directly. Whether that's because we see the consequences of our actions play out in real time, or because we receive rebuke, as the letter writer did, we're forced, finally, to see what we've done. Our letter writer would have happily remained oblivious to his behavior and its consequences if his ex had not contacted him and spelled it out in clear language. (We'll look more at the process of rebuke in the next chapter.)

Many times, when people are told that they have caused harm, a defensive, self-protective impulse kicks in. We often deny either our actions or their impact, particularly if we have caused great harm—or if we believe that *doing a harmful thing* is the same thing as *being a bad person*. If someone interprets the statement "You said something racist" to mean "You are an irredeemably racist person," they might well resist the critique, seeing it as a condemnation of their whole self. But walking the path of antiracism is riddled with mistakes and new learning; acknowledging the mistake of saying something racist does not mean we are irrevocably racist, doomed to this fate. It's rather the opposite, no? Doubling down and getting defensive makes it much more likely that you'll just keep doing the thing. If you can't face and work to repair your mistakes, you certainly won't learn from them.

This all-or-nothing mentality elides the fact that we are all imperfect people, that we all do things that cause harm, that we all have repair work to do—even if we mean well, even if we too have been hurt, even if, even if, even if. When we respond to someone offering us the gift of rebuke—and it is a gift—we have the opportunity to learn and grow and rectify our errors. Defensiveness, however, shuts out the possibility of attending to the pain we have caused. And we miss the chance to work on becoming the kind of person who does not cause pain in the future—not because we have been silenced or shamed, but because we care, because it matters, and because we don't want to be the kind of person who causes pain.

When the comedian Amy Poehler received a letter telling her that she had—unwittingly, but nonetheless viciously—mocked a disabled girl in a sketch on *Saturday Night Live*, she, as she told it,

> told everyone about it and asked everyone to say it wasn't my fault. I threw the note in the trash like it was evidence of a crime. I stomped around for a bit and then pretended it went away . . . I made a lot of noise because I felt bad about hurting someone's feelings and I didn't want to get quiet and really figure out how I felt. I was afraid to lie down and put my hand on my heart and hear the tiny voice inside me saying that I had screwed up.[6]

In a society that has oppression of certain people built into its structure, those who have any kind of privilege (white people, for example, or wealthy people, or men) say and do things that support the dominant power structures at least some of the time—intentionally or not, out of malice or out of ignorance, or out of a perspective poisoned by the normalization of ideas that are racist, ableist, transphobic, fatphobic. This sometimes applies even to those without a certain kind of privilege, as well—women are capable of making sexist choices, those struggling to get by can reinforce classism, gay people can say or do homophobic things, and so on.

Of course, it's impossible to regard these as individual behaviors that do not function inside an oppressive, interlocking set of systems. It is the presence of power that transforms prejudice into racism, that transforms bias into misogyny, and so forth. And, as the Black writer Brooke Obie puts it, within oppressive systems, single acts of oppression have "the power to not only destroy an individual, but put an entire group of people on notice about what harm awaits them and [to witness] the lack of accountability for their perpetrators. Harmdoers have to understand the full extent of the harm they're causing in order to get to repentance, reparation and hopefully radicalization"[7] for a more just society. Proper redress of damage committed with the context of systemic oppression must take into account that larger context and potentially more widespread impact.

So, as you know by now, the first step of repentance is understanding and acknowledging the harm that has been caused. The "Dear Prudence" letter writer, to his credit, did not react to the message from his ex as an opportunity to shut him down, deny his claims, or gaslight him—to manipulate his ex-boyfriend into questioning his conclusions about the relationship. He began to take responsibility: "I was chilled, and reading his descriptions of what I put him through made me realize I was abusive. I'd never physically hurt him, but I'd controlled his actions, isolated him, and even encouraged his eating disorder. I was, as another ex put it, a monster." He listened, he heard, and evidently he even consulted with a different ex about his own behavior as part of the effort to better understand both his actions and their impact. And he spelled it out in a letter that was, as he knew it might be, published in a national publication.

The steps of making amends and becoming transformed are revealed in the next sentences of the letter: "I paid his therapy bills and put myself in therapy for as long as I could afford it and am still currently in a great group for abusive men trying to change their behaviors. I've made a lot of progress but still have a long way to go." Paying therapy bills is good amends work. The letter writer can never undo what he did to this ex, but he can certainly do his part to help the ex recover from their relationship and move forward. And we see the letter writer's earnest endeavors to transform himself; he did therapeutic work and participates in a program designed to help people who have perpetrated this kind of harm to make different choices in the future. He doesn't indicate whether he apologized sincerely, both to the ex who contacted him and the second ex, the one who described him as a "monster," so that part of the process remains unclear.

But, even with all this excellent repentance work under his belt, our letter writer discovered that making profound and definitive change is actually really difficult. His letter continues, with his reason for writing in.

> The issue is my current boyfriend. We started dating eight months ago . . . We are now talking about moving in together (his lease expires soon), and I feel like I will be doing a terrible thing if I let him move in with me without fully disclosing my past, not least since I think my worst controlling behaviors came out when my last boyfriend moved in with me. He knows my last relationship ended badly, and I told him I didn't treat my ex well and that it was my fault but didn't go into any detail. He's never asked beyond that. What should I tell him? I desperately don't want to say to this wonderful, compassionate man, "By the way, my last boyfriend needed therapy after dealing with my psychological abuse and stalking tendencies. I'm really sorry about it, though!" because obviously he will leave me. But do I owe him this? Should I just not be in a relationship at all? I don't know what to do and sincerely want to behave better than I have in the past. I will take whatever advice you give me on this.

Up to this point, he has faced, courageously, some hard emotional truths about himself and responsibly taken up the financial obligation of covering all that therapy. Real, powerful work. And here, in his question, we see what is at stake for him in owning his actions and being accountable for them: how vulnerable he would make himself, how he might risk his current relationship, his larger fear of being forever without a romantic partner.

As you may remember from the last chapter, some of the demands of the deep work of transformation might include "crying out in tearful supplication, giving alms according to one's means, distancing oneself exceedingly from the thing causing the sin . . . to change one's identity and . . . conduct . . . and exiling oneself from the place of residence . . . because it leads them to submissiveness and to be meek and humble-spirited."[8] Exile from one's place of residence. Changes in one's identity and conduct. That is, pulling up anchors that might make it all too easy to repeat past behaviors.

Rabbi Menachem Meiri, a thirteenth-century commentator (known as "the Meiri" in Jewish circles), writes that "changing your identity" really means "overcoming anger, jealousy, hatred, competitiveness, unhealthy frivolity, greed, and pursuing luxury"[9]—traits that Maimonides explicitly says also require a process of repentance.[10] "Indeed," Maimonides writes, "these iniquities are more serious and difficult than those that involve action, because when a person is immersed in these things, it is harder to separate from them."[11] Immersed in them—like a fish that knows only the waters of anger, competitiveness, greed.

That image of immersion becomes even more powerful when we think back to the beginning of the letter: "I was always kind of aware that I treated my boyfriends badly, but I didn't see it as a big deal. I'd just blame it on my violently abusive upbringing and act as though that excused everything I did." This letter writer has been swimming in certain kinds of hardship and pain his entire life. We can only guess at the messages he received as a child about his worth and lovability, can only wonder whether or how those messages were transformed into anger, jealousy, hatred, competitiveness, or greed—some of them evinced in his own descriptions of his past behavior. Sometimes we are immersed in these traits because of our childhood, sometimes because of trauma, sometimes because of ongoing social oppression, sometimes for any one (or more) of a myriad of other reasons.

We all have at least some—if not all—of these destructive traits, in various amounts. They are, the Meiri asserts, the things that cause us to do harm in the first place. These tendencies don't tend to just vanish by themselves, of their own accord—they often remain entrenched unless we are willing to undertake risky, vulnerability-inducing work. They are part of our identity. Most of us would prefer to stay in situations in which we feel solid, powerful, and in charge; few of us enjoy feeling "meek and humble-spirited." But that's just the thing. Real repentance work puts real things at stake. We have to face all of the ways that we rationalize our choices, all the ways we let ourselves off the hook, all the ways that the very water in which we swim causes us to hurt others.

In order to change and become the kind of people who do not cause harm as we once did, we must take genuine risks. Because it is so easy—so profoundly easy—to slip into old paradigms, often without thinking, even when we want very badly to change, as our letter writer clearly did. As Daniel Lavery, writing as "Dear Prudence," noted, the letter writer's reluctance to tell his current partner about his past behavior is, in fact, an extension of that very same past behavior. Lavery said,

> This is another form of controlling behavior masquerading as vulnerability and fear: Your fantasy is that if you can control your boyfriend's access to information about your past behavior, you can guarantee you'll keep him. If you follow that instinct, it'll likely be the start of a slippery slope back into trying to control, isolate, and demoralize your partner.

The letter writer has taken some great strides on the path of repentance. But he's still not taken the radical measures needed to transform completely, to become the kind of person who does not cause the same harm the next time. It's easy to see how he might abuse his new partner—not because he consciously wants to hurt him, but because these old patterns are so painfully difficult to break—as shown by his reluctance to even share information about his past with his current boyfriend.

Lavery's advice about how and why to break these habits is spot on, in my opinion:

> I do think that you should tell him, not least because he has a vested interest (not to mention a right) to have that information before deciding whether to move in together or continue this relationship. You should also tell him because if you don't, you'll feel furtive, guilty, and shameful the moment he moves in, as if you're getting away with something you shouldn't be, and that will color the way you treat him and yourself. Worse, you'll grow paranoid and agitated worrying that he'll find out through some other means. If you don't tell him and the two of you move in together, it simply won't work. Your peace will vanish, a distance will spring up between the two of you, and your sense of having changed for the better over the past year will begin to slip away.
>
> … The goal should not be to bury it but to be open, honest, clear, and specific and to develop new behavior and healthy ways of dealing with fear, anger, and your desire to control others. If you sincerely want to behave better, then you'll have to make different decisions. That starts with what you say to your boyfriend right now and not deciding you know what's best for him without his knowledge or consent.

Real repentance, real transformation requires real vulnerability, real risk. There are no guarantees that our letter writer's relationship will survive this disclosure. But the alternative is no alternative—not if he wants to stop inflicting the same suffering again and again and again. And by arriving at the place where he had once caused harm and making different choices this time, our letter writer can become a true master of penitence, someone who is no longer the same as the person who had once done such grave damage.

I want to soften some of what we've been talking about. That is to say: Yes, the work of repentance is often described in terms that place heavy demands on the harmdoer (which is all of us, at different times, in different ways). But that doesn't mean that it can't also be gentle.

The reason to do repentance work is not because you are BAD BAD BAD until you DO THESE THINGS but because we should care about each other, about taking care of each other, about making sure we're all OK. Taking seriously that I might have hurt you—even inadvertently! even because I wasn't at my best!—is an act of love and care. It is an opportunity to open my heart wider than it has been, to let in more empathy, more curiosity about how my choices or knee-jerk reactions have impacted you, have impacted others. To care about others' perspectives. To let your experience matter, deeply, to me. To look at another person—or a community, or a team of people—and say: Where are you? What are you feeling and experiencing now, and how might I have (even unwittingly) brought you pain or difficulty? And to care about making that as right as I can.

It's an act of concern. And facing the harm that I caused is an act of profound optimism. It is a choice to grow, to learn, to become someone who is more open and empathetic.

It's also important to remember that sincere repentance work isn't the same as self-flagellation—in fact, the latter can become a convenient way to stay stuck in inaction. We probably all know at least one person who, when told they have done something harmful, will go deep into their *feelings* and their *reasons* and the ways they were acting out of their *pain*, and they feel *so bad* and they know that it's so *not OK* and on and on. And yet—they don't focus on the needs of the person they hurt, and they don't do the work to change.

It's also useful to note that accountability and punishment are not the same thing. (Sometimes being accountable involves facing significant consequences, to be sure, but they are two distinct concepts.) As Danielle Sered notes in her powerful book *Until We Reckon: Violence, Mass Incarceration, and a Road to Repair,* "Forms of punishment that do not include the human reckoning of accountability and the human grappling of remorse rely exclusively on extrinsic motivation—a threat from outside. One of the effects of accountability is to help foster people's intrinsic motivation, which manifests in part as remorse."[12] That is to say, we can think of punishment as coming only from the outside, and accountability as inviting or pushing people to do the work from within. Accountability can feel vulnerable, scary, and even painful, but it has integrity and allows us to move forward. It moves us out of avoidance, blame, and denial, and into the reality of what we've done—we finally face it bravely and begin to learn and grow from the experience. It's not always easy or comfortable, but it's crucially important—for us, for those we've hurt, and for anyone we meet in the future.

It can be tricky, of course, to know where the lines are—some people (many, I'd suggest) are apt to let themselves off the hook too early and don't regard the damage they've done with the appropriate level of seriousness. This is another common pitfall in repentance— not worrying enough about the person who has been hurt and too much about ourselves and our own desire to assuage our conscience or protect our reputation.

The work of repentance is, in many ways, the work of looking out- side ourselves, looking with an empathetic eye at what we have done, letting it matter to us, and trying earnestly to figure out how we can both meaningfully address it and ensure that it never happens again. This is, in some ways, an act of tenderness, of extending ourselves to care for others, of giving ourselves the time and attention we deserve to grow, of investing in our own learning and capacity to heal.

Because repentance is, I believe, in part, a kind of self-care. When we do the work, we give attention to our own broken places, our own reactionary impulses, our own careless ignorance. And it's a way of saying, "Hey, self, you need some attention. Let's give you some help becoming the kind of person you want to be."

What do you need? Some learning on the issue at hand? Therapy? Time to call your sponsor? Talking this through with a trusted friend? Other supports? Who and what else can help you cross the bridge between where you are now and where you want to be?

This process reminds us that the person or people we hurt matter, matter profoundly, and that we must give them all the attention and care and love and concern that we hope those who hurt us will extend our way. (But we can't wait on those who hurt us for us to begin our own work.)

If it helps, imagine a scenario in which the people who have hurt you come to you in exactly the way that would appease you best, make you feel most loved and cared for and seen—do that as a starting place, as you consider the people you have harmed. Which is not to say that what you need and what the person you hurt needs are the same thing—remember, this work demands that we ask where *they* are, to center *them*, not to impose our ideas of what we want onto them. But this exercise can help, at the beginning of a repentance journey. Open that heart a little more, find that place of concerned empathy.

You might also look to your internal compass to find the places where it feels there might be dissonance, disharmony, a sense of embarrassment or guilt because of choices you made, things you said or did. There's no need to beat yourself up—just notice them. They're there. It's OK. You are not bad; you are just a fallible human, like the rest of us. Then let yourself look with deeper curiosity at those places of dissonance: What happened? Why? What's that about? Who do you trust who can help you unpack what was going on? But start first with curiosity.

And then, after you've spent some time there, begin thinking about how your choices might have impacted other people. Don't assume you already know or can easily arrive at the answer. Instead, extend your empathetic curiosity to wonder how a certain situation might have felt from their perspective. This work is serious, to be sure, but it's not impossible. You can do it. Even now, just extend your empathetic curiosity, your love and care, a little more. As you do this—and as you continue, step by step, along the path of repentance, you will find that you are growing in the process, slowly crossing that bridge from who you have been, developing ever-greater capacity for love and care. Leveling up.

As Rabbi Abraham Joshua Heschel put it,

> Should we . . . despair because of being unable to retain perfect purity? We should, if perfection were our goal. However, we are not obliged to be perfect once and for all, but only to rise again and again beyond the level of the self. Perfection is divine, and to make it a goal of [humans] is to call on [human beings] to be divine. All we can do is try to wring our hearts clean in contrition . . . To be contrite at our failures is holier than to be complacent in perfection.[13]

One all-too-common pitfall along the path of repentance involves trying to do this work while still holding on to power and control in a situation. You can understand the temptation—it's a lot less emotionally risky to do so, and can be even less risky when situational or structural power is factored in, such as when the penitent has a higher professional status than the person they harmed or has significant social privileges that the person they hurt does not. There is, indeed, a danger in using a set procedure for something as internally and interpersonally profound as repentance. Once you know the steps, just checking them off, one by one, like items on a to-do list, might seem appealing. But without doing the deep inner work, the process may be an empty exercise. And the way to ensure that deep inner work is taking place is to focus on the needs of the person harmed, on the healing that might be done.

It's a tricky balance. Too much emphasis on the internal life of the perpetrator can get us mere feelings, maybe even some pithy words, without the concrete actions of repair and change. But there is also a danger of emphasizing the deeds themselves without true transformation.

Maimonides makes it pretty clear that both are required—internal work and external repair. But sometimes even people who know their *Mishneh Torah* can find themselves trying to fudge their way through the process.

When Rabbi Haviva Ner-David was a student, pursuing rabbinic ordination, she was tasked with organizing some lectures by visiting scholars. She extended an invitation to someone well-qualified to speak on the topic at hand, not knowing that there was bad blood— some unspecified history of enmity and unkind feelings—between a faculty member at her program and the speaker.

When Rabbi X, as she calls him in her memoir, *Dreaming Against the Current*, found out about the invitation, he called up Haviva (as she was not yet Rabbi Ner-David), screamed at her, and then hung up on her.

Haviva knew that Rabbi X had been wrong to yell at her like that—she truly had no way of knowing in advance that there were issues with the visiting lecturer. But she placed value on both the student-teacher relationship and on the healing of rifts, so, a week or so later, at the holiday of Purim, she sent the director a little basket of treats—as is customary—with a note explaining that she hadn't known of the situation between the two senior scholars and asking him to forgive her mistake. He did not respond.

She didn't hear anything from him about this for several years. Then, one day, on the eve of Yom Kippur—the Jewish Day of Atonement, the very end of the season of repentance—Rabbi X's administrative assistant invited her to his office. She went in, only to find three of the director's rabbinic colleagues standing there with him.

She was being ambushed.

Maimonides had written, "Even if they offended their neighbor only in words, they must appease [the injured party] and implore until they are forgiven. If [the injured party] refuses, they should bring a committee of three friends to implore and beg of them; if they still refuse, they should bring a second, even a third committee."[14]

So yes, technically, the writings of Maimonides (like the Talmud,[15] on which he's basing his ruling) say that a penitent should bring three witnesses to an apology. (Though, you'll note, the *Mishneh Torah* quote I just cited specifies that the penitent is first supposed to ask forgiveness in a one-on-one interaction, and only if that interaction is unsuccessful is a person supposed to return with backup. Rabbi X, here, went straight to assembling a committee.)

Look at all the verbs in these few short lines of Maimonides—to appease, to implore, to beg. The person who was hurt must be appeased. And if they are not appeased, the person who did harm must come back again, and again, to figure out what must happen to make it right—though as this case illustrates all too well, this text can be misused to bully the victim rather than care for them. And the language escalates a little bit, as well; the first thing that's supposed to happen is a sincere, private apology—with a focus on "appeasing" the hurt party. If the harmdoer is unsuccessful, they need to realize that they perhaps haven't attended well to the person who was hurt and must work harder, until the victim feels that they've gotten closure and healing. (We'll talk more about apologies, as well as forgiveness and its limits, in Chapter Seven.)

In my opinion, the real reason we're supposed to bring witnesses to a second or third attempt at an apology is about support or accountability. First, go try to clean this up yourself. But if that attempt doesn't go well, perhaps we need some trusted representatives of the community to help hold space, make sure the harmdoer is really doing what's needed in the interaction, maybe notice cues the victim is giving off that the harmdoer is missing that could be helpful in healing the wound. Or maybe those other parties can be there to have everyone's back and to help move a broken situation toward more wholeness, if that's possible. Perhaps their role is to be a go-between, bridging the gap between victim and harmdoer, asking the victim privately what they need, serving as an accountability team akin to what happens in restorative justice contexts (which we'll discuss in Chapter Six).[16]

Needless to say, this notion of bringing witnesses can easily be used in problematic ways, as it was for Rabbi Ner-David as a rabbinical student. She was set up, brought into an emotionally fraught situation without warning or consent, a student suddenly trapped in the office with someone who had positional power over her, and three of his colleagues—all of them senior to her in professional ranking, all people whose goodwill she'd need later in her career, and all men in a still all-too-patriarchal culture. From the very beginning of this encounter, which was supposed to effect healing, she—the aggrieved party—was made to feel pressured and coerced.

That's not how it's supposed to go.

So Haviva arrived at Rabbi X's office and found his colleagues standing there. Without any introduction or framing, he mumbled the word, one word.

"*Mechila*," he said to her. Forgiveness.[17]

She was taken aback. After the screaming and ignoring, he now decided to ambush her with a rabbinic court and demand her forgiveness? There was no confession of harm—not one that she heard, in any case—and she had no idea if he had learned anything or made any sincere personal changes. She didn't hear any regret in his voice. He simply instructed her to forgive him.

She looked at him.

"No," she said.

He repeated the word again. "*Mechila.*"

She refused him a second time, then a third time, and walked out.

Rabbi X's actions were not focused on repair. It was more like a paint-by-numbers repentance process. It sure didn't heal anything.

Even if Rabbi X had done sincere confession and transformation work—let's give him the benefit of the doubt that he tried to do these things, even if Rabbi Ner-David did not know that—he did not approach her privately, which ought to be the first step. And Maimonides is clear that the three asks before witnesses are meant to be a process: "If they still refuse, they should bring a second, even a third committee."[18] A second and third committee—different people, each time, not three questions asked in rapid succession. This implies, to my mind, that the penitent is being urged to think through what might have gone wrong in the first (and maybe second) attempt.

A process—one that unfolds over time, whether a week or a month or several years—enables the perpetrator to ask questions: Why didn't healing happen? In what way did I do this incorrectly? What wounds might be present? What power dynamics? What did the victim need that they didn't get? What was holding me back from giving those things? What kind of personal or emotional risk was I not taking? How might I have been replicating the same dynamics that caused the harm in the first place? How might I be playacting the work of repentance while actually staying on the safe side of the bridge? With whom can I safely examine the previous interaction or two, to better understand what went awry and to figure out how to initiate a better process next time?

Remembering that repentance is a process is important. People do not change easily. Sometimes when we're actively trying to change—quickly, dramatically—shifts don't happen at the cellular level in the way that they need to. Instant change is usually not true change. One thinks of the letter writer—even months of therapy and active efforts to grow weren't enough to stave off the temptation to conceal his abusive past from his new boyfriend. Our harmful actions generally come from some place of brokenness and dysfunction inside us; healing takes time for both perpetrator and victim, in different ways. Meditation and therapy and rehab and reading all the books in the world won't change us if we aren't willing to make serious changes in our environment, our habits, and our ways of being. Literally or metaphorically, we need to be willing to exile ourselves from who and how we have been. And it doesn't happen overnight.

Years later, Rabbi Ner-David remembered the incident and decided to contact Rabbi X. She wrote an email to him "expressing [her] feelings of having been emotionally abused by him and by his use of the Jewish religious legal system and ritual to absolve himself without doing the inner work."[19] She wasn't sure what, if anything, would happen. This time, though, she got an effusive reply. Since getting her email, he had done some real reflecting about the incident and finally understood why his original behavior and his attempts to railroad his student into forgiveness were so egregious. The two had a meaningful exchange and then, finally, each found catharsis and healing.[20]

He should have reached out to her. But I'm glad they finally found closure.

I believe that in almost every case, Maimonides' steps of repentance are the right ones to take. But at certain points, particularly around apologies and making amends, special thought and care are needed.

The Mishnah teaches that "for transgressions between a person and another, Yom Kippur [the Day of Atonement] does not effect atonement until [the one who caused harm] has pacified the other person."[21] Maimonides, in developing this idea, wrote that someone who harms another person "is never forgiven until they make restitution of what is owed and begs the forgiveness of the other person."[22] This is true in most cases, to be sure, but I suggest that some nuance is also essential if repentance is (as I believe Maimonides understands it to be, and as I certainly do) to be centered on care for, and preventing further harm to, the victim. So we must make sure to ask: What should we do when trying to apologize may cause more damage than healing?

In Judaism, we have a series of prohibitions against saying or doing something if it would hurt another person, and this can include apologies that might cause, rather than alleviate, pain. One example cited in the literature is about gossip—if a person gossiped about someone else, and the person who was the target of the gossip was unaware of this fact, *and* if it would hurt this person to be told that they were, in fact, the subject of this conversation, then the gossiper has no right to cause this person pain by asking for their forgiveness.[23] It seems clear to me that this idea would necessarily extend to other situations that might cause pain or trauma to the victim of harm.

A corner of the world that has been particularly thoughtful about this question is the Twelve-Step Program, a methodology for recovering from addiction. Pioneered by William Griffith Wilson (referred to in sobriety circles as Bill W.) in his founding of Alcoholics Anonymous, the program focuses on identifying and naming harm, making amends, and apologizing. Its work toward deep change is perhaps the contemporary framework of repentance closest to that of Maimonides. Certainly, the Twelve-Step Program has helped many, many people looking to transform their relationship to addiction. (Though, it should be noted, some of its core assumptions have been critiqued as problematic by those who claim that its focus on powerlessness and individualism can harm people with socially marginalized identities and deny structural injustices that shape many people's lives.[24] In the next chapters, we'll look at how the Maimonidean approach can help effect not only individual repentance but also address such change at the levels of culture, major institutions, and our nation as a whole.)

In any case, the twentieth- and twenty-first-century work of AA has, in some places, brought nuance that is simply not visible in Maimonides' twelfth-century law code. The complexity of making amends is one of those places. The ninth step of the Twelve-Step Program specifies that a penitent person should refrain from making direct amends "when to do so would injure them or others." There are times when going directly to the person harmed, for making apologies and amends, could cause more hurt than healing.

As my friend Ella—sober now for more than fifteen years—notes about this process,

In my opinion, [some] situations that are particularly tricky are the ones where the victim doesn't know about the harm. I was super flaky at one job but got away with it because my boss and I had different schedules. The company went belly up and was long gone by the time I was making amends. My sponsor and I discussed it and decided that no, it was not appropriate to reach out to this person and say "Hi. I feel bad about how I pulled the wool over your eyes." Ditto the friend who told of an ex showing up to make amends, "I'm sorry I never really loved you." In these particular cases, direct amends would be/were more harmful, however they may make the addict feel better about 'fessing up but don't actually right a situation. For me, the correct thing was to be scrupulous about my timekeeping at work (which later resulted in contacting a different former employer about a similar issue and offering to make up time by volunteering for the number of hours I estimated I had padded my timesheet with).[25]

There are ways to walk the path of repentance that don't add to the hurt already inflicted, and they need to be considered carefully. It's not unusual for the penitent to be tempted to focus on the closure or absolution they long for, rather than the needs of the victim. They might continue to apologize and bring up past harm even when the victim is ready to move on. They might insist on sharing information that an unwitting victim didn't have in order to clear their own conscience, even if it causes the listener unnecessary pain. The perpetrator might seek out a victim who would be upset or even traumatized to hear from them—sometimes persisting even after the victim has set a boundary. None of these things are signs of true repentance. These actions aim to alleviate the penitent's feelings of remorse rather than doing the work of true repair—that is, caring for the needs of the person or people harmed. Sometimes the penitent must understand that they won't get the catharsis they so badly want, and that the most loving gesture that they can offer the person they've hurt is to leave them alone and find a way to live with the lack of closure.

At the same time, the person attempting to repent also needs to check themself and their hesitation about not contacting the person to whom they owe amends. Is the hesitation really because reaching out would harm the person further? Or is it avoidance, born of a desire to save face, a reluctance to engage directly with someone who is hurt and possibly angry? Is it an attempt to let themself off the hook? Christina, whom we met at the beginning of this chapter, was reluctant to reach out to Eva, her direct report—she told herself at first that it was because too much time had passed, but when pressed more deeply, she found she was afraid of what the conversation might reveal. Now, it might be that, after some true weighing of the facts, reaching out to Eva might *not* be the best approach in this case, that it might cause more harm than healing. But Christina would never be able to get clarity about the right path forward until she acknowledged her own fears about the process.

Deciding the correct course of action must always hold the twin poles: the desire to be held fully accountable and care and concern for the needs of the victim. Certainly, we all, when we mess up, want to feel forgiven and absolved. But real repentance demands that we concentrate not on our own emotional gratification but rather on re-pairing, to the best of our abilities, the hole in the cosmos that we have created.

The next story illustrates a number of the dangers we've just dis-cussed—excessive adherence to only the formal aspects of repentance, hesitation to take full ownership of the harm caused, and most of all, a focus on the desire to unburden guilt rather than the needs of the victim.

This is about sexual assault, and it might be difficult for some read-ers. Consider this a trigger warning. The story was published online, in *Vice*, anonymously (presumably as a form of self-protection).[26]

A while ago, I got a phone call around 1 a.m. This is pretty typical for someone who is friends with comedians. It was an out-of-town area code, which is also typical. Then I heard the voice on the other end.

"Is this [my name]?" I shivered. I knew that voice.

"Yes."

"This is Brian. Do you remember me?"

Yes.

Let's pause here for a moment. Brian called her, without warning. No email or text to see if she would be open to a conversation, no consideration of how hearing from him out of the blue might impact her, whether she'd want to prepare herself in some way or have the opportunity to decline contact. And he called at 1 a.m.—he very well could have woken her up, disturbed her sleep, made it difficult for her to return to sleep, gotten her when she was disoriented and not thinking clearly. These are not choices that facilitate healing.

> Brian (I've changed his name for this story) proceeded to tell me why he was calling. He was an alcoholic. He was in a 12-step program. He told me he knew what he did to me was wrong—that it wasn't OK. But he never went into detail about what he did. So I'll explain: Brian used to be my friend. He was also my rapist.
>
> After his long diatribe about recovery, there was an awkward pause.
>
> "I hope it's OK that I called you."

Brian opened the conversation by focusing on himself, his own situation. He went on a "long diatribe" about his own needs, his own internal work. Again, this wasn't about her. He acknowledged that he had harmed her but did not explicitly name that harm. Did he understand, really, what she had suffered at his hands, and since? Did he really have any inkling of an understanding of how this affected her? This is why the confession of harm is so crucial—it forces the person who has done wrong to engage, explicitly, with their actions and the probable impact.

He seemed to understand that, in fact, it might not have been OK to call and force her to respond to him in real time. But rather than think about how to handle his desire to reach out, given that contact might not be welcome, he made the choice to do the thing that would most quickly relieve him of his own guilt.

What could he have done instead? Jaclyn Friedman, an author and activist with decades of work focusing on sexual violence and consent, advises, "I would say, if someone profoundly wanted to make amends, that they should first do a lot of checking in with themselves—and ideally a mental health professional, clergy, ethicist, etc.—about their own motives. And if after that they still think they're doing it to amend the harm they've done, and not to make themselves feel better, I would recommend a very indirect approach, heavy on, 'You will never hear from me again if you don't want to.'"[27] In this case, an email might have worked well. In it he could say that he would like to speak to her to apologize, but that he understands that this contact may not be welcome. If that is the case, she is welcome to block his contact information and make no response. He would have to live with the lack of closure; that's on him. In a different scenario, he could ask a mutual friend to inquire gently of her whether this contact would be welcome or not. Friedman clarifies this point: "There should be nothing that demonstrates the offender has information the victim didn't know they had. No tracking down their address and sending a letter. *Definitely* nothing sent to the victim's place of work. Which gets back to my original thought, which is: This is generally just not a good idea at all because the potential risk to the victim is so much greater than their potential reward."

Brian needed to understand that, given the nature of the trauma he inflicted, making amends indirectly may have been preferable. He could have done things like financially supporting survivor services, learning bystander intervention, pressuring local leaders and government representatives to address any backlog in the processing of sexual assault evidence-collection kits (often known as rape kits) and prosecuting offenders with more speed and efficiency. Friedman offers a caution about the manner in which those who have committed sexual assault might make amends indirectly: They should not have direct contact with survivors, for a host of important reasons connected to the survivors' well-being.

These are not the choices Brian made.

The story continues:

The words "It's OK" crept out of my mouth. It wasn't OK. But I felt frozen with fear. I'd fantasized about confronting Brian for years, but when the opportunity finally presented itself, I was shocked into silence. I didn't think his voice would affect me like this. I had to get him off the phone immediately.

"I hope you can forgive me."

"It's OK," I said again and hung up before he could say another word. My stomach was churning. I was so upset.

No, not upset. I was livid. I thought about what Brian had said. Yes, he was truly sorry—but for what, he didn't specify. He might not even remember. He didn't call me because he was sorry. He called me out of the obligation to apologize—step nine.

Worst of all: He was calm. Like he arrogantly expected to be forgiven.

Then I thought about what he said and realized I do not forgive him. Not at all.

I checked my phone. His number was saved. I was afraid that if I heard his voice I'd freeze up again, so I texted.

"I do not forgive you," I wrote.

"What you did was unforgivable. You raped me."

She continued, describing in graphic detail the actions Brian had taken the night of the assault and the impact they had on her. Brian had not been willing to do a proper accounting—a proper confession—and so he imposed on his victim the burden of explaining to him what he had done. He confronted her unawares, put her in a situation where she felt that she needed to say something, anything, to get him off the phone. This is not healing. This is not repair.

This may be a good time to emphasize, yet again, that the Maimonidean approach regards forgiveness and repentance as separate processes that may or may not intersect. The problem here is not that the author of this piece did not forgive Brian—she may, someday, and she may not; he may hear about it, though likely he will not; she is not obligated to share with him her feelings on the matter. Whether she ever does is independent of the question of whether he has done real, meaningful, important repentance work.

It's Brian's problem that he did not do this as he should have. We did not see full willingness to own the harm caused; we did not see care and concern for his victim or a meaningful making of amends and an apology. We don't know whether he has, in other ways, done deep work to become the kind of person who will not commit the same offense again, but we can make a guess, based on the evidence. In this exchange with his victim, he shows us that he's still the guy who is focused on his own interests and experience and regards his victim not as a whole person—one with needs and a perspective that matter profoundly—but rather as an object to be acted upon or apologized at. He is acting out the dynamics that enabled him to commit the assault in the first place. He's not listening. He's not interested in what will harm this woman and what will keep her safe.

Again, he could have done profound, painful, humbling work to understand what drove him to assault in the first place. He could have focused on teaching boys and men not to rape, on becoming an educator about consent, on taking an active part in dismantling rape culture and creating a world in which more survivors are believed and more perpetrators are held accountable. And if he had done that, he might have found himself more sincerely and fully on the path of repentance.

Greg grew up in the 1980s in a suburban part of a conservative red state. His milieu was parochial, one that supported and encouraged his homophobia. "I don't really remember how it started or what I learned, but I do remember making a comment in middle school about going gay bashing," he reflects. He's now "appalled and disgusted" to think that those words had ever come out of his mouth, but they did. As he moved into high school, he continued to refer to homosexuality as something that "just isn't normal."

He was in his early twenties when he got a phone call from his mother, who said, "Your brother has come out, and your father has disowned him." Greg's father suggested that his brother, Ryan, consider conversion therapy or look into "pills that you can take for that." The family fell apart, and the crisis forced Greg to try to understand what it means to be gay, both generally and from a religious point of view.

Over the past twenty years, both Greg and his father have grappled with the harm they caused Ryan. Ryan's father has apologized, knows he may never be forgiven for his statements and choices at such a critical moment, but he has worked to become a staunch supporter of Ryan both personally and professionally—even bankrolling some of Ryan's *very* queer, sometimes sexually explicit avant-garde photography. Things have improved between Ryan and his father so much that Ryan and his husband chose to shelter in place during the first part of the COVID-19 pandemic at his father's home.

And as for Greg—well, he knows that he too caused Ryan real pain all the years that he spouted homophobia, totally unaware of how his brother might hear and receive his derogatory statements, as well as when it took him time to make sense of how same-sex relationships might fit into his religious worldview. "We've had conversations," Greg said.

> I've tried to apologize for my actions, and my brother has said, "But you said it. The damage is done." It's a stab in the heart, but it's true. Other times we've cried together and hugged. My repentance doesn't erase what happened. Even if a wound heals, there's still a scar. And even if scars fade with time? There's still a scar.

Ryan concurred. "I was aware of Greg's homophobia before I was aware that I was gay," he told me. "I wish he and my father had the power to erase my trauma, but they can't."

But even so, Ryan said, Greg "is an entirely different person than he was then, with entirely different sensitivities. He's done a lot of growing and a lot of apologizing and we've talked through things as well as we ever could. And this growing is a continuous process for him."

Greg has repented and changed, and he makes different choices now.

A few years ago, he was in a job interview with a religious organization and told the hiring committee that his support of LGBTQIA+ people would impact some of his choices at work, if he were to serve in that role. (He got the job.) His kids have, for years, referred to Ryan's husband as "uncle," which he considers "a beautiful thing," and his family has long paused TV shows with married gay couples to talk about how of course two men can be married, like Uncle Ryan and Uncle Jim.

But more than that, Greg's teenage daughter recently came out as gay. And if Maimonides teaches that perfect repentance is arriving at the place of harm and making different choices, Greg has had the opportunity to rise to the occasion. He embraces and loves his daughter, exactly as she is, and swells with pride while telling me about the fact that she's taken on a leadership position in a local organization for LGBTQIA+ teens.

Greg is no longer the person that he was. And while he's right that he can never erase the pain he caused his brother, he has done the brave work of crossing that bridge to become someone else entirely—someone who is not only an ally of and advocate for LGBTQIA+ people and families, but someone whose skin is in the game.

As Ryan puts it, "He learned and grew. And that's what you hope for. Seeing someone be a better person is the best thing. For me, that's more important than the apology." Greg makes different choices because he is different now. And his family is so much more whole as a result.

CHAPTER THREE

HARM IN THE PUBLIC SQUARE; OR, ACCOUNTABLE TO WHOM?

We scroll past images of harm and abuse every day. An elderly Asian American woman is kicked and beaten while onlookers do nothing to intervene. A white woman screams, "Go back to your country!" at a family speaking Spanish in a restaurant. Another white woman tries to call the cops on a couple of Black six-year-olds with a lemonade stand. Yet another revelation is dropped about a powerful, famous sexual abuser supported by a team of people who knew what was happening all along.

Each day, it seems, we are exposed to at least one new story or video or other kind of evidence of human beings hurting one another, sometimes doing horrific damage, cases in which we are neither perpetrator nor victim. We, the witnesses, take in the harm, absorb it. Are impacted by it, to some degree, though not in the same way that the victim is. (Of course, we may be significantly more impacted if the harm targets or victimizes someone based on an identity or experience that we share.) Maybe it shapes the conversations we have online, or at work, or around the dinner table. Maybe it triggers places of deep trauma in our own lives. Maybe we ingest it and, without pausing to process what we've encountered, try to just go about our day.

When offenses are revealed in the public sphere—a video gone viral, a celebrity news item, a politician's misdeeds uncovered—what does the path to repentance demand? Does the perpetrator of harm have to account for the millions of eyes and ears taking in their actions, and if so, in what way? We, the witnesses, are not necessarily the direct recipients of hurt. But we're impacted. Our whole culture is.

In Chapter One, we discussed the Mishnah's teaching that a person who causes interpersonal harm must "appease their friend."[1] The Jerusalem Talmud—a collection of rabbinic teachings from the land of Israel, finalized by probably the early fifth century—teaches that "one who commits slander never gains forgiveness."[2] This position is codified in later Jewish law to mean that the injured party is not ever required to forgive.[3] (We'll discuss forgiveness in greater detail in Chapter Seven.) Why slander, of all things? The standard explanation for this is that the damage is irrevocable—there's no way for a penitent to correct their lie to all of the people who have heard it.[4] In other words, if damage spreads far and wide, and if it's likely that the perpetrator will be unable to ensure that every witness to or recipient of the harm hears the correction, it requires different consideration than other mistakes.

What would the Jerusalem Talmud have said about harm that wasn't technically slanderous, but that was traumatizing, toxic, potentially of a piece with larger systems of oppression, and could be recorded on a device carried around in everyone's pocket and reach millions of people with the push of a button? I wonder if we might consider this text as teaching a broader principle—that once harm is released to the public in a way that can't be contained or recalled, it necessarily carries a different kind of weight.

In the Laws of Repentance, Maimonides singles out a few transgressions as especially grievous; among them are those "leading the public to sin."[5] Think of the impact when an author, with millions of devoted followers, tweets something transphobic.[6] Or what might happen when a video is published, showing a beloved, championship-winning athlete committing a graphic, horrific act of domestic violence.[7] How about the widespread effect when a doctor publishes a deliberate scientific fraud, with falsified data, in order to incorrectly assert that there is a link between vaccines and autism?[8] Or the fact that 20 to 30 percent of mass shootings were "inspired by past events that were heavily publicized in the media"?[9] The ways that people share stories and proof of harm these days has the potential to increase both the number of people causing harm and the degree of harm caused, leading the public to sin.

Public acts of wrongdoing are older than the Jerusalem Talmud, but today we seem especially vulnerable to them. Damaging information, and disinformation, spreads faster and more widely than ever. Technology has continuously transformed communication—from the printing press to newspapers, radio, television, and now the Internet. On the one hand, in the online age it's even easier for information and disinformation, photographs and videos, to get around, and quickly. And on the other, it has enabled people to respond to it in a totally different way.

Though the Internet—run, as so much of it is, by a handful of immorally rich men in charge of corporate monopolies—is not exactly a democracy, it has democratized the public conversation to some degree. People who have not traditionally had access to the power or the platform of a major public media outlet now can be heard, and amplified, in a way that was heretofore inconceivable. And this has impacted not only the ways in which we witness and receive harm, but also how we respond to it and invite repentance.

The phenomena referred to in the popular media as "callout culture" and "cancel culture" are in fact, attempts—often by those without significant social influence—to address harm that has been caused.

Calling out is, in effect, the public rebuke, frequently done online, of someone who has caused or been perceived to have caused harm. As the white queer writer Sian Ferguson notes, "Calling people out allows us to hold people—particularly those who have privilege over us—accountable for their oppressive actions."[10] It directly confronts such a person and lets others know that this person should be held accountable. According to the Black feminist activist Loretta Ross, "Callouts are justified to challenge provocateurs who deliberately hurt others, or for powerful people beyond our reach." She says, "Effectively criticizing such people is an important tactic for achieving justice. But most public shaming is horizontal and done by those who believe they have greater integrity or more sophisticated analyses. They become the self-appointed guardians of political purity,"[11] sometimes on the basis of only scant information.[12] Indeed, callouts can be excessive and disproportionate to the harm caused; they sometimes lack sufficient data and context. Certainly, that's something that happens.

Yet the Black *New York Times* columnist Jamelle Bouie makes an important point:

> There have always been these negotiations in the public sphere about what people can say, and those have always been mediated by who has power and who doesn't ... What I think is novel about the present is that it's people who, under ordinary circumstances, may not necessarily have power. [Those] who, 20 years ago, may have been voiceless all of a sudden have a forum for voicing displeasure and that actually has weight on the institution.[13]

For both Bouie and Ross, the power dynamics matter—and much of what is derided by the media as "callout culture" is actually a process of trying to speak truth to power (to borrow a famous phrase from a 1955 Quaker pamphlet on nonviolence).[14]

Sometimes the callout-repentance loop doesn't have to be a particularly big drama. Not long ago on Twitter, I saw someone post, "I deleted a book recommendation thread because the authors I highlighted in it are, to my knowledge, all white. That was a mistake entirely of my own making (I did not consult with any of the authors or publishers in advance) and I recommit myself to doing better. I'm sorry."[15] What had happened was pretty obvious: He had tried to do a nice thing by recommending a bunch of books, and one or more people had pointed out that he—a white man with a certain amount of cultural influence—had amplified only white voices, thus perpetuating the historical and systemic exclusion of people of color in literary and theological spaces. So he deleted the thread—addressing the harm—and tweeted the apology, which perhaps serves as both public confession and apology; he didn't harm any person in particular to whom he owed restitution. (Perhaps posting a new thread highlighting thinkers of color or donating to an organization supporting marginalized authors might have been a good step toward making amends.) And he's made it clear that he's learned from the experience and will make different choices in the future. Presuming that he does do so, this act of public repentance seems genuine and complete.

Sometimes it takes time for a callout to have impact. The grassroots organizer Gwen Snyder shared such an experience on Twitter: "Not sure what happened to the person who was in my mentions all last year calling out my ableist language—I didn't take the agitation at first & didn't engage but she got me, it sunk in eventually. It's a good reminder that agitation is rarely wasted, even if it seems that way."[16] Learning can happen, if slowly, and sometimes responses on a public platform like Twitter are the only means for people who don't know each other to communicate on significant issues, and can be a way to impact others' thinking and actions.

And sometimes a callout can have an effect based on a single exchange. During the Black Lives Matter protests in the summer of 2020, the journalist Dorothy Tucker—who is Black—was speaking to a protester in Chicago, who was also Black. Tucker, as one viewer put it, "asked a question and the protester rejected the framing of the question and spoke at length about why the framing was problematic. As I listened I held my breath at how [Tucker] would respond to what could have been viewed as being chastised. [The] reporter took a beat and said, 'OK. Thank you. I accept that education.'"[17] While this example may not hit every last one of Maimonides' steps in repentance, it nonetheless fits right in with the framework. Tucker publicly acknowledged the validity of the protester's objection—it happened on the air, during the interview. With one clean, elegant sentence, she stated that she was wrong and committed to doing differently in the future—all the while modeling grace and professionalism. Thank you, I accept that education.

This concept of public rebuke differs from what is known as calling in, a concept that originated with the queer Viet/mixed-race disabled writer Ngọc Loan Trần.[18] This approach is meant as a gentler, often more private way of letting someone know that they have erred—"a practice of loving each other enough to allow each other to make mistakes," as Trần put it.[19]

Calling in generally is used in a specific context: where the harm was caused by someone with whom one shares preexisting ties or community. By contrast, calling out may happen in spaces or in contexts where people do not have any sort of connection or bond—it might happen across spaces rather than just within them. (It also happens within community spaces, to be sure.) This may also explain why calling out seems like a newer phenomenon; the Internet in particular has made speaking across communities much easier, and so the likelihood of harm being named visibly, in online spaces, is much higher. Needless to say, harmdoers are not entitled to police the reactions of those they harm by requiring or demanding gentleness. There are subtleties and nuances around what method of rebuke best suits a situation, as we'll see, and all harmdoers have the opportunity to receive rebuke with the same grace that the journalist Dorothy Tucker did.

That said, the practice of calling in closely mirrors much of the Jewish literature on rebuke, perhaps because it too presumes that all those involved have the shared bonds of a caring community. Maimonides uses Leviticus 19:17–18 as his source text: "You shall not hate your kinsfolk in your heart. Reprove your kin but incur no guilt because of them. You shall not take vengeance or bear a grudge against your countryfolk. Love your neighbor as yourself." Implied in the verses and suggested even more strongly in the Talmud,[20] and then the *Mishneh Torah*,[21] is the notion that the reason it's important to rebuke another person is for *the victim's own emotional and mental well-being.* "If one person commits a sin against another person," Maimonides says, "the one sinned against should not remain in silent hate against the sinner."[22] If someone harms you, you must tell them, so that you don't nurse the grudge or feel consumed by resentment. It is, in fact, a significant statement of care for the person who has been harmed—the focus is not on the perpetrator's spiritual development (though that, of course, is in the mix somewhere), but on the victim's emotional health.

Maimonides continues:

The one who sees their fellow stooping to sin or following an un-
righteous path is obliged to return them toward the good, and to
let them know that they are actually sinning against themselves in
pursuing wicked deeds ... The one who rebukes their fellow ... it is
essential that the rebuke be administered only between them both;
and they should speak to them calmly, employing soft language ... If
[the person doing harm] receives it attentively, it is well; if not, they
should rebuke a second, even a third time.[23]

Note the change in language here. For Maimonides, the victim of
harm should rebuke when (and only when, I'd argue) it might help
them let go of resentment. However, when someone "sees their fellow"—that is, when they witness harm as a bystander, their role is
different. The third party's work is about helping to "return [the harm-
doer] to the good," pushing them to grow in ways that might not be
comfortable and reminding them that the harm they're causing not
only potentially hurts others but is self-destructive. The victim's job
is to take care of their own spiritual health; the ally's job is to get into
the trenches with the perpetrator.

All of this, of course, presumes that there is a relationship and
shared values here. Maimonides is describing work done in community—a sense of connection and similar beliefs that may or may not
be applicable in the situations in which the need for rebuke arises
in our society today. For example, rebuke sometimes happens across
significant lines of difference, such as unequal levels of power or privilege, different degrees of personal familiarity, or many or few shared
assumptions.

Maimonides is adamant that, most of the time, public shaming is
not of value—rebuke should, when it can, happen privately:

A person is obliged to guard themselves against putting their fellow
to shame publicly, regardless of whether they be young or old; not
to call them by a name that would cause them to feel shame, or tell

them something that would cause them shame. However, all these refer to matters touching the relationship between two people; but if it
concerns heavenly matters, if the sinner does not repent after being
rebuked privately, they should be shamed publicly, and their sin should
be proclaimed, and harsh words should be used in their presence, and
they should be shamed and cursed until they repent and take up the
good path, just as all of the prophets in Israel did with the wicked.[24]

Many times this is true. Someone didn't know better! They're more
likely to listen and not get defensive if you speak to them privately.
Protecting the victim doesn't mean we run to injure the harmdoer!

And shame can powerfully inhibit repentance. The writer and researcher Brené Brown somewhat famously defines guilt as the feeling
that I *did* something bad and shame as the feeling that I *am* bad.[25] So
being told that we have—wittingly or not—hurt someone else in a
way that triggers our self-preservation instincts—"I'm not bad!"—may
make it harder for the soul-searching work of repentance to even begin.
(And, as discussed in the introduction, the tendency to conflate our
actions and our innermost self is particularly strong in our culture.)

Of course, as the psychotherapist Martha Crawford notes, we have
a lot of power to decide how to respond to rebuke, when we're on the
receiving end:

> We don't know how to process guilt in the way we used to, and so all
> we're left with is public censure and shame, which can just escalate.
> You know, you see people sometimes who really do seek forgiveness
> or simply accept responsibility. And you can feel it. You can hear
> it in their voice. Right? They didn't implode and collapse in shame
> and beg the world to rescue them from how terrible they feel about
> themselves. They didn't accuse anyone. They didn't become defensive.
> They said, "I'm a . . . human being and I failed this way, and I'm taking
> it seriously and it matters to me, and I'm going to learn something
> from it."[26]

No matter how rebuke is issued—even if it's delivered in ways
that feel unnecessarily harsh to us, for example, or inappropriately

publicly—we can choose to receive it with humility and to regard the opportunity to begin the work of repair as a gift. We have been given a chance to learn, to grow, and to become better. One rabbinic text teaches that, in fact, rebuke is a necessary part of any healthy process: "Rabbi Yosi ben Chanina said, 'A love without rebuke is no love.' Resh Lakish said, 'Rebuke leads to peace; a peace where there has been no rebuke is no peace.'"[27] Thank you, I accept that education.

Sometimes rebuke cannot, however, be limited to the private sphere. When harm happens in more public spaces, there is great value in making sure that both victims and witnesses hear someone name that harm. Important healing and learning can happen when, at a party, a bystander says, "That was a really racist comment" in front of all the people who heard it, the moment it's uttered, or in reply to the status update, right there on Facebook. The time taken to speak to someone privately may have an effect on both direct victims and other witnesses, causing them to feel that others at the party (or online, or elsewhere) agree with the racist statement, or that permission has been granted for others to make similar comments. Addressing the problem in the moment can be an act of care for those hurt by it and a prevention of harm with regard to other potential perpetrators.

This is not trivial. Public rebuke can encourage others to speak out against oppression and can help harmdoers to see that bystanders are willing to take action.[28] It is also true that an often useful principle—that "rebuke should happen in private"—can be weaponized to silence criticism or the naming of injustice. And let us not forget that disagreement is different from rebuke—someone expressing, in public, an idea that differs from yours is not the same thing as telling you that you have done something wrong. Our public discourse might be healthier if we were clearer on these distinctions and used them with more intentionality. In any case, there is a time and a place for public rebuke.

That said, people sometimes jump into public rebuke when a direct message or phone call, suggesting that someone course-correct, would be less shaming and easier for the harmdoer to hear. Calling in is preferable when it makes sense in context—and is also often more effective from the perspective of getting harm meaningfully addressed. This approach may, in many cases, be more likely to encourage someone onto the path to repentance. But so much depends on the situation, on power dynamics, on relationships or lack thereof, of the nature of the harm; those involved are certainly not always obligated to prioritize a harmdoer's comfort and growth. Our duty, first and foremost, must be to those harmed, and when we ourselves have caused harm, we have a moral obligation to hear rebuke with an open mind and heart, no matter how it is delivered. But sometimes we—the concerned third parties in community with those harming and harmed—can also offer enough love to help others grow from mistakes. There are a number of ways that we can foster the process of repentance work so that everyone can become the kinds of people who actively repair their own harm and work for a better world. We can be thoughtful about deciding when to use which tools.

Rebuke is a call to accountability. And there are ways in which the repentance process itself calls for us to be responsive—that is, it invites others to help in the process.

Maimonides writes that in any case of interpersonal sin, it is "praiseworthy" to confess the harm publicly—that it is "commendable for one to let the public know their iniquities."[29] This might be because there's a presumption that the harm itself took place in public, and thus the repair must have this public dimension as well.[30] Or it might be that, even if a penitent did a hurtful thing to another person in a more private space, the public confession and declaration of intent to do repentance work can be a powerful way to invite accountability. In some cases, this confession may feel quite freeing—liberation from worry that everyone will find out about the harm and the clarity that comes from facing what has been done. If you want to be different, you must not only face the truth of who you are but also make yourself vulnerable, expose your weaknesses, and ask for help in making different choices. Public confession demands being specific about the harm that you've caused. And it helps you become accountable not just to specific individuals but to the community at large.

The comedian Louis C.K. was named early on in the revelations that came when #MeToo broke. He was given, in a way, a form of public rebuke; in 2017 five women told the *New York Times* that he had masturbated in front of them without their consent or had forced them into situations where they felt obligated to give consent.[31]

His public statement in the wake of the story was imperfect, to be sure; his repeated focus on his perception of the women's "admiration" of him was condescending, debatable, and irrelevant. But he did at least acknowledge the harm that he had caused, writing, "These stories are true." He noted that he regretted his actions and would "step back and take a long time to listen."[32] As public confessions go, it was certainly one that evinced a real need for more *cheshbon hanefesh* (soul-searching), but promised at least an opening to the work of repentance. And it was an invitation to accountability—he shared his awareness that he had done wrong and made clear his intention to try to become different. It was not the completed work of repentance, but it was a signal to us, the public, that we should expect to see changes in his speech and behavior moving forward.

And in this case, public confession was necessary—Louis C.K.'s deeds had become public, and, as a well-known entertainer, his response would—for good or bad—impact the larger ongoing conversation about #MeToo, rape culture, and consent. Because the harm he caused was not private in nature, the repair work he was obligated to do needed a public dimension.

The grassroots organizer Gwen Snyder distinguishes between "personal" and "public" relationships. The former are like those described in the previous chapter—the intimate bonds between people in private space in the realm of work, family, friendship, and so forth. In contrast, "public relationships are what we hold in front of each other, with each other. Those public relationships are how we model the world we want to live in."[33] This is where the work of accountability for harm becomes particularly important. We have choices to make about how we respond to the harm we scroll past—whether we let it mean something, and whether we let it inform our choices and our actions moving forward.

When harm happens in public—or becomes public—everyone who learns about it has a choice to make about whether to condone the harm, rationalize it, ignore it, or let it mean something. Do we say that it's OK to confirm the appointment of a sexual abuser to high judicial office, knowing that this may affect how related cases might be adjudicated and discourage victims from coming forward in the future? Do we amplify the white teens who rip off, for clout and fame, the dances created by Black teens on social media without crediting them, knowing that doing so harms the young Black artists and reinforces a larger pattern of white appropriation of Black culture? What does it mean to stream the music of—and thus enrich—a once-beloved postpunk icon who has begun expressing increasingly fascist ideology on social media? Our responses to public acts of harm are statements about what kind of society we want to live in. When we call to the work of repentance those harmdoers whose actions have broad cultural impact, we are acting as allies to those who have been harmed.

So what happens if the person who was rebuked doesn't take up the opportunity to be accountable? What if they are unwilling to do the work of repentance and transformation? Our contemporary society has developed some tools to address that: highly imperfect tools with good intentions—attempts to speak to the obligations of unrepentant perpetrators of harm. "Cancel culture" is defined in the dictionary (because yes, the phrase has become so ubiquitous as to merit a dictionary definition) as "the popular practice of withdrawing support for (*canceling*) public figures and companies after they have done or said something considered objectionable or offensive."[34] That is, meeting problematic behavior with social consequences. And though the practice is sometimes criticized for punishing relatively minor infractions with harsh social ostracism, or offering no path toward repentance and repair, it doesn't always play out that way (in fact, it almost never does). Almost all of the people who have allegedly been "canceled" continue to thrive professionally, and almost all who were publicly condemned for their speech or actions had opportunities to show evidence of real repentance work but chose not to.

Snyder underscores how public rebuke is related to work for justice, using religious language to talk about the nature of harm (even though she herself does not identify as religious):

> When we sin publicly—meaning, damage the threads of caring commitment that bind us to society as a whole—the natural consequence should be alienation from that society. A just society is a system that values and supports those threads of implicit caring commitment, and rejects sin—meaning, again . . . behaviors that damage those threads . . .
>
> In public relationships, justice calls on us to model the world we wish to live in, and demand the same of others. That means demanding that the person who committed the sin and [who then] self-isolated participate in accountability and perform the bulk of the labor of repair. I believe we always offer that path to redemption, towards coming back into relationship rather than withering in isolation. But the bigger the sin, the more labor that repair and healing requires . . .
>
> And we need to always remember that public restoration can't demand the labor, participation, or forgiveness of the injured as part of the restorative process. Forgiveness is a personal act. It doesn't have a role in public relationship. Sin is something we can forgive in private relationship. In public relationship, we can only justly address sin by using accountability practices to heal and repair what was broken as best we can.[35]

In other words, it simply makes sense to distance someone who causes harm from the situation in which they cause harm. And that person should absolutely be invited to do the work of repair—which will, necessarily, be proportional to the force of the injury. Whether or not the harmdoer accepts the invitation to do this labor of healing and restoration is, however, up to them.

A just model of repentance in public spaces should allow for the fact that, sometimes, this work takes a while; someone might take two steps forward and one step back as part of a long process of growth and progress. And that part of accountability can involve reminding someone of their stated intentions, even if they're not able to live up to them very well quite yet.

In a loving, caring community, public confession can be a way of asking for help, knowing that the road might be long and rocky.

But all too often in our culture today, the public confession, sometimes written by a frazzled publicist and deployed by a public figure, is used as a get-out-of-jail-free card, as if the confession should suffice, without the work of repair or transformation, to bring this figure back into the fabric of society. And if this doesn't happen right away, the person might protest the lack of immediate forgiveness: "I SAID I was SORRY!" This is where, perhaps, our culture's overemphasis on forgiveness and underemphasis on repair can really hurt us. It invites someone who has caused damage to do more damage, without asking them to properly clean up their mess.

Evidently Louis C.K. had attempted, haltingly, to apologize to at least two of his victims before the *Times* story broke, but he did so without taking full responsibility for his actions. Instead, he dismissed his behavior as "a bad time in his life." Furthermore, he was unable to keep his acts of misconduct straight; when he called one of his accusers, he apologized for an entirely different situation than the one that involved her. He also told her that he used to "misread people," which she felt "implied she had done something to invite his behavior."[36]

Louis C.K.'s actions had serious consequences. The careers of each of the women he abused suffered as a result of his choices,[37] and at least two have had to scrub their social media accounts because of the severe harassment that came their way when they spoke out about what he did to them.[38] But no robust plan for restitution was forthcoming from the comedian. Amends, presumably organized with the victims' consent, might have included financial reparations made directly to them, donations to organizations that provide education on sexual and gender-related violence, or active efforts to bolster these women's work or to lift up women comedians in general. It's not as though there is only one correct approach. But he took no approach at all.

And personal transformation didn't happen, either. That "step[ping] back and take a long time to listen" turned out to be about nine months (not long, given the inner work needed). Then he began his return to the ego-stroking, power-filled limelight that made abuse so easy to perpetrate in the first place. He started with an unpublicized set at a comedy club,[39] and not long after that he went on a full-fledged comeback tour,[40] followed by the release of a comedy special on his website.[41] If the goal of repentance implied in his public statement had been made in earnest, we'd expect to see a shift in priorities, an investment of wealth or time in work protecting victims of assault and harassment, creating policies that would better prevent abuse, or doing entertainment work that centered women comedians or attempted to dismantle rape culture. Instead, Louis C.K. made another grab at fame and status, this time doubling down on his newfound identity as someone who causes harm.

His 2019 material included jokes about people with intellectual disabilities, survivors of school shootings, the enslavement of people of African descent, the Holocaust, Asian men, gender-nonconforming teenagers, and, yes, the victims of his own misconduct.[42] And his 2021 tour, the ironically titled *Sorry*, included fatphobic and transphobic jokes and bitter complaints about the social consequences that he experienced for his actions—comparing sheltering in place during the COVID pandemic to his own short-lived exile.[43] Again and again, he chose to "punch down"—making marginalized people (including his actual victims) the butt of his jokes, rather than "punching up" at those in power, as he once did, or reflecting meaningfully about his choices and the impact that they had.

His public confession might have seemed to be a step toward accountability, but his actions show that, well, he is unwilling or unable to do repair work. Instead of helping to mend the harm to his actual victims and the ripple effect caused when his abuse became part of a larger cultural narrative, he made the choice to pump more hate and intolerance into the world.

This is part of the reason why Gwen Snyder insists that alienation is a natural social consequence for those who refuse to do the work of repentance and repair. As she puts it,

> Accountability isn't about canceling, it's about healing. Like, sometimes people in our communities are so hurt by something that's

been done that we have to ask the perpetrator to leave, because those who have been hurt can't heal in their presence. In digital spaces, that can take the form of cancellation . . . [Certainly,] it can be as or more healing for impacted people when we see the person who caused the injury take ownership of the sin, acknowledge its impact, and do the labor of restoration . . . But when the injurer not only refuses to apologize but refuses even to admit to the reality of the injury, it starts to look a whole lot like they not only don't care, but are deliberately working to justify continuation of the behavior.[44]

Someone who refuses to be accountable for their actions not only leaves those first threads damaged, but also, without at least beginning to make an earnest effort to learn and grow, remains the same person who hurt others to begin with. And while that impulse to hurt might take different forms at different times, it's still there, causing harm, again and again and again.

At the ethical level, a path toward repentance is always available. It includes understanding the harm we have caused and doing the work of repair and restitution, to whatever degree possible. Louis C.K.—and so many like him—can always, on any day, make the choice to grow and become better. He might have already begun that work, and I just haven't heard about it. Or maybe he will begin it tomorrow, or in ten years, or never. I don't know.

We as a society are not obligated to reward harmdoers with more opportunities to gain wealth, prestige, power, celebrity. It's possible that some or all of Louis C.K.'s victims have forgiven him. But the impact he has had on our society as a whole has not been healed, and a streaming network ready to earn money certainly can't make decisions on behalf of his victims. In fact, given that part of doing repentance is accepting consequences of your actions, diminished professional prospects and alienation from a caring society for this comedian would be understandable and logical consequences of his choices, given that he refuses to do the work of caring. There are many talented people whose work should be elevated; we as a society can choose to invest in furthering their work instead—thereby sending a clear message that we do not tolerate sexual abusers or rape culture.

Derek Black is the son of a prominent white supremacist. His father, Don, is the founder of the neo-Nazi website *Stormfront* and has been a Grand Wizard in the Ku Klux Klan and a member of the American Nazi Party. Derek, whose godfather was the neo-Nazi politician David Duke,[45] was homeschooled in this toxic ideology and was instrumental in helping his father start *Stormfront*; by the time he was twenty-one, he was hosting a white-nationalist radio show that broadcasted five times a week on a local Florida radio station. Black wasn't just a white supremacist—he was something of a white supremacist celebrity.

Around the same time, he decided to study medieval history, so he enrolled at the New College of Florida—a liberal arts school—which was a four-hour drive from his parents' place. This was his first time away from home.

He kept quiet about his beliefs and his radio show, on which he would talk about white genocide and how Jews were destroying the world. At college he befriended a Peruvian student named Juan, began studying with an Orthodox Jew named Matthew, and started dating Rose, who was also Jewish. For a while he led a double life, but in April 2011, a student discovered who Black was and posted about him on the online campus forum. The reaction was swift and intense, as one might imagine. As his biographer, Eli Saslow, wrote, "The fallout was even worse than [Black had] feared. These were smart people whom he respected, and now they were calling him an 'idiot,' 'a hatemonger,' a 'Hitler' and a 'fraud.' He sat for hours . . . and watched as each new classmate joined in on the [online] thread, his relationships disappearing one message at a time."[46] His Jewish girlfriend, unsurprisingly, broke up with him.

By every measure, Black was canceled. But then something interesting happened.

In late September of that year, Matthew Stevenson—his Orthodox friend—and Stevenson's roommate Moshe Ash invited Black to Shabbat dinner. "Maybe he'd never spent time with a Jewish person before,"[47] Stevenson thought. Black had not had any other social invitations since being outed and ostracized, so he decided to go. And then those friends invited him back, again and again, Friday night after Friday night, as Black got to know them better and moved outside the perceptions and stereotypes that had enabled his ideology. A woman named Allison, whom he met through the dinners, began to challenge his thinking more explicitly in one-on-one conversations, pointing out the ways in which he was misusing statistics, arguing from faulty premises and the like. Little by little, his understanding began to change, and over the course of several years, he realized that "everything [he] believed about human nature was totally incorrect."

The next question he asked himself was "What do I do about this now?"[48] Despite his desire "to move to Bermuda and never be heard from again,"[49] Black understood that he needed to take responsibility.

Are oppressed people obligated to take upon themselves the labor of trying to reform those who have not only done damage, but done damage that affects them? Let me be clear: no. Stevenson and Ash's actions were extraordinary, as were those of the friend who then challenged his thinking more directly—and they did not come without social and emotional cost. Stevenson noted, "That's two years of every week, coming over, spending hours; receiving, frankly, a lot of criticism by other people on the campus—not everybody, but certain people on the campus, for what I was doing, including friends who had been coming to these dinners previously and stopped coming because they didn't want to be around Derek." Stevenson and Ash would also regularly question whether they were doing the right thing and whether it was worth it, whether it was impacting Black's thinking in any way.[50]

It should also be noted that this approach is not effective as a systemic tactic. As the journalist and activist Molly Conger, best known for chronicling government meetings in Charlottesville, Virginia after the deadly "Unite the Right" rally in August 2017, put it, "Deradicalization [away from extremist viewpoints] is possible, but it is a slow, difficult, and personal process . . . On a societal level, focusing on derad[icalization] as the primary tool to fight hate is like bailing out a flooded basement with a teacup while the storm still rages outside."[51]

So no, I am not, in sharing this story, suggesting that all marginalized people go out and try a DIY approach to converting those who spread hate; rather, I think it is important to look at Black's tale in light of the cultural narrative that suggests that once a person has crossed certain lines, they are irredeemable. His story shows that repentance—true, earnest, meaningful repentance—is possible even for people whom our culture might regard as beyond hope.

On July 15, 2013, Black sent an email to Mark Potok of the Southern Poverty Law Center, an organization dedicated to fighting hate and bigotry. Here is part of it:

> I have decided to write now after thinking about the implications extensively, and I am requesting that this letter be published and available to the public in full . . .
>
> I have resolved that it is in the best interests of everyone involved, directly or indirectly, to be honest about my slow but steady disaffiliation from white nationalism. Over the past few years, I have been disentangling myself from white nationalism. While the radio show I founded ended in January of 2013, over the course of the prior year I only appeared rarely and typically only when emergency required that someone fill in for the other hosts. I haven't posted on *Stormfront* in 2013, and I only posted once in all of 2012—then to give a report on my dad's media appearance. I am closing my *Stormfront* account . . .
>
> I acknowledge that things I have said as well as my actions have been harmful to people of color, people of Jewish descent, activists striving for opportunity and fairness for all, and others affected. It was not my intention then, and I will not contribute to any cause that perpetuates this harm in the future. Advocating for redress of the supposed oppression of whites in the West is by its nature damaging to all others because of the privileged position of white people in these societies. Promoting a victim complex for whites does not recognize the oppressed experiences of others not in the position of a white person in society, and that's what my efforts have done . . .
>
> Advocating for white nationalism means that we are opposed to minority attempts to elevate themselves to a position equal to our own. It is an advocacy that I cannot support, having grown past my bubble, talked to the people I affected, read more widely,

and realized the necessary impact my actions had on people I never wanted to harm.

I realize not all will instantly believe me, or may perceive this as a seemingly abrupt change when it has been instead a gradual awakening process. I understand that my words don't suddenly heal all wounds caused by my actions or my encouragement of others. Time, however, will demonstrate my full lack of involvement.[52]

It's a powerful example of the confession step. The full letter goes into greater detail about the various destructive impacts of white nationalist ideology and the harmful ways it perpetuates the systemic and individual oppression of those with less structural power, as well as how Black himself perpetuated that ideology. He clearly and explicitly owns the harm he has caused, requests that the confession be made public, and indicates that this letter is only the beginning of a longer process of making amends and undergoing change.

In fact, he even changed his name, swapping his middle and first names.[53] The reasons were a mix of the practical and the symbolic— the former, in order to make the things he had said about white nationalism harder to find through a Google search. (Of course, he is now famous for renouncing that path, but he wanted his future as a teacher not to be overshadowed by his past statements.) But that wasn't the only reason behind this decision. He told me that "renouncing white nationalism felt like such a huge life change that was otherwise not really reflected in the world, so I wanted to mark that. I wouldn't want to carry the metaphor too far, but I was definitely thinking about monks who change their name when they convert."[54]

Remember Maimonides? "Among the ways of repentance are [for the harmdoer] ... to change their name, as if saying: 'I am now another person, and not that person who perpetrated those misdeeds.'"[55]

He apologized personally to Matthew, Rose, and Juan, though he knew that, as he put it, "It's impossible to apologize to everyone I hurt ... because I basically hurt the entire world."[56]

His amends work involves both public activism and private scholarship, offering up his story as a case study that can be used in the fight against white supremacy. He has allowed his life—which, yes, is a story of redemption, but is also a humbling tale about the harm he caused—to be featured widely in the press to educate the public about the manifestations and harms of white supremacy in American society.[57] He is dedicating his life's work to combatting damaging thinking about race; currently at work on a PhD in medieval history, he is focusing in part on how race has been used to define and divide.

The transformation has happened. He is no longer the person he was. He is someone different now.

It's important, here, not to gloss over the ways in which his being cancelled was part of his repentance story. As Saslow noted, "There was civil resistance on campus by a group of students who organized a school shutdown and shut down the school and sort of cast Derek out and made it clear to him how awful and how hateful and how hurtful this ideology was."[58] If his peers' overwhelming response to learning about Black's white nationalism was to treat it as no big deal, if Black had not suffered meaningful social consequences of his actions and made him profoundly vulnerable, it's not clear how receptive Black would have been to the Shabbat dinners, or how they would have gone.

But, needless to say, that's not the core point—the people who separated themselves from him were not background actors on his path to enlightenment. These students, many of whom were BIPOC, or Jews, or both, made the choice to distance themselves from a deeply dangerous person. His cancellation was a boundary that they needed to set for their own safety, as a moral refusal to condone his words and choices, and as a step in creating a campus culture that felt more just to them.

As Black put it,

> I worry that my story gets told as a piece of evidence that the only way that you change people's minds is by having friendly conversations with them, when it's clearly not true. It's essential that you speak up loudly and condemn something that's wrong . . . The context for those [Shabbat dinner] conversations was that an entire community of people that I had gotten to know for a semester before they knew who I was, and who I respected, clearly had come to a very intelligent

conclusion that what I was advocating was morally wrong, was factually wrong. And I found that very unpleasant, and I didn't want to listen to it . . . I don't think I would have talked my way out of this belief system without those private conversations with somebody that I trusted, in the same way that I wouldn't have ever entered into those private conversations if I hadn't had a community who were very clear that what I was doing was threatening to their livelihood. But that reaction that they had made me say, "Clearly, it's happening; so, why?" And that's why I went into those conversations. And I really worry that someone will hear the fact that I had quiet conversations over two years and then, ultimately, abandoned my ideology, as proof that being loud and saying, "I condemn that in my society," is counterproductive, when I don't think it is. They're both essential.[59]

We need to set a very, very high bar for repentance, particularly for people whose social influence and reach—and harmful impact—are significant. It is possible for someone who has committed cancellation-worthy harms to come back from that, but they should not be automatically given a free pass because they (or their publicist) wrote a regret-filled statement of apology. But that doesn't mean that there's no way back. There is, and we know what to look for. If someone is truly, earnestly doing the work, we will be able to tell. Black is proof that it's possible, in both word and deed. Repentance is conceivable even for those who have caused profound harm with wide-ranging public implications. Derek Black can never completely undo the damage that he caused, but he has been trying to repair and heal, to whatever extent that he can, and to become someone different.

Black observed, "I said things that tried to energize racist ideas and get people to be more explicit about it. And then people who listened to that and who believed it—some of them committed horrible, violent acts. And what is my culpability and responsibility for how these things went out into the world? And they continue to bounce around in the world, and I can't take them back."[60] And yet, he has done, and will likely spend the rest of his life doing, what is in his power to make things as right as he can. That in itself should give us all hope for what is possible.

CHAPTER FOUR

INSTITUTIONAL OBLIGATIONS; OR, WHAT IS OWED

It was a special night: a gala, celebrating the fiftieth anniversary of SAR, the Salanter Akiba Riverdale Academy, a well-known Jewish private school in New York. Rabbi Yitz Greenberg, a widely respected scholar and one of SAR's founders, got up to pay tribute to the school. He spoke warmly about what it was like to realize the dream of creating a school that valued the uniqueness and holiness of each child, that taught respect and kindness, that nurtured children's curiosity and helped them grow. And then his tone changed. "Now, for all of this excellence, I must acknowledge a tragic failure," he said.

> This year, an investigation showed that four decades ago, we had a faculty member who abused students. He was not prevented from acting, and although he was sent away, he was not held accountable for his actions. We failed to protect those students, and we feel that pain. We feel their pain. This is a sin for which there is no forgiveness, and even if thousands more were treated right, this is no consolation. Each child is of infinite value, so this is an infinite failure. We have taken strong steps to ensure that this will never happen again, and we will keep this painful memory before us constantly to spur us to love more deeply, nurture more richly, to embrace life more fully for every student at SAR, today and tomorrow.[1]

Stanley Rosenfeld had served as a teacher and assistant principal at SAR for three years in the 1970s. He abused many students—at least twelve, though perhaps many more. At least two other members of the school faculty and administration were aware of this fact, and he had been accused of sexual abuse at two previous schools where he had been employed—a fact, as noted in one lawsuit, the school would have uncovered if an adequate background check had been performed.[2] SAR did nothing after being made aware of Rosenfeld's conduct; he left the school only after a complaint of abuse was reported to the principal.[3] The school even rehired him for a brief stint in 1986. Rabbi Joel Cohn, the assistant principal in 1986, asked Rabbi Yonah Fuld, the associate principal during Rosenfeld's tenure in the '70s and head principal by the mid-1980s—if there were any concerns regarding Rosenfeld. Cohn recalled that Fuld responded, "For a short amount of time, I think it's OK."[4]

In late 2017, a former student emailed the current principal of the school, informing him that he had been abused by Rosenfeld at SAR.[5] The school launched an internal investigation, which took most of a year. The administration then shared the report with school stakeholders, writing in an email, "We want to extend our most sincere gratitude to the individuals who came forward to report instances of inappropriate behavior and abuse . . . We remain heartbroken that our alumni suffered abuse while in SAR's care, but we also are deeply inspired by their bravery."[6]

But the investigation and email statement weren't enough. When Rabbi Greenberg was asked to speak at the gala, he made it clear that he would have to address the Rosenfeld case. He told the administration and the board that he would say something about it and that "it will have to be an acknowledgment of failure and guilt and taking responsibility."[7] His remarks at the gala were given with these stakeholders' blessing, though all parties involved knew that accepting blame, rather than evading it, might make them more vulnerable to lawsuits. As Greenberg put it, "The board understood that it had to take the penalty,"[8] that it had a moral obligation to make the school open to the possible legal and financial implications of owning the harm that it had caused. (And, in fact, around the same time, New York passed the Child Victims Act, which extended the statute of limitations for abuse claims, leading at least three former SAR students to sue the school for its neglect in addressing Rosenfeld's actions.)[9]

True repentance, as Greenberg put it, "has to acknowledge, not to fudge or make believe. There were things I could have said that would make the school look a little better, but this [speech] was really the *vidui* [that is, the confession step of repentance]. The school supported it, and was prepared to take responsibility." The confession, he said, is important as "the extra spur to create protocols to make sure this would not happen again."[10]

And yet, "this" did happen again—at least in the sense that someone dangerous made it onto staff. A mere nine months after Greenberg's speech, federal authorities arrested SAR's recently hired associate principal, Jonathan Skolnick, on child pornography charges. Here was an opportunity to arrive again at the place where harm had happened and make different choices. After the Rosenfeld investigation, staff had been rigorous in their screening procedures; an FBI special agent noted at the time of the arrest that there was nothing SAR could have done differently to prevent Skolnick's being hired, calling him "a wolf in sheep's clothing."[11] *The Riverdale Press* wrote, "The reaction of SAR leaders to Skolnick's arrest—immediately firing him and communicating with parents and students—is like night and day compared to how the Rosenfeld accusations were handled."[12]

This seems like a tidy case of institutional repentance, doesn't it? You can see the elements: public confession, apology, transformation, different choices made. Except that, particularly when institutions are involved, the work of repentance is almost never tidy.

I spoke with one of Rosenfeld's victims, who wondered why the investigation did not reach out directly to the obvious possible victim pool, male alumni who had been students in the seventh and eighth grades during Rosenfeld's tenure; they included the victim I spoke with and six others who had come forward to the press.[13] "How valid is this investigation if the target audience isn't being included?" he had asked at the time. He was livid that the school's cover letter for the corroborative investigative report thanked victims for coming forward but did not apologize for the institution's role in enabling Rosenfeld's abuse, which he felt was critical to the work of accountability. And then, when Greenberg did finally offer a public apology, he addressed a room full of people who were not, themselves, necessarily impacted by Rosenfeld. This victim said, "Part of me felt positive about what [Greenberg] said to the group that night, felt it was heartfelt, but in the end, I say to myself, 'Who is he speaking to? Was I there? Did they invite me to be there? Did they invite the other twelve victims?' They were speaking to a room full of people who knew nothing about this."[14] SAR apologized—but not directly to the people that the institution had hurt. And that, in the end, turned out to be a critical oversight. As Maimonides reminds us, the perpetrator of harm "must appease [the injured party]."[15]

"I still feel disappointed and angry," he told me.[16] He is suing the school.[17]

Most of us are part of many institutions—places of work, our own and/or our children's schools and universities, houses of worship, community organizations, sports leagues, social networking websites . . . the list goes on. And these institutions can and do perpetrate harm. Sometimes, that harm impacts us as individuals—as stakeholders or beneficiaries of those institutions, or as those excluded or hurt by them—and sometimes it can impact our local or national culture. An employee's harassment claim is shunted aside by the CEO, senior team, and board. A school system disproportionately disciplines and expels Black students. Companies hire suppliers that they know break local wage laws or even commit human rights abuses in order to keep prices down. An ostensibly feminist coworking space allows transphobic comments, by one member against another member, to stand. Websites permit antisemitic hashtags to trend, allow vaccine- and election-related disinformation to be deliberately spread, and refuse to ban white supremacists who repeatedly violate their terms of service. Some hospitals discriminate against disabled people when rationing care during a pandemic—undervaluing their lives, often with fatal consequences.

How can and should we think about the work of repentance when not a single person, but rather a body, made of many actors with different roles is causing harm? Some are decision-makers, some exert explicit or implicit pressure to make certain choices or simply produce results, and others are complicit, tasked by their bosses to carry out horrific, or unjust, or simply suboptimal orders. What does the work of repair look like then? What, if anything, changes when those who are in charge today weren't personally responsible for harm caused in the past? How can we as a society push the organizations that impact our own communities to do better? What are the obligations—and limits to the obligations—of the individuals in charge, and what does repentance look like when undertaken by an institution?

Shira Berkovits, an attorney, psychologist, and president of Sacred Spaces—an organization that helps institutions in the Jewish community "prevent and respond to sexual abuse and other abuses of power"—noted that many institutions struggle to acknowledge the harm they have caused. "When institutions are most likely to get it right," she says, "it's because they're doing [repentance work] when the harm is happening, and they have great humility—they're actively seeking advice and trying to get it right." In terms of reckoning with the past, she says, "I've seen language like, 'We will put [such-and-such measures] in place to prevent this in the future,' which is not the same as saying, 'We did wrong.'" Institutions often prefer proactive measures focused on moving forward, she says, over the earlier stages of Maimonides' repentance work—public acknowledgment of harm and making apologies and amends—because, all too often, they believe that "the last step makes you look good and the first steps make you look bad."[18] However, Dr. Berkovits noted, "It would be a provocative lens for organizations to understand that doing the first steps [in the work of repentance] makes you look good," that actually owning the harm caused can go a long, long way toward not only healing and repair, but also toward institutional responsibility and moral leadership.

Investigating the nature—and, perhaps, the limits—of institutional obligation offers a great opportunity to look at larger questions around amends and damages. Jewish law is pretty clear about liability for physical harm. For example, as mentioned in Chapter One,

Maimonides (as usual, taking from Talmudic sources) writes, "If a person wounded their fellow, [the harmdoer] must pay [the victim] compensation on five counts, namely: injury, pain, medical treatment, forced idleness, and humiliation."[19] Separate sums to compensate for the injury itself, for the pain suffered, to cover any costs of medical care, to reimburse lost income if the victim is unable to work because of their injury, and, on top of it all, compensation for the humiliation suffered—for emotional distress, as we'd call it today.

This is a pretty radical departure from how we think and talk about damages today, which is usually defined in practice as "the minimum an organization can do to get away with the harm they perpetrated and make the issue vanish." Jewish law is concerned not with covering the bare minimum, but with figuring out what might make the situation at least more just, if not wholly healed. Suffering matters. The impact on one's ability to work matters. Both emotional and physical pain matter. Therapy bills, paid time off during an investigation, the ability to work from home when things are fraught, flextime, a generous damages package, whatever is needed—not to make the problem go away, but to attend to the victim's needs during and after the harm. And this concerns only the making of amends. Maimonides, of course, presumes that all of the other parts of the repentance process will be present and accounted for. Making things better isn't (just) about financial compensation. It must be a holistic effort.

And that is, so often, where things go south in institutional reckonings. Guila Benchimol, a criminologist who consults with institutions on preventing and addressing harm and misconduct, told me,

> A lot of times you'll hear individuals say, "I wanted the company to do good but I couldn't get them to do it." What is prioritized is monetary value, not the human values of care, ethics, and compassion. The CEO and HR have to get on the same page about policy and procedure and about communicating these to employees—there's this disconnect.
>
> If you want good process, you have to bake it into your whole system. We spend so much money ensuring that we're doing everything legally, but do we employ ethics commissioners? What would it look

like to have someone on speed dial to help us think through how to respond to complaints or investigation findings in ways that were both legal and ethical? In ways that took into account not just the harm that was caused but its far-reaching impact—on individuals, on companies, on communities?

It's not about simply ticking off the boxes so we don't get sued. If we are seeking to truly do right and help heal, then maybe we should be asking, "How far should or could we go?" rather than "What is the least we need to do?" They may sound similar, but the answers to these different questions rest on the perspective they are coming from. The former is about moving toward another while the latter constrains us to think about ourselves.[20]

An institution is a body made up of donors, board members, senior staff, junior staff, and perhaps other stakeholders—members, students and alumni, users, patients, congregants, or others. When harm is caused by an institution, often multiple people make choices about how that claim reported to HR will be handled, or how to word the press release, or what to share (or not share) on the website. When we talk about institutional harm, we need to talk about the individual obligations of the actors who are making choices as well as the obligations of the institution as a whole. If the president of a large organization makes the choice to bury a complaint, the institution as a whole is liable—and continues to be liable if that president leaves to take a job elsewhere. (That former president would also be obligated to do the work of repentance and repair on an individual, ethical level, in my opinion—but their new organization would not be; the old organization that caused the harm would be, however.)

As we talk about institutional repentance, I should note that the question, "What boxes can an individual perpetrator tick off in order to make it possible for them to return to institutional or communal life?" is the wrong question. An individual who has done real repentance work will, naturally and organically, find their way back, because their remorse and efforts to repair will be so evident that victims will not be able to help but feel that this person is on their team. But the decision must come from those most impacted.

We can look at someone like Rabbi Yosef Blau, who, after understanding his complicity in enabling a sexual abuser to continue working as both a high school principal and youth group leader, has dedicated much of his life and work to helping Orthodox Jewish institutions implement policies that decrease the possibility of abuse and creating cultural change, such as believing survivors and refusing to tolerate abuse and abusers.[21] Or consider Kelly Clark, a recovering alcoholic who, after becoming a lawyer, was relentlessly transparent about the harm he had caused before sobriety, even posting a "letter of disclosure" on his firm's website and blogging about his path of transformation.[22] Clark became a champion for victims of abuse, representing survivors in lawsuits against institutions like the Catholic Church and the Boy Scouts of America—but he would take on cases only if he felt the process could be beneficial or healing to victims.[23] These are people who understood the pain they caused and worked tirelessly to do better—not to complete a checklist so that they could get prestigious institutional appointments back, but because doing the right thing mattered to them.

In a victim-centered approach, the question is not, "What are the things harmdoers must do so that an institutional ecosystem that depends on them can return to normal?" Rather, it asks: "What do victims need, and are they getting those things?" How would a victim feel about running into her abuser at a conference? Seeing him pop up on a video call? Navigating his presence at the gala dinner of the organization where she works? If he is doing the work of repentance, he would want, for example, not to retraumatize her by accident. He would want to give her time and space for healing. And if he had really shown remorse and a willingness to be different, perhaps she'd be OK with his presence at that conference, and she could tell him that herself. But certainly an anxious board member should not be the person to make this call, no matter how much the organization would like to make use of a former hero's talents or a prominent donor's money.

If they're really doing the work, it will be clear, eventually. Don't worry about that part, not now.[24]

That institutions are not individuals does not mean that people do not have relationships with them. Kelly Clark, the lawyer mentioned previously, represented many victims of child abuse in litigation against what he referred to as "institutions of trust." He noted that houses of worship, school districts, and organizations like the Boy Scouts derive great benefit from people's trust in the institution and its staff, and indeed, they "do not hesitate to claim credit when one of their employees or agents does something laudable."[25] The problem, of course, is when things go sideways. As Clark wryly noted, all too often, "as soon as it comes time to step up and clean up after one of their own, these organizations cut and run like so many thieves in the night."[26] All too often, when confronted with the news that the institution, or someone within it, caused harm, those with power in that institution choose to deny it, dismiss it, or otherwise refuse accountability. They worry about bad PR rather than caring for the needs of those who have been hurt.

This is a gross violation of the trust that people invest in, and that has been cultivated by, these institutions. An organization's response to harm caused while a person was in its employ or care—whether a workplace, hospital, university, house of worship, school or any other space—has a lasting impact on how easily or quickly victims heal from that harm and whether it causes them additional pain or even lasting trauma. The psychologist Jennifer Freyd's research has found that what she calls "institutional betrayal" can cause emotional, mental, and physical health problems and can have a significant impact on the development and intensity of post-traumatic distress.[27] Other studies have discovered that those who have experienced institutional betrayal have higher rates of PTSD and depression, and one found that such victims even had higher odds of attempting suicide.[28] Harm caused by an institution, either as a direct result of its own actions or its mismanagement of a stakeholder's need for care or redress, is real. As the psychologist Paul Mattiuzzi notes, attempting to rely on an institution for support carries inherent risks. "Filing a complaint carries the risk that you will be doubted, blamed, refused help and denied protection. People take that risk because they trust the institution to 'fix it and make it right.'"[29] When that trust is violated, the hurt can cut deep.

Of course, this is not the only possible path.

Dr. Benchimol notes, "People don't believe that an apology will make such a difference. They don't realize how far acknowledging and apologizing can go."[30] This reflects Kelly Clark's experience as well. He found that, despite the fact that our society often measures civil justice through verdicts and financial awards, acts of institutional repentance can be profoundly healing for survivors. Often he found that his clients sought an unequivocal apology—not a "letter of regret" or a letter "acknowledging the victim's pain and suffering" or the "wrongness of the abuse," but a full owning of the harm caused and an apology for it. (This may have been where SAR went wrong, in the story at the beginning of this chapter.) Clark also noted the power of symbolic gestures made by institutions—memorial gardens at Catholic institutions in tribute to survivors of child abuse, masses offered on behalf of victims, and the like, "especially in settings like the Catholic Church, where liturgical symbols are so important." Other amends he has found impactful have included paying for victims' counseling, policy changes, assurance that similar abuse will not happen moving forward, swift and just means of dealing with similar incidents that arise, and the maintaining of archives (files and other relevant evidence), accessible to the public as a form of public confession and to invite the kind of accountability that might prevent something similar in the future.[31]

In the end, true institutional repentance—like all repentance—requires not only addressing the harm immediately present, but also ensuring that when the opportunity arises to commit the same sin another time, it is possible, and perhaps much easier, to make a different choice.

Although the traditional approach to medical malpractice has been "deny and defend"—that is, pretend that nothing happened and defend doctors' choices and actions—more people are looking into other models. "You have to normalize honesty to create a culture of continuous improvement," said Richard Boothman, who launched a new approach to unanticipated patient outcomes at the University of Michigan Health System in 2001. "Litigating a case for three years and telling everybody, 'Don't talk about it and don't change anything,' is immoral and counterproductive," he added. "I don't serve my organization well by defending care we shouldn't be defending."

Instead, he pioneered an approach that focuses on "prompt investigation of errors whose findings are shared with victims, apology, and compensation for injuries."[32] And this transformation in approach to harm means that there's a different kind of responsiveness to patients; as Boothman says, "Today we're often at the bedside as soon as things happen."[33] Acknowledgment of harm, apology, reparations, and an investigation that can determine what went wrong, making it possible to avoid the same mistake in the future—that's it. That's the work of repentance, right there.

And not surprisingly, this repentant approach has other impacts. At the University of Michigan, for example, this policy of transparent investigation, apology, and compensation cut malpractice lawsuits in half.[34] Studies indicate that this tends to be the case generally—that when medical institutions are willing to apologize and otherwise take responsibility for clinical wrongdoing, it cuts the incidence of lawsuits by at least 43 percent.[35] But, as Boothman himself notes, "The whole point of this isn't to drop malpractice costs, it's to drive patient safety."[36] By changing how it responds to harm, the institution has transformed its capacity for preventing future harm. Each time the University of Michigan Health System figures out why something went wrong, they make it safer for the next patient coming through their doors. They set up systems to make it less likely that they will repeat the mistake. Each time the hospital arrives at a place where they once did harm but now do better, they perfectly enact Maimonides' path to repentance. This work is ongoing, but when institutional structures are set up to meaningfully address and improve upon past actions and choices, an organization can succeed. It is possible. What is needed is the institutional will to attempt it and the right processes for that particular organization.

This is why Dr. Freyd has turned her attention to what she calls "institutional courage"—that is to say, "an institution's commitment to seek the truth and engage in moral action, despite unpleasantness, risk, and short-term cost. It is a pledge to protect and care for those who depend on the institution. It is a compass oriented to the common good of individuals, institutions, and the world. It is a force that transforms institutions into more accountable, equitable, healthy places for everyone."[37]

What is particularly striking, and useful, about Freyd's definition is her insistence that institutional courage isn't "all or nothing": "I think of institutional courage as a complex, intersecting set of behaviors that are best classified on a spectrum. It's really not a black or white issue, so I wouldn't categorize a single institution as 'courageous' or 'not courageous.'"[38] It can be easy to get discouraged by the demands of repentance and repair, to say, "If we can't do it perfectly, we shouldn't bother at all." But in many cases, doing better is a continual process. It can be about taking the first courageous step and finding our way into the next. And about being willing to listen when we are called to do more than we already do.

Several years ago, Citigroup—the banking and financial services company—announced its intent to bring more women and more Black, Indigenous, and people of color workers into senior leadership positions[39]; in response, their shareholders pushed them to release data on their unadjusted or "raw" pay gaps. The company revealed that the median pay for women was about 71 percent of men's compensation and that the median pay for people of color was 93 percent that of white people. (They did not mention the median pay for women of color; note that the phrase "women and people of color" erases the specific experiences of Black women, Indigenous women, and other women of color, who tend, statistically, to be paid even less for the same work than white women or men of color—and certainly less than white men. Additionally, Citibank did not share information about employees who did not fit within the schema of binary gender.)[40] The bank also shared that, although women make up more than half of Citi's workforce, they comprise only 37 percent of senior positions between the levels of assistant VP to managing director. Several months later, Citi publicly pledged to increase the representation of women and people of color at senior levels by 40 and 8 percent, respectively, within the next several years, and to take steps to create policies related to the hiring and retention of these groups.[41]

As Citigroup's CEO, Michael Corbat, wrote, "Problem solving can't start without an honest assessment of where you are. Transparency breeds accountability."[42]

And yet, Corbat himself was criticized for the fact that his salary was 486 times the median employee pay at the bank, one of the most extreme ratios of this kind in banking.[43] He defended it, suggesting that this ratio factors in the lower salaries of employees in places like Mexico and the Philippines, where the cost of living is much lower. One does wonder, however, how much easier it might be to get to salary parity for his other workers by adopting a slightly less extreme executive-employee pay ratio. How much money might that free up? What other systems and structures could help the bank become the institution that it hopes to be? What means of redress might this bank create for employees looking to advance or wondering if they are being paid fairly? What things could Citigroup do to become, as the University of Michigan Health System did with regard to malpractice, unrecognizable as the company that had enabled those pay gaps in the first place?

The work of calling our institutions to do better is messy, and it's not linear. Some institutions will be more courageous and will do repentance work with more integrity, naturally, because it's the right thing to do. But in many cases, this process will be long and fraught with difficulty; improvements in one area may or may not lead to improvements in others. We must constantly urge the organizations and institutions in our lives along the path of repentance, to show them that the way forward can be an ongoing process of more transparency, more accountability, more amends, more taking ownership, more structural change, more focus on care for those who were harmed and those who are most impacted. The University of Michigan hospital gets better at caring for its patients each time it handles a situation involving malpractice. Because, crucially, it has set up the systems necessary to make that possible.

The question of who is liable, and for how long, and for what outcome comes into stark relief when we look at the ways in which universities have begun to grapple with their own legacies of slavery and racial discrimination. Without a doubt, it is easier to consider organizations' obligations to individuals who have been harmed in the recent past than to grapple with their participation in oppression that is both systemic and historical. Yet some institutions are beginning to find their ways—with varying degrees of success.

Jewish law makes it clear that if the person who caused harm did not pay appropriate damages and is now deceased, the victim can collect from the perpetrator's heirs,[44] and that remittance of debt applies even when both the party owed and the party who owes are deceased.[45] Obligations left unfulfilled in the life of a particular person must be fulfilled by descendants.

Some institutions have begun the work of public acknowledgment of harm. But I hope that, if you have read this far, you might feel a bit wary about a project that appears to begin and end with acknowledgment. (This does not mean that there are not scholars doing crucial work in most of these spaces; the question at hand is about how we evaluate *institutional* attempts at repentance for active participation in unspeakable horror.)

In 2006, Brown University published a report on the ways in which the school's founders benefited from the slave trade; they also created the Center for the Study of Slavery & Justice. In 2009, the College of William & Mary responded to calls from students and faculty to address its former ownership and exploitation of enslaved people, as well as its complicity in Jim Crow segregation; they did so by establishing The Lemon Project: A Journey of Reconciliation, which includes courses, symposia, and a paid summer research fellowship.[46] In 2017, Rutgers University renamed some of its buildings after its first Black alumni and Sojourner Truth, who was once herself enslaved by the university's first president.[47] The University of Virginia,[48] Harvard University,[49] and other schools have built memorials to the enslaved laborers forced to work on their campuses. Harvard[50] also undertook major projects focused on studying "the enduring legacy of slavery in our university community,"[51] and the University of Virginia has convened Universities Studying Slavery, a consortium of forty colleges and universities that support one another in addressing "historical and contemporary issues dealing with race and inequality in higher education and in university communities as well as the complicated legacies of slavery in modern American society."[52]

The political scientist Angelique Davis—who is Black—had a look at various legislative resolutions apologizing for slavery (and, sometimes, for subsequent centuries of injustice) and drew this conclusion:

> These apology resolutions . . . serve to covertly thwart reparations or other racial justice for [B]lack Americans while providing the illusion of substantive racial progress. Through general calls for reconciliation, recognition, and healing they give the appearance of recognizing the harm while doing nothing to repair it. In addition, they provide a form of "catch 22" for those who are the subject of these apologies as those who call for further action can be characterized as ungrateful whiners who are looking for a handout.[53]

Although university initiatives and legislative resolutions are not the exact same thing, one can see how in the former case, projects aimed at making apologies or acknowledgments might "covertly thwart reparations or other racial justice for [B]lack Americans while providing the illusion of substantive racial progress" and make it more difficult for those seeking more substantial redress to attain it.

Some institutions have begun to move into something a little more like making amends, though many of these efforts are not uncomplicated. In 2019, the Episcopalian Virginia Theological Seminary apologized for its exploitation of the labor of enslaved people and its participation in segregation. It also announced a $1.7 million fund for reparations to address "particular needs" of the descendants of those the seminary enslaved and to create programs that "promote justice and inclusion."[54] Georgetown University announced a plan to raise $400,000 a year for "community-based projects like health clinics and schools" to benefit the descendants of the people who were enslaved and sold by the school. And Princeton Theological Seminary (PTS) announced a $27.6 million endowment to fund a faculty position focusing on "the legacy of slavery and the African American experience," a review of existing curriculum for manifestations of bias and white privilege, and scholarships for descendants of enslaved people; the school also pledged to support underserved local communities. John White, the dean of students at PTS, framed this move very explicitly in the language of repentance. "The report [that Princeton Theological Seminary conducted on its relationship to slavery] was an act of confession," he said. "These responses are intended as acts of repentance that will lead to lasting impact within our community. This is the beginning of the process of repair that will be ongoing."[55]

But the fact that an institution makes a confession and, potentially, even also something like amends does not guarantee that harm is no longer being perpetrated. William & Mary's Lemon Project engages students to work in a volunteer capacity—so some of its efforts at reconciliation around the legacy of enslaving people is done by leveraging unpaid labor. Georgetown students criticized the school for a plan that "contain[ed] no clear criteria, accountability measures or transparency with regards to construction or implementation."[56] And for all of its memorials and commissions, Harvard, at the time of this writing, is still actively profiting from slavery. In the 1850s, a well-known white Harvard biologist, Louis Agassiz, commissioned daguerreotypes of Renty and Delia, an enslaved father and daughter, as part of his racist endeavor to prove that white people were biologically superior to people of African ancestry. Harvard—at least up to the date when this book was sent to the printer—still owns this photograph and continues to use, and profit from, images of Renty and Delia. Tamara Lanier, a Black descendant of "Papa Renty," as he was called in her family, sued Harvard for wrongful seizure of the photos and profiting from them. As the case made its way to the Massachusetts Supreme Judicial Court in late 2021, three dozen descendants of Agassiz signed a letter in support of Lanier, telling Harvard, "For too many years, we have ignored Agassiz's role in promoting a pseudoscientific justification for white supremacy . . . Now is the time to name, acknowledge and redress the harm done by Louis Agassiz."[57] The biologist's descendants sought to do the work of repentance, but Harvard, for all of its commissioned studies of "the enduring legacy of slavery in our university community," has not, at the time of this writing, shown full willingness to do the same. Even if this school does come around, that gap between the memorials and the lawsuits is real—and invites larger questions of who else has what kinds of gaps, and what kinds of institutional courage it will take to address them.

And beyond these types of failures, many related programs and initiatives do not fundamentally address the larger context of systemic racism. For example, Black students at Princeton Theological Seminary suggested not only that $27 million was insufficient for the nature and extent of the harm perpetrated by the institution, but that the school also had an obligation to address how it "used theology to justify the institution of slavery."[58]

Kelly Brown Douglas, a Black Womanist theologian and dean of the Episcopal Divinity School at Union Theological Seminary, wrote a searing piece on the limits of this approach—apology, study, even reparations—to repent for an organization's participation in such profound evil. For, she writes, "The fact of the matter is—after the money has been paid ... for scholarships and other programming—systems and structures are not disrupted. Life goes on as usual—and these institutions continue to benefit from the ongoing legacy of white supremacy to the detriment of people of color."[59] This is all the more stark, she suggests, when an institution can, if it was not built with the labor of enslaved Black people, declare itself exempt from examining the ways in which it is currently complicit in upholding white supremacy.

The Rev. Dr. Brown Douglas outlines three key aspects of the work a faith community must do toward reparations—which, she implies, is not merely about paying money (as the term has come to mean in common parlance) but about holistic work toward repair, insofar as it is possible. The work, she writes, demands truth-telling that "confronts the ways in which the past remains alive in the present," how white supremacy is upheld both philosophically and culturally in institutions. It demands fostering a moral identity by "confront[ing] what it means to be a beneficiary of white supremacy and its legacy," by working to eradicate white privilege and its manifestations, and by transforming institutions and spaces so that they can be "a sanctuary for all people."[60] In a church, she suggests, this last principle might look like interrogating choices in music, programming, curriculum, use of images, such as a Black Jesus, and bilingual worship. In the context of Jewish communal life—including the agencies and foundations that set our communal priorities—many of the same things would come into play, including, of course, addressing the ways in which majority white Jewish spaces perpetuate racism and majority Ashkenazi spaces perpetuate assumptions that exclude Sephardi and Mizrahi voices, traditions, and paradigms of living (what we call "Ashkenormativity"). In our synagogue spaces, we should center the voices and leadership of Jews of color and Jews from communities around the globe who can expand and at times perhaps even upend traditions and practices considered normative in American Jewish spaces. All of this work must happen with the leadership and active involvement of Jews of color and Sephardi and Mizrahi Jews (some of whom may of course identify as Jews of color), so that all choices are made with care, thoughtfulness, and cultural sensitivity. Though the Rev. Dr. Brown Douglas doesn't state this explicitly, I imagine she would agree that an organization ought to consider the racial and cultural makeup of its employees and stewards, especially senior staff and board leadership.

In other words: Remunerative amends aren't enough. There must be public confession, a profound looking inward, a grappling with the ways in which racism continues to manifest, and a whole-scale transformation that makes it impossible to continue repeating the harms of white supremacy. How the institution now looks, who runs it, the programs it offers, and how it offers them are now, at the DNA level, antiracist in approach and execution. It is impossible to keep repeating the same sins if you yourself are different. And this work is the responsibility of every institution that, in whatever way, upholds white supremacy (which is to say, all of them)—not only those that participated directly in the atrocity of slavery.

And that, in the end, is the work. To become different. Whether in a hospital or a bank, a school or a house of worship, a tech startup, a nonprofit, or any other institution, the work of repentance remains the same. How it might be executed, who must be thoughtfully brought on board, what it might look like when the transformation is complete may be wildly different from institution to institution, but the guiding principles remain the same. What must be found is the will, and the bravery, to move forward.

CHAPTER FIVE

ON NATIONAL REPENTANCE; OR, THE TRUTH AFTER ITS TELLING

The work broadens in scale, it gets wider and wider. Private individuals. Public figures. Institutions. But how far can repentance extend? And what are its limits? Can an entire nation repent? Does that even exist in the realm of the possible?

For Maimonides, the answer is yes. A collective body can—and should—repent for collective sins:

> All of the prophets commanded concerning repentance; the Jewish people will not be redeemed save by repentance. Indeed, the Torah long since assured us that in the end, at the close of the period of exile, the Jewish people will turn to repentance and be immediately redeemed.[1]

Here, Maimonides is referring to the end of the diasporic exile of the Jewish people that began with the destruction of the Second Temple by the Romans in 70 CE. While there's much that can be said about his understanding of redemption through the lens of today's world, what's relevant for our purposes is that he envisions the necessity of an entire people seeking repentance together. Though he does not speak about a nation-state (which did not exist in the twelfth century), he is nonetheless clear that repentance can, and sometimes must, be a large corporate project undertaken by a whole people, together.

The larger the scale of harm—and the greater the number of people obligated to address and repair that harm—the more critical the first step of repentance is. In every situation, minor or major, intimate or public, the work of confession forces the penitent to acknowledge fully the harm that they caused. It forces them to resist the temptation to minimize, to gloss over, to skip a reckoning with what actually happened, how it happened, by whom, and why, and to avoid rushing to fix it, whatever "it" might be. Critically, without the confession step, that "it"—the nature and scale of the harm—can be left undefined and ambiguous, even if "it" is often abundantly clear to the person or people harmed.

In the case of national repentance work, confession—the public telling of the truth, the naming of an atrocity committed by a government on its own people, or on others—becomes absolutely critical. It may be that some people were heretofore unaware of the nature or extent of the harm, and the confession serves to alert them. It may be that those who did indeed know wished to elide, ignore, or discount what happened, to deny their own complicity, or to focus on their own experiences of pain. It becomes much easier to avoid real accountability, to sidestep the critical work of change, if the full truth is not told. Addressing what happened may challenge those who hold power in critical, necessary, and just ways—and this may be exactly why those who are culpable wish to avoid the conversation altogether. Confession empowers those who were harmed by validating the truth of their experience, and also empowers those who were unaware, by giving them the opportunity to demand change from their government and society. Confession also, I believe, empowers those who caused harm, by inviting them to grapple with their actions and do the work of repentance, to whatever extent possible. How can we change if we don't know who we are? If we can't face what we have done?

This chapter will look first at two countries that have done real work in trying to face, reckon with, and repair horrific brutalities perpetrated by their governments. Then we'll examine some of the open questions and possibilities available to one country that has not yet deeply entered this work.

We know already that the steps of repentance are public confession, working on transformation, amends, apology, and making different choices in the future. And we know that the larger the body that perpetrated the harm, the more actors involved, the more complex this work will be. Can any nation do repentance work perfectly? I'm not sure; I have not seen it. Does that mean that there is no work that can be done? Of course not. And I continue to believe that Maimonides' repentance framework can be profoundly useful, here as elsewhere, in informing our attempts to name, address, and repair, to the fullest extent possible, profound—even unforgivable—harms.

This may be a good place to revisit my claim that issues of forgiveness are separate from those of repentance. "Can and should a nation repent?" is a very different question than "Can and should that nation be forgiven?" Repentance is an ethical and often practical necessity, even in cases where forgiveness is not merited or may not be extended. We will discuss forgiveness at length—including forgiveness for great atrocities—in Chapter Seven.

But first, let us examine national repentance and the critical role of speaking honestly about what has happened.

South Africa's Truth and Reconciliation Commission (TRC) is one of the most oft-cited examples of a country's attempt to uncover and name profound national harm. While certainly not the first commission of its sort—there have been more than forty truth commissions worldwide since the 1970s—the South African TRC is certainly one of the most well known. It was formed in 1995, just after the first election in South Africa's history in which citizens of all racial and ethnic backgrounds were permitted to participate.[2]

Several critical issues informed the shaping of the commission. The TRC was created in the belief that the country could not possibly move forward without facing the harms of apartheid, the brutal system of state-sponsored institutionalized racial separation and white supremacy that reigned in South Africa from 1948 until the early

1990s (and that existed, less formally, within the colonialist structure of government before 1948).³ Many of the horrors of the apartheid era—collective expulsion; forced migration; the bulldozing, gutting, or seizure of homes; restrictions on day-to-day movement; forced removal into rural ghettos; dispossession of land; coerced labor through administrative and statutory regulation; the banning of political parties and organizations and detention without trial—were sanctioned by the government.⁴ Some monstrosities were less "official" but were nonetheless perpetrated by government officials. They included arson, the bombing of the headquarters of the South African Council of Churches, firing on anti-apartheid protesters, massacres, torture, assassinations, the brutal murders of activists, and of course, creating conditions of terror, poverty, and desperation.

In negotiations to end this era, the old (apartheid) government demanded blanket amnesty as a condition of the peaceful transfer of power. And the TRC needed to encourage absolute truth-telling. As such, the TRC decided to make amnesty conditional on the telling of truth—a person wouldn't be eligible for a pardon unless they fully disclosed all of the facts surrounding any human rights abuses in which they played a part. The hearings were televised, so these disclosures would be public. One of the three committees of the TRC was tasked with formulating a system for reparations to, and rehabilitation of, those most harmed. This setup allowed, as the Indian-Ugandan scholar Mahmood Mamdani put it, "individual amnesty for the perpetrator, truth for the society, and reparations [from the government] for the victim."⁵

This did not mean that the TRC offered amnesty indiscriminately. Of the seven thousand people who applied for amnesty, only about 10 percent received it; others remained subject to both civil suits and prosecution by the state. But the policy of offering amnesty in exchange for truth was not uncontroversial. The survivors of several activists murdered by the apartheid government filed a lawsuit, claiming that the TRC's amnesty clauses infringed on their rights to pursue justice through the court system, but they were not successful.⁶ Ntsiki Biko, widow of the murdered Xhosa activist Steve Biko, was one of the plaintiffs. When one of the police officers involved with her husband's death testified to the Amnesty Committee of the TRC, she told journalists, "His testimony is nothing new. I think he is lying more than he did at the inquest. I have been saying this all along—they are going to lie even more so they get amnesty. I feel bad."[7] In the end, the police involved in her husband's case were denied amnesty, but four years later the minister of justice declined to prosecute them due to the time elapsed since Biko's murder in 1977 and, he claimed, insufficient evidence.

Those who supported the decision to make amnesty conditional on truth-telling argued that doing so enabled the country to undergo a process that would have been impossible otherwise, and many believe that the concessions offered around amnesty helped prevent civil war.[8] Structuring the process as they did also provided the government with useful testimony: Lower-ranking perpetrators were given amnesty in exchange for testimony that included identifying those higher up who issued unlawful or unjust orders.

The hearings were meant to be an opportunity for a certain kind of healing that might not have been possible had the TRC chosen more conventional models of punitive justice. As the white American legal scholar Martha Minow notes, unlike the prosecution of human rights violations in a court setting—such as the Nuremberg trials—this opportunity for victims to hear and tell the truth "without interruption or skepticism" could be crucial for survivors of trauma. Furthermore, she suggests, it allowed for the possibility of a "coherent, if complex, narrative about the entire nation's trauma, and the multiple sources and expressions of its violence."[9]

And, in fact, this aspect of the commission illuminates something important about the public confession stage of repentance. For, as Pumla Gobodo-Madikizela, a Black South African psychologist serving on the TRC's human rights committee, put it, hearing the full truth about the harms committed is a way of telling victims and survivors, "You are right, you were damaged, and it was wrong."[10]

So often when harm is committed—on the individual, institutional or national level—there is a desire by perpetrators to minimize, to mitigate, to downplay. To gaslight the victim. Public confession invites the perpetrator to accountability—but it also, crucially, validates the victim's experience. And it can provide the victim necessary information—for example, the TRC process enabled the families of murder victims to obtain critical knowledge about what had happened to their loved ones, allowing them to grieve and obtain closure. And in some cases, they were able to give a loved one a proper burial.

For Archbishop Desmond Tutu, the activist and theologian of mixed Xhosa and Motswana heritage and the TRC's chairman, a critical piece of this airing of the truth was to ensure that every member of South African society—particularly those who benefited from apartheid by virtue of their whiteness—could be clear on what had happened, and would be neither ignorant nor feign ignorance. By televising the hearings, he would ensure that everyone understood: "This is the horror that was apartheid. And those who supported the system must know what they supported. Those who claimed they did not know cannot very well say so now. They know."[11]

For Archbishop Tutu, the possibility of repentance was a critical part of the commission's work and the society he hoped it would engender. As he put it, using the language of his Christian faith, "Those who committed the most ghastly [crimes] have the capacity to be different. They have the capacity to be saved. If you become deterministic and say, 'Once a perpetrator of evil, always a perpetrator of evil,' then let us shut up shop."[12] But as he understood it, this repentance work should not be limited to those confessing to profound brutalities; it had to encompass all recipients of economic and social privilege. He suggested that the white South Africans who were, to whatever degree, previously ignorant of some of the evils of apartheid were very much "the ones who ought to be saying, 'We benefited from an unjust system, what can we do to show that we have contrition?'"[13] He believed that the TRC could begin the process of widespread, national repentance, which could foster the changes the country so badly needed.

This work was meant to include a program of government reparations to make amends for victims' suffering, but the effort proved to be deeply fraught. In the end, the TRC determined that only those victims who testified about their experiences would be eligible for individual financial compensation. This likely increased the number of testimonies, but it meant that many people harmed by apartheid—whether in specific or systemic ways—did not receive any official reparations. Furthermore, not even the officially designated recipients received the full amount they were due. The committee had recommended that each victim or family that had testified—about twenty-one thousand people—receive a sum of roughly $3,500 each year for six years, paid for by taxes on both the public and the corporations that were unjustly enriched by apartheid. But instead—after considerable delays—the South African government made a much more modest one-time payment.[14] The community reparations programs proposed by the TRC to uplift Black communities specifically were eventually built out by the government as part of broader development programs meant to impact all South Africans—thus diluting both the moral and practical impact as a reparative measure after apartheid.[15] The commission had also recommended a wealth tax to generate revenue from those who had benefited financially from apartheid, but the government never implemented it.[16]

The TRC's choice to treat apartheid as a discrete harm with individual victims, rather than a mass oppression perpetrated by the state against a critical percentage of its population was considered by many to be a major failure; something that failed to help facilitate reconciliation on a widespread social level, despite Tutu's hopes to the contrary.[17] So many of those impacted were not named as victims, and their needs and concerns were not addressed.[18] Furthermore, eliding the systemic nature of the harm also meant that those who benefited from apartheid could ignore the ways in which their privilege and actions had contributed, and may still contribute now, to inequality and injustice in South African society.[19]

There were other problems with implementation as well. Not everyone with a grievance was heard; few of the perpetrators who were denied amnesty were prosecuted for their crimes; post-TRC South Africa did not become the bastion of justice and equality that so many had hoped for. Though more Black South Africans were able to move into the middle class with the lifting of apartheid's economic sanctions, the country's white population nonetheless disproportionately benefited from the post-sanctions increase in the GDP. Particularly outside the country's major cities, significant racial disparities in both income and opportunity remained.[20]

Eugene Baron, a Black South African theology professor and minister, argued that one obstacle to more reconciliation across society was the fact that the TRC demanded truth, but not repentance, from those to whom it granted amnesty.[21] One can certainly question whether or not this would have been strategic or effective—after all, it is easy for someone seeking amnesty to recite apologetic words without doing the real internal work of repentance. But, Baron argued, the TRC's emphasis on forgiveness and reconciliation without demanding repentance from the perpetrators of atrocity implicitly pressured Black South Africans to forgive unrepentant perpetrators for the great harm that they did. He also suggested that perpetrators should have been obligated to take part in the work of making amends, to have "active involvement in the reparations and the healing of the wrongs committed" by contributing financially or by some other means to their victims or by donating to the TRC's pool of reparation funds. And, most of all, he was concerned that the process didn't help perpetrators unpack their crimes from a moral standpoint, to face the depth of their breaches of ethics. Such moral understanding, he believes, could impact their attitude toward their past actions and open the door to transformation. Sounding not unlike Maimonides, he wrote, "This change of heart needs to materialise through the future actions of the perpetrator."[22]

This repentance did not happen, and neither did the profound, and profoundly hoped for, social transformation. Archbishop Emeritus Tutu reflected in the South African *Mail & Guardian* in 2014, "Today, as we reflect on the commission's contribution to reweaving the fabric of our society, we do so . . . against a backdrop of a hopelessly inequitable country."[23] He lamented his country's widespread social violence, especially against women and children, its gross economic inequality, failing education system, corruption, and government excess. The reason, he argued, is the TRC's "unfinished business":

The level of reparation recommended by the commission was not enacted; the proposal on a once-off wealth tax as a mechanism to effect the transfer of resources was ignored, and those who were declined amnesty were not prosecuted . . . The tardy and limited payments of reparations to victims of human rights violations eroded the very dignity that the commission sought to build.

The commission played a magnificent role in facilitating the telling of the story of the true horrors of apartheid. I believe truth is central to any healing process because in order to forgive, one needs to know whom one is forgiving, and why.

But healing is a process. How we deal with the truth after its telling defines the success of the process. And this is where we have fallen tragically short. By choosing not to follow through on the commission's recommendations, government not only compromised the commission's contribution to the process, but the very process itself.[24]

Telling the truth—as Maimonides would frame it, confession—is a critical first step for every nation that seeks to address the harm that it has caused. But without the other pieces of the puzzle—the reparations, the apology, and the work to become different in deep, systemic ways, to set up structures that necessarily create a new kind of reality—it is not enough.

We must also find meaningful ways to deal with the truth after its telling.

Remembering, once again, that doing the work of repentance presumes neither forgiveness nor atonement, it is nonetheless worth asking about the obligations of repentance if the victim is not present, if the victim has died, if the victim has been murdered. Regardless, the perpetrator is obligated to do what is possible—in public, and with an awareness that a debt may be carried down the generations until it is paid. As Maimonides teaches us,

One who sins against another, and the other person dies before they asked their forgiveness, should bring ten people to the grave and say:

"I have sinned against God and against this certain person because I did such and such to them." If [the harmdoer] owed [the victim] money, they should give it to the [victim's] heirs; if they don't know of any heirs, they should leave the money with the court and confess.[25]

Confession, in public. In Judaism, a gathering of ten people is considered a quorum, a critical mass that marks a context as communal. If the victim is no longer alive, then public (rather than private) confession is no longer "praiseworthy,"[26] for Maimonides, but, rather, a prerequisite. Our obligation to the truth changes when the person or people harmed are unable to stand as witness themselves, unable to hold for themselves the story of what really happened.

That which is owed belongs to the heirs. If the heirs are unknown, then that which is owed sits in public trust—but it no longer belongs to the perpetrator.

Our obligation to repentance outlives those to whom we are obligated.

In 1951, West Germany declared that "unspeakable crimes had been committed in the name of the German people which entails an obligation to make moral and material amends"[27] and pledged to make reparations to both the newly formed State of Israel, which had absorbed half a million survivors of the Holocaust, and to Jewish organizations that aided survivors with resettlement and recovery. Two years later, West Germany established a program to compensate those who had been harmed "because of their opposition to National Socialism or because of their race, creed, or ideology."[28] In German, this program is known as *Wiedergutmachung,* "to make good again."

This commitment was far from the end of West Germany's repentance for the Holocaust, nor was it uncomplicated; it was the beginning of a messy, decades-long process of trying to reckon with, understand, and make sense of the genocide perpetrated by the German government and its citizens, on and beyond German soil.

The concept of reparations for the Holocaust did not originate with the West German government. The Jewish community had begun demanding amends for the theft of Jewish property and revocation of Jewish citizenship even before World War II had officially begun, and certainly before the nature and scale of the genocide had been understood. After the war, the newly formed State of Israel estimated that six million Jews had been murdered and $6 billion in property had been seized.[29] The idea of accepting reparations was, however, highly controversial. The Israeli government's deliberations about it led to protests, and even rioting, as Israelis—including but not limited to many of the recently resettled Holocaust survivors—argued that such payments were tainted, were blood money; accepting them would be tantamount to absolving the Nazis for their unforgivable atrocities and enabling West Germany to find a legitimate place in the family of nations.

West Germany's own motivations were certainly mixed at best. At the time, Chancellor Konrad Adenauer argued that payment of reparations would help West Germany regain international legitimacy, understand the horrors of the Nazi regime, and choose a different future.[30] (The sincerity of this last motivation is fairly questionable, given that Adenauer employed former Nazi officials high up in his own government,[31] granted amnesty to Nazi criminals who had been sentenced in court,[32] restored back pay and pensions to Third Reich civil servants, and sabotaged Jewish efforts to track down and capture Adolf Eichmann.)

Despite this focus on legitimizing the country, Adenauer faced opposition both within his own cabinet and from the public at large. In the early 1950s, a survey found that only 5 percent of West Germans admitted feeling "guilty" toward Jews, and only 29 percent agreed that West Germany owed restitution to the Jewish people.[33] For individual survivors, financial reparations were initially somewhat accessible, but as time went on, the criteria for receiving them became increasingly stringent and varied widely across programs to the point of seeming arbitrary. Rules shifted over the years as to the proof accepted, hardships suffered, and income at the time of application.[34] Since 1951, Germany has paid at least $89 billion in reparations,[35] which, on the one hand, is a significant figure. And on the other, well, that's a fraction of what it has spent on the pensions of military veterans, including former members of the Waffen-SS, who, unlike survivors, did not have to prove that they made less than $16,000 ($25,000 in today's rates) annually to qualify for funds.[36]

More to the point, while financial reparations may be important in the work of repentance, they are hardly sufficient—particularly for harm on the scale of the Holocaust. And in fact, despite the Allies' half-hearted efforts to force the West German people to confront and take moral responsibility for the horrors of Nazism,[37] the dominant public attitude for many years after the war was the sense that most Germans were victims duped by a small gang of ideologues, sent off to fight, and bombed by Allies, all in ignorance of what was really happening.[38] In 1949, a poll revealed that half the population regarded Nazism as "a good idea, badly carried out."[39]

In the 1960s, that attitude began to shift, at least in some ways. The 1958 trials of former members of the Einsatzkommando in West Germany were followed, in 1961, by the trial of Adolf Eichmann in Jerusalem and those of Auschwitz death-camp personnel in West Germany in the mid-1960s.[40] Younger Germans—those born during or after the war—began to accuse the previous generation of participation in the horrors of the Third Reich. In 1968 student protests broke out in West Germany about, among other things, the fact that former Nazis still held a tremendous amount of political power in the country.[41] Notably, however, this initial attempt at a reckoning was, as the East German–born historian Katja Schatte suggests, focused on "specific student life–related issues, like the ways in which Nazi ideology continued to shape higher education," both philosophically and in terms of who continued to hold power—including professors who had been aligned with the Nazi Party.

But, Dr. Schatte notes, the people protesting "were not just students, they were literally being raised by [family members who had been] bystanders and perpetrators" of the Holocaust, with the occasional exception of those whose families had been in the Resistance or had themselves been targets of the Nazis. It was certainly a lot easier for these student activists to critique what was happening on campus—to point fingers—than to go home and have the more personal, and painful, conversation with their own parents and grandparents about what *they* were doing during the war, what they knew, what they believed, what they perpetrated, whom they abetted, and how they might have been complicit in the long-range project of genocide.[42] So these protests stopped short of a true reckoning in German society—the protests were about "them," not about "us." This conversation was, however, pushed forward with the airing of a miniseries on the Holocaust in 1979, which prompted about ten thousand Germans to call in to the TV station in post-broadcast segments—some expressing shock or shame, many telling their own stories of crime and collusion in the Nazi regime.[43]

In the 1980s a new ethos emerged, based on an understanding that, as Thorsten Wagner, a German-Danish historian and executive director of Fellowships at Auschwitz for the Study of Professional Ethics put it, the work of building a "functioning, stable democracy and civil society required confronting this history head on,"[44] with a deeply self-critical approach. In many ways, this was a grassroots project with an antigovernment ethos. Activists and artists developed city walks on which they revealed traces of Nazism and undertook projects laying bare how town officials collaborated with the Nazis or memorializing local sites of atrocity. This era also saw a new level of accountability from top leadership. Federal President Richard von Weizsäcker gave a speech in 1985 commemorating the fortieth anniversary of the end of World War II that was powerfully reflective; it certainly may be considered at least part of a public confession. But it might not have had such a strong impact if the country as a whole had not been, piece by piece, over the previous twenty-five years, trying to find ways to speak of unspeakable harms. "The greater honesty we show in commemorating this day," he said, "the freer we are to face the consequences with due responsibility." He refuted the notion that Germans were unaware of the genocide as it took place:

> Who could remain unsuspecting after the burning of the synagogues, the plundering, the stigmatization with the Star of David, the deprivation of rights, the ceaseless violation of human dignity? Whoever opened his eyes and ears and sought information could not fail to notice that Jews were being deported. The nature and

scope of the destruction may have exceeded human imagination, but in reality there was, apart from the crime itself, the attempt by too many people, including those of my generation, who were young and were not involved in planning the events and carrying them out, not to take note of what was happening. There were many ways of not burdening one's conscience, of shunning responsibility, looking away, keeping mum . . .

All of us, whether guilty or not, whether old or young, must accept the past. We are all affected by its consequences and liable for it. The young and old generations must and can help each other to understand why it is vital to keep alive the memories. It is not a case of coming to terms with the past. That is not possible. It cannot be subsequently modified or made undone. However, anyone who . . . refuses to remember the inhumanity is prone to new risks of infection . . .

And, critically, he related understanding and taking responsibility for the past to specific contemporary policy choices:

If we remember that [disabled] persons were put to death in the Third Reich, we will see care of people with [mental illness] as our own responsibility. If we remember how people persecuted on grounds of race, religion and politics and threatened with certain death often stood before the closed borders with other countries, we shall not close the door today on those who are genuinely persecuted and seek protection with us.[45]

These are, indeed, powerful words—and yet Chancellor Angela Merkel was the first German head of state to actually follow through with opening the country to refugees in any meaningful way, thirty years later.

We see, again and again in German history, a complex dance between avoidance and confrontation, between doing and naming, between performance and engagement, between intention and action. It is not straightforward, it is not linear, and it has suffered from crucial omissions. For example, Germany's attempts to engage in a post-

Holocaust repair process has not included LGBTQIA+ people, those who were compelled to perform forced labor, or the Romani communities who face systematic and violent discrimination in Germany to this day. And other harms perpetrated by the nation have not received the same level of critical attention, such as colonialism and the Herero and Namaqua Genocide of 1904 to 1908, in what is now Namibia, which involved the slaughter of 65,000 to 100,000 people, up to 80 percent of the Indigenous population at the time. Germany did finally formally acknowledge the atrocity as genocide in 2021.[46]

Reckoning with the Holocaust was also complicated by the fall of the Berlin Wall in 1991 and East Germany's subsequent reintegration with West Germany. East German leadership had long encouraged its citizens to identify with Communist opposition to Nazism, thus enabling that population to avoid reckoning as deeply with its own complicity with the Nazis before and during the war. Notably, though, East Germany was much more rigorous, if imperfectly thorough, in removing Nazis from positions of institutional power.[47]

Nonetheless, over the course of the second half of the twentieth century, Germany (and before that, West Germany) did make significant, if incomplete, choices toward ensuring that the evils of the Holocaust were not forgotten and absolutely would not be repeated. The evidence included the memorialization of the crimes and horrors of the Holocaust (widespread), education (robust, as far as the Holocaust is concerned),[48] military policy (generally pacifistic),[49] and refugee policy (significantly generous, as of 2015).[50]

Of course, the story is not simple—right-wing populism is once again on the rise, in Germany as elsewhere worldwide—despite the extensive education, despite the attempts to organize a society around "never again." Islamophobic incidents have been increasing since at least 2009, according to Muslim German leaders, and some assert that the government has not always addressed it with the seriousness needed. There has also been a rise in antisemitic hate crimes in recent years—up 15 percent in 2020.[51] Centrist Germans have been reluctant to engage in needful ways about racism and other forms of hatred and intolerance in contemporary German society. As Mithu Sanyal, a German author of Indian and Polish descent, put it, "For a long time, nobody wanted to hear about anything race related . . . There is this thinking that race is a construct, so there can't be any racism. That was the end of the discussion. Racists are Nazis and we're not Nazis."[52]

Has Germany repented completely for the Holocaust? Could it ever, fully? Of course not. Has it done everything that it could to repent? No, not that either. But, particularly when compared to many other countries that have committed great atrocities, it has done, at least, better. Like South Africa, Germany shows us what might be possible, even if these countries have not, themselves, entirely gotten there.

Though Germany has proceeded through many of the steps of repentance, it has not done so in the order that Maimonides suggested, and has often done them in ways that are fraught or complex. Might some of Germany's problems in reckoning with the Holocaust have been alleviated by engaging in Maimonides' steps in order—with, for example, a willingness to first truly face the harms caused and then consider appropriate redress? It's possible. Certainly, Holocaust survivors needed money and justice immediately after the war, even if German society was not yet able to engage, in a meaningful way, with the harms it had committed. Or would postwar Germans have been able to look more directly at the atrocities they'd abetted if the Allies had been willing to push West Germans further, or if the choice to rebuild society had included fewer . . . well, Nazis? We will never know.

In any case, even though it has been imperfect, inelegant, and insufficient, a reckoning and a naming of harms has been undertaken; work to become different has progressed; amends, apologies, and different kinds of choices have been made. This has taken decades and generations. It has required both agitation at the grassroots level and bold steps from national leaders, but it has been done, and in a deeper way than many other countries can claim.

A few things to note about the two national stories juxtaposed thus far in this chapter. First, Germany's process reminds us how many decades this work can sometimes take. Archbishop Tutu's assessment that his country had fallen "tragically short" of the TRC's goals was written nineteen years after the TRC convened. After that number of years on its own trajectory, Germany had barely begun to face the nature of its genocide. The full story of grappling with apartheid has not yet been written; perhaps there are better chapters still to come. Further, Germany's reckoning primarily concerned harms committed, in the past tense, to people who had almost entirely been murdered or jettisoned from its borders. The questions Germany needed to ask of its society and ways it needed to repair were, in many ways, much more theoretical than those of South Africa, where significant systemic restructuring is required to undo the centuries of oppression imposed by 10 percent of its population upon the other 90 percent—and where inequality is ongoing. Which is not to say that the TRC's work was ultimately meaningless. If the South African government had followed through on the TRC's recommendations, as Archbishop Tutu noted, it could have made all the difference. That said, I caution us to resist simplistic narratives about which nations have done what kind of repentance work, and why.

I ultimately agree with President von Weizsäcker that neither individual nor nation can achieve moral perfection, and Germany most certainly has not done so. But despite the many shortcomings in its process of reckoning, Germany does show us that repentance work can nonetheless be undertaken on the national level. At the same time it may prove that repentance at the national level is likely to fall short.

During much of my conversation with the historian Thorsten Wagner on the complexities and nuances of this reckoning, he cast a deeply critical eye on most of the ways that Germany, and Germans, did not do the work as well as they could have. And yet, in the end, he concluded:

> Yes, I think Germany is a success story. Yes, I think it was painful and slow and had a lot of shortcomings, but at the end of the day I think what came out was beautiful and a success story ... but let's not think that this [repentance and transformation] is a given, a constant, something that we just have. It took a lot of blood, sweat and tears to get here, and it can be gone like nothing. It must be a constant struggle.[53]

The Talmud requires that a person confessing says the words, "We have sinned." But Maimonides' formulation of the ritual confession—as he codified it in his Day of Atonement liturgy—reads not merely "We have sinned," but rather "We and our ancestors have sinned."[54] (This is now the standard formulation found in prayer books.) An anonymous German commentator, writing in the fourteenth or fifteenth century, said, "A person is obliged to mention their own sins, and the sins of their ancestors. Now why should one confess the sins of their ancestors? Because a person is held accountable for holding on to the deeds of their ancestors."[55]

We are held accountable for the harm that was done before our time—for all the injurious deeds that we have held on to, for all that we have not actively worked to undo.

Let us turn now to a place—not the only place, to be sure, but one of them—where national repentance is very long overdue, and unpack what might be possible, were we to take Maimonides' work to heart.

The genocide and displacement of Native Americans is one of the two great founding sins of the United States. The other, of course, is the enslavement of peoples of African descent—and, as with the treatment of Indigenous peoples, that history of oppression continues today in a myriad of ways. Questions concerning just reparations for Black Americans must address the specifics of their history and experience. But in this section, we will focus on what is owed to Indigenous peoples (some of whom are Black, to be sure). While there are more stories in more parts of the United States than can be covered in one chapter, I think we can learn a great deal about the larger issues at play, and what repentance could look like, by focusing on one community, in one place: the Dakota of Minnesota.

From the very beginning of settler colonialism in Minnesota, harms were heaped onto the Indigenous population, including fraudulent and coerced treaties with deceptive, exploitative, and unethical terms that were repeatedly violated, causing suffering, harm, and hunger.[56] In 1862, Minnesota's governor, Alexander Ramsay, who was white, declared that the Dakota people should be "exterminated or driven forever beyond the borders of the state."[57] He went so far as to offer money for the scalps of Dakota people.[58] That same year, the Minnesota state government confined more than sixteen hundred Dakota women, children, and old men in an internment camp on Pike Island and held a mass hanging of thirty-eight Dakota men on the order of President Abraham Lincoln, the largest one-day mass execution in US history.[59] In April 1863, the US Congress abolished the Dakota reservation and declared all treaties with the Dakota people null and void, and the Minnesota government began to expel them to Nebraska and South Dakota. And for those who did not leave, the project of forced assimilation and cultural genocide came in the form of boarding schools, which lasted until 1953, operating under the horrific slogan "Kill the Indian, save the man."[60] (Though we are focusing on the story of the Dakota people here, know that displacement, forced assimilation, and cultural genocide stretched across the United States and Canada and affected many Indigenous peoples, and continue to affect their descendants today.) The Dakota land base started at fifty-four million acres; by modern times they occupied around 0.006 percent of that.[61]

While these atrocities can never be fully repaired, there is work that can and should be done. One powerful approach comes from a Dakota professor and activist named Waziyatawin, whose book *What Does Justice Look Like?* lays out a clear vision for what might be possible. Strikingly, it also follows many of Maimonides' stages of repentance. I don't believe that this is because she was aware of or influenced by his work; rather, it speaks to the effectiveness of this framework and the wide-ranging power it can have.

A major theme of this chapter has been the critical role of public confession—of truth-telling—in repentance work for harm caused at the national level. And for Waziyatawin too this is certainly the case:

> To many Minnesotans truth telling may seem an unnecessary educational goal because there is no awareness of a denial of truth . . . This means that well-intentioned people, who ordinarily would be

horrified at the notion of being complicit in the coverup of genocide and the ongoing denial of justice for Indigenous Peoples, have done just that.[62]

She calls for a widescale truth-telling process that mobilizes both Dakota and white communities and includes the passing of formal resolutions, the collection of testimony, broad-based educational campaigns, and more.[63] As with South Africa's Truth and Reconciliation Commission and Germany's intermittent attempts to face the Holocaust, public confession is a crucial first step. And, Waziyatawin suggests, it may open the door to liberation for everyone involved.

> Truth-telling has the potential to alleviate the burden that all of us carry—Dakota people who carry historical trauma and the pain of ongoing oppression and [w]hite Minnesotans who carry the burden of maintaining oppressive systems ... Truth-telling allows us to relieve those burdens and take the next step towards justice.[64]

I think about the thousands and thousands of people who called in to the TV station after Germany aired the Holocaust miniseries in 1979 to tell their stories—how they must have felt, for almost thirty-five years, as they carried stories of participation in the horrors and atrocity that they had dared not name; and how they may have felt after speaking the unspeakable.

Of course, the critical role of confession is in its potential to liberate victims of great harm—it marks an end to the denial of their experience and an affirmation of the legitimacy of their suffering. It can offer answers, context, information about what happened or why that might be key to healing, and it can bring something too long hidden into the open. But I agree with Waziyatawin—it can also be liberating for the perpetrators. It engages the possibility that what was done was not what had to be done; it enables those who acted wrongly to engage with the immorality of their actions; it opens the door to accountability and repentance, to becoming different. We cannot change the past, yet we can change the future, but only if we are honest about what has been—and who was harmed, and who caused that harm.

This truth-telling is needed in many contexts, in all places where great harm and suffering have been caused. And it can open up space to consider what next steps might be needed—like the TRC in South Africa, which had a committee dedicated to formulating concrete, reparative steps. One imagines such a process being useful in the United States around the horrors of its immigration policies and practices, including separation of family members; with the Israeli occupation of Palestinian territory and other aspects of the Israeli-Palestinian conflict; in the genocide of the Rohingya people in Myanmar; in the persecution of the Uyghur people in China; in Cyprus, in Kashmir, in Chechnya, and elsewhere around the world.

This might be particularly true in places where groups perceive competing truth claims about historical events, such as with Israel/Palestine. A truth commission that began with a specific scope could be a first attempt to gain communal consensus. One wonders if beginning with a public detailing of everything that happened in Israel/Palestine in 1948, for example, could open the door for additional space to unpack other events, whether in 1929, 1967, 1987, 2000, 2014, 2021, and all the years in between and beyond. It could begin with the personal testimony of Israelis and Palestinians, archival documentation, and more. Or, perhaps it could start with and expand upon the much more recent work of Breaking the Silence (an organization of Israeli veterans who tell the truth about the Israeli army's activities under Occupation), Al-Haq (an independent organization that details human rights violations of Palestinians by both Israeli and Palestinian institutions), the Parents Circle–Families Forum (a joint Israeli-Palestinian organization of those who have lost family members to the ongoing conflict), international NGOs and monitors, and the work of Israeli and Palestinian historians, sociologists, and many others who have been working for decades to document the many truths of what has happened and what is happening now. So much is known, even if it is not all spoken, and not all in the same place.

But as the lessons of South Africa and Canada (the latter discussed in Chapter One) show us, making space to tell the truth isn't enough. Recommendations must be followed. Structural changes must be implemented. Restitution must be provided.

And, particularly on the national level, truth-telling must not be a single event but rather a part of the ongoing work of becoming different, of transformation. As Waziyatawin argues, the suffering and genocide of the Dakota people must be a central part of Minnesota education, which includes everything from what is taught in schools to the words that the Minnesota Historical Society chooses to use.[65] This education could pave the way for profound change because "adult citizens in the state cannot conceive of justice for Dakota people, because they do not even recognize the injustice . . . Minnesotans have the capacity to make radical change once they understand the history and the need to work for justice."[66] This resonates with the thoughts of Archbishop Tutu: "Those who claimed they did not know cannot very well say so now. They know."[67]

But a critical part of that transformation work is also part of the process of making amends. That is to say, it is impossible to become different when systemic injustices are continuing to be perpetrated. In this case, the exile of Dakota people from their ancestral homelands is a key part of that harm. Indeed, the #LandBack movement has gained considerable traction across Indigenous nations and, critically, non-Indigenous governments in recent years. In 2019 the city of Eureka, California, returned two hundred acres of Duluwat Island to the Wiyot Tribe—in addition to the forty they had restored in 2004—giving the tribe near-complete ownership of the island.[68] In 2020 the Essalen Tribe was able to reclaim about twelve hundred acres of land near Big Sur, California.[69] That same year, the US Supreme Court ruled that three million acres of land, nearly half of Oklahoma, is Native American territory. However, in 2021 the attorney general of Oklahoma filed a petition with the Supreme Court, asking that this ruling be overturned and any application of the decision be narrowed.[70] (One of the great challenges of writing a book on contemporary topics is that some issues remain extremely live right up to the last moment when edits can be made. You, dear reader, likely know where this last case stands, even though I, at the moment of writing, do not. I hope SCOTUS upholds the original *McGirt v. Oklahoma* ruling and the principle of Indigenous sovereignty.) In 2021, over nine thousand acres in Washington State were returned to the Coleville

Confederated Tribes, from whom the land had been taken in 1892; over $4.5 million was raised by private donors through a conservation organization to purchase the deed.[71]

Waziyatawin looks not necessarily to divest white Minnesotans of their private land holdings so much as to find other ways to enfranchise the Dakota community today. (This is one opinion; other Indigenous leaders may encourage pushing non-Natives to engage more personally around the idea of land ownership and reparations, and much depends upon one's definition of "private land holdings.") She notes that about 22 percent of Minnesota is comprised of federal and state agency lands, tax-forfeited lands, and metro-commissioned lands—which add up to almost twelve million acres.[72] Almost three million of those are due to tax forfeiture. It is entirely possible, if logistically complex, for the state and federal government to designate those lands for Indigenous reclamation. In addition, it is possible for individuals to choose to bequeath all or some of their land holdings to Indigenous communities, as Bruce and Marion Cumming did in 2007.[73]

Minnesota is in the process of reconsidering its past positions on tribal territory. In February 2020 Minnesota's Black, non-Indigenous attorney general, Keith Ellison, formally backed the Anishinaabe claim to sixty-one thousand acres of land along part of Mille Lacs Lake, and in December 2020 a federal bill written by two Minnesota legislators was passed to restore eleven thousand acres of Minnesota land to the Leech Lake Band of the Ojibwe.[74] And in early 2021 the Minnesota Historical Society returned 114 acres of land to the Dakota people of the Lower Sioux Indian Community.[75]

In 2018 Minnesota elected its first Indigenous person to executive office; Lieutenant Governor Peggy Flanagan is Ojibwe. Among other efforts, she has spearheaded the creation of the Office of Tribal State Relations to focus on both understanding tribal governments and their sovereignty and on respecting and honoring treaty rights so that, as she puts it, the work "continues long after we're gone, [even when there is not] *Anishinaabekwe* as lieutenant governor. It just becomes the work that the state does ... When we have Indigenous folks at the table, we are changing those systems for the better."[76]

The goal of land restoration is not possession and ownership for its own sake—the idea of land "ownership" is in itself a colonialist construct. Instead, the goal is enabling a return to traditional practices in ancestral home space and the renewal of culture, language, spiritual expression, healing methods, rites of passage, folkways, governing structures, agriculture, and so much more that had been forcibly taken away. It would be, for Waziyatawin, space to reclaim the "values and ways of being that make us distinctly Dakota. It would be a rejection of the values and ways of the dominant society that are harmful to our people, our lands, and our ways of being. This commitment to being Dakota would constitute nothing less than the rebirthing of our nation."[77]

Would this transformation, and at least partial land restoration, constitute full repentance? Maybe not. Can a country ever fully repent for mass genocide and destruction? As with Germany, the answer is no, and all the more so in a settler-colonialist state; the United States won't ever return to a pre-1492 place. Does that mean that a nation does not have the obligation to continue to try, in all of the ways that it can, to make right what it has destroyed? Of course it is obligated. Of course it must try to do this work in all the ways that it can. And even if complete restoration is impossible, transformation is not. Repentance does not unbreak what has been broken so much as interrupt the cycle of repeated harms—which stretches from first contact to the Trail of Tears, from Wounded Knee to the Dakota Access Pipeline. Our refusal, as a nation, to name and face the original harms perpetrated against Indigenous Americans means that we commit them again and again. If we were willing to invest in the work of repair and transformation, however, another future might be possible—for tomorrow and for, perhaps, seven generations from now.

While I was writing this book, I gave a (virtual) talk about some of these issues at a university. One of the students asked how we could get a country unwilling to face its own evils to begin to do the work of repentance, and she cited the legacy of slavery in America as a specific example. There are two possible answers to this question: one of them more optimistic and the other less so.

On the one hand, the East German–born historian Katja Schatte suggests that "the honesty required for actual repentance is irreconcilable with the modern nation-state project" and that "much of the viability of the modern nation-state has to do with its ability to incorporate dark periods in widely digestible ways, generally at the expense of the victims and their descendants."[78] She's not wrong. And this statement might account for many (or maybe even all) of the places where the work of repentance is ignored, denied, limited, or circumscribed on the national level.

And yet Germany's history shows us doorways to another possible path. It's notable that two significant turning points in its own halting reckonings with the Holocaust were grassroots movements—the student protests of the 1960s and the hyperlocal art and history projects of the 1980s. Both times, in different ways, people self-organized to make noise that was sufficiently loud and disruptive to force the country to respond. Also, the students of the '60s eventually became the adults in power in the '80s. This means that the leaders of the student protests—the ones who agitated and advocated and moved the conversation ahead, who engaged their peers and pulled them in—wound up having an outsized influence. Some of those peers found their way into roles that enabled them to impact institutional priorities.

Even without detailing the (formidable) history of antiracist activism in the United States, a look at its most recent wave—the Black Lives Matter movement—shows how grassroots activism has moved the national conversation, and, yes, policy, around systemic racism, policing, and racial justice. Many city councils have reduced police budgets, removed police from schools, and/or made tactical rule changes in an effort to reduce police brutality—not yet the far-reaching structural change that many have asked for, but real wins that may have a lifesaving impact.[79] And more than that, movements such as BLM help shape the national story and move the national consciousness, even if those changes are not always immediately manifest. For example, Gallup polling indicates that fewer Americans now believe that Black and white people have equal opportunities than has been the case since it began tracking the issue in 1963. Similarly, the perception that the job market is racially equitable is lower than it has been in forty years.[80] More of the country is finally seeing what has been true all along. We can hope that this understanding may become an entry point into the next chapter of our nation—and the development of not only more *allies* fighting white supremacy, but what a 2014 *Indigenous Action Media*'zine referred to as "accomplices" who are "complicit in a struggle towards liberation."[81]

And, of course, the importance of those working to shape the cultural conversation cannot be overstated as well. In Germany, that critical miniseries on the Holocaust starred Meryl Streep and James Woods—a very Hollywood production, to be sure, but its screening ignited a national dialogue, which opened the door to a new kind of reckoning. On the sins of American slavery and systemic racism, one can consider the impact of Ta-Nehisi Coates' 2014 article, "The Case for Reparations," for bringing the reparations movement into the mainstream public imagination,[82] and Michelle Alexander's *The New Jim Crow* for giving traction to the conversation around mass incarceration. Nikole Hannah-Jones's creation of the 1619 Project for the *New York Times* spurred a crucial new engagement with US history—as well as a terrifying backlash, as those determined to continue committing the sins of white supremacy passed laws prohibiting the teaching of accurate history, of telling the truth, of public confession, of engaging with harm.[83] And yet. That is so much impact for a handful of projects to have—even the backlash is proof of its power. There are many more art makers, authors, and directors whom I wish I could name here, since there are so many critical voices. The work of changing the national understanding, opening the national heart, chipping away at the national determination to "incorporate dark periods in widely digestible ways" does not happen overnight or by dint of a single event or creator's work. For centuries our country has invested in many harmful systems and narratives, and there are many who are deeply attached to maintaining power through them. There is work to do.

There is also movement. Is it enough, is it fast enough? No. Can whole-scale systemic change be effected, the kind that comes in time to make a difference? It's already too late, far too late, except insofar as tomorrow has not yet been written, and can yet be written for more wholeness, more justice, more integrity, more truth. As in South Africa, what is at stake is not only a historical reckoning but the entire structures on which the country has been built—literally. And that is, indeed, a very threatening prospect for those who benefit from white supremacy. And if done properly, our nation's transformation will be a very ongoing process indeed. As the Black and Borican speaker and facilitator Dana White put it, "The truth is this country, white people, could only begin to pay us what's owed. It would take lifetimes. It's not a onetime payment."[84]

Will the United States ever hold a Truth and Reconciliation Commission for slavery; for structural racism; for Indigenous land theft, genocide, and oppression? Will it ever look with curiosity at what making amends, repair, and true transformative change might look like?

I don't know. I hope so.

In 1985, a group of primarily Black theologians in South Africa came together during a particularly draconian period of apartheid to write the Kairos Document, a powerful treatise of liberation theology. In it, the authors make their terms clear: "No reconciliation is possible without justice. What this means in practice is that no reconciliation, no forgiveness and no negotiations are possible without repentance."[85]

CHAPTER SIX

JUSTICE SYSTEMS; OR,
WHAT CONSEQUENCES FOR HARM?

When we think about repentance and accountability, we must also think about consequences. We must consider what the goals of these consequences are, and what kinds of impacts they have—and whether or not those consequences are ultimately beneficial to the harmed party or parties. And we must consider whether they facilitate or hamper the ability of perpetrators to grapple with, and ultimately to do repentance work on, the harm that they have caused.

In short, we must talk about criminal justice.

At the time of this writing, the American criminal justice system holds three million people in state and federal prisons, local jails, juvenile detention centers, and other carceral facilities.[1] Since 1970, the US prison population has risen by 700 percent, far outpacing the growth of the general US population or its crime rates.[2] The United States incarcerates more people than any other nation in the world; our country holds 25 percent of the world's prisoners, despite representing only about 5 percent of the world's population.[3] There are a number of reasons for this, including (but certainly not limited to) mandatory minimum sentences and "three strikes" laws, as well as a tendency to imprison people for things that do not lead to incarceration elsewhere. Half a million Americans are in prison for nonviolent drug-related offenses,[4] many of which are connected to issues of addiction; there are six times as many arrests for possession than for sales of drugs. These high numbers also include those with mental health needs; about half of prisoners have mental health concerns before incarceration (to say nothing of the psychological impacts of imprisonment), and an estimated 10 to 25 percent of those incarcerated suffer from severe mental illness.[5] Many people are currently behind bars for things that have been deemed criminal, but that are, at their root, an expression of other kinds of needs. As the racial justice activist and organizer Mariame Kaba puts it, "All that is criminalized isn't harmful, and all harm isn't necessarily criminalized. For example, wage theft by employers isn't generally criminalized, but it is definitely harmful."[6]

Poverty is both a huge driver and a consequence of incarceration; one study found that those in the bottom 10 percent of American income distribution are twenty times more likely to be imprisoned than those in the top 10 percent.[7] About 70 percent of prisoners in California were in foster care during their youth.[8] And, of course, racism is a tremendous factor in systems of mass incarceration. Black Americans make up 40 percent of the incarcerated population despite being only 13 percent of the United States population; they are imprisoned at five times the rate of white Americans. This tendency to mete out punishment to Black Americans begins early. Black students are three times as likely to be suspended and expelled from school as their white counterparts—despite studies showing that they do not misbehave at higher rates—and there is a strong correlation between being subject to these harsh punishments and the likelihood that a student will end up in the juvenile justice system. In addition, increased policing in schools has meant that some arrests are actually happening *at* school. Black students are at least 2.5 times more likely to be subjected to a school-related arrest than their white counterparts are.[9]

Much has been written about the devastation wreaked by mass incarceration, and the injustices and abuses perpetrated through and by it—including, but not limited to, the psychological torture of solitary confinement; the prevalence of violence and sexual abuse in the prison system; the overcrowding and neglect (particularly acute during a deadly pandemic); the failure to adequately treat people who are mentally ill; and the lack of access to education and other programming.

The system is not necessarily concerned with justice. When Adnan Khan was eighteen years old, he agreed to take part in a robbery—to grab some marijuana and run as part of a fake drug deal, with the understanding that no weapons were to be used in the crime. But things didn't go according to the plan. The person assigned to be the getaway driver began punching the person they were trying to steal from—turns out the driver was having a schizophrenic break—and then he used a knife to kill their target. Because Khan was involved in the robbery, he too was considered liable for the death of this man and was sentenced to twenty-five years to life in prison. He became an activist, protesting unjust sentencing and cofounding an organization focused on that goal from inside San Quentin. (He has since been released.) As he put it, "Holding someone accountable isn't built into our carceral system. The district attorney never wanted me to be accountable, he wanted a conviction. Two different things."[10]

The desire for a conviction leads to many miscarriages of justice. Part of the problem is the extraordinary number of arrests that take place now, which far outstrips the number of trials the system can handle. The need to process cases, often coupled with a county's desire to offer statistics that show that they are "tough on crime," urgently pushes the DA, in many situations, to move cases out via plea bargains. And on the other side, in many places a cash bail system penalizes those who do not have the resources to free themselves while they await the evaluation of their innocence or guilt. According to the Prison Policy Initiative, approximately 70 percent of people in jail at any point in time are being held in pretrial detention on minor charges which should not involve incarceration, because they do not have the funds to post bail. Those who find themselves in this position often feel forced to plead guilty to crimes they did not commit—to take whatever deal is on offer—since the alternative, waiting in jail in the hopes that a trial will prove their innocence, is not much of an alternative. This is especially true given that defendants who are imprisoned before their trial are four times more likely to be sentenced to prison than those who are released prior to trial.[11] It's important to note that judges have the power to raise, lower, or waive bail amounts, and that on average, Black and Latino men are forced to pay 35 and 19 percent higher amounts in bail, respectively, than white men are. And if the bias present in the system is not yet clear: 69 percent of pretrial detainees are people of color.[12]

When a person is convicted for a crime that caused harm to someone (unlike, say, drug possession or other victimless crimes), the current carceral system does little to facilitate the work of repentance and repair, and in many ways actively hampers it. If one of our goals as a society is to encourage those who have caused harm to take responsibility for and grapple with their actions, to do as much as they can toward repair, and to become the kinds of people who do not cause harm in the future—well, the prison system as it stands now isn't it.

Most people in the system, including harmdoers, are encouraged to plea bargain (copping to one thing in order not to be charged with something else) in order to help move cases along. Cynical deal making, rather than a nuanced reckoning with harm and its impact, becomes the priority. When a case does go to trial, the person indicted is often encouraged to plead "not guilty"—the direct opposite of owning their actions. Time spent in a carceral facility generally includes absolutely no support for reckoning with the impact of harm caused and its moral implications. Those who are imprisoned are often forbidden any contact with their victims, so any kind of apology or direct making of amends is off the table. People who are incarcerated are removed from family and community—the structures of support and accountability that might help foster growth and change. And those who do feel remorse for their actions have almost no way to make amends.

As Melody Ermachild Chavis, a private investigator who works on trials for death-row inmates, put it, "I've spent 35 years closely witnessing the extreme suffering of perpetrators—[it is like they are] hung up on a hook in the hall, twisting in the wind with regret, with no way out of it."[13] (Some, or perhaps even many, of those condemned to death are innocent, and some complex cases do not call for repentance. But some do.) In situations of harmdoing that take place outside the carceral system, a repentant perpetrator has the ability to channel feelings of regret into useful, reparatory action, either through direct relationship with the victim or by preventing similar harm. Accomplishing these goals is much more difficult, if not impossible, in the contemporary criminal justice system.

Ermachild Chavis told me the story of an eighteen-year-old who had shot a gun in the darkness, accidentally killing a municipal official. The first time she met him, the first words out of his mouth were "Can I tell [his family] I'm sorry?" His attorneys told him no, we can't contact the family—it might backfire, and this family has the ear of the DA, so your attempts could negatively impact your sentencing. As Ermachild Chavis reflected, "A big piece of his suffering was in his inability to apologize and make amends. Which of course then makes it [even harder] to make the community whole, for anyone to do any healing."[14]

And while incarceration is, at least on the face of it, meant to be the punishment for crime, those imprisoned are often punished further after release. Formerly incarcerated people often experience discrimination in housing and employment (even in places where such discrimination is illegal),[15] and in many places, they are denied the right to vote.[16] These measures further hamper the repentance process. If a formerly incarcerated person is unable to find work after eight months, they have a 33 percent likelihood of recidivism and re-incarceration; that proportion jumps to 50 percent likelihood after a year, and 70 percent after three years. At least one in four of the people who go to jail will be arrested again within the same year—they are often dealing with poverty, mental illness, and issues with substance use, and these problems may only worsen during incarceration. Those who do find employment make, on average, 11 percent less than those without a record; their ability to make a living wage and save for unforeseen emergencies is hampered.[17]

As Danielle Sered, in her masterful book *Until We Reckon: Violence, Mass Incarceration, and a Road to Repair*, observes, "On an individual level, violence is driven by shame, isolation, exposure to violence, and an inability to meet one's economic needs—factors that are also core features of imprisonment. This means that the core national violence prevention strategy relies on a tool that has as its basis the central drivers of violence."[18] And, indeed, research supports this assertion: Prison ultimately causes a measurable, statistically significant increase in crime and violence; locking people in a system defined by these drivers of violence does, indeed, increase the likelihood that they will cause greater harm in the future.[19] Imprisoning people doesn't necessarily make our society safer.

Excessively severe consequences for harm are such a clear barrier to an honest and thorough repentance process that the fourteenth-century Spanish rabbi Yom Tov Asevilli expressed concern that too harsh a punishment might lead someone back on the path to sin— even if they had done, or wanted to do, sincere, whole-hearted repentance work.[20]

Ermachild Chavis told me, "My clients would say, 'My dream would be to work with youth, to tell them not to join a gang,'" to do the work of transforming themselves and preventing future harm, "and I would think, 'Nobody is going to let you do this.'"[21] The system as it stands now does not, apparently, want the repentance work of incarcerated or formerly incarcerated people. It sets up a myriad of obstacles to it.

Critically, the system as it exists also doesn't serve the needs of victims—who, after all, should be at the center of any justice or repair process. Sered asserts that, in her many years of doing work related to criminal justice, she has found a number of clear patterns in what survivors of violence want. They want, she suggests, validation that what happened to them is wrong. They want answers as to why this harm came to be, why they were targeted—to help them build a coherent narrative, to make sense of what happened to them. They want some power and control, to have a say in what happens as a result of the harm caused to them—a necessary corrective after the experience of powerlessness and trauma. They want their voices to be heard. They want the resources needed for their healing and safety. And, Sered notes, "Every single survivor we have spoken to has wanted one thing: *to know that the person who hurt them would not hurt anyone else.*"[22]

These things are difficult to obtain in the current criminal justice system. Victims do not usually have the opportunity for face-to-face conversation with their assailant because contact between survivors and perpetrators is limited. Since 94 to 97 percent of convictions end in plea bargains,[23] often involving admission to having committed different or lesser crimes, most victims do not see their day in court nor have a chance to make statements that might influence sentencing. The factors that hamper a meaningful repentance process lead to high rates of recidivism after release, so the desire to ensure that others are not hurt by their perpetrator may not be met. And the criminal justice process can retraumatize victims, adding to their suffering rather than ameliorating it.[24] As the Talmud scholar and justice activist Rabbi Aryeh Cohen puts it, "Treating the victim as an object . . . by sidelining her in the judicial proceedings in a contemporary state prosecution— reenacts the original offense against her humanity."[25] Indeed, a recent poll of victims of violent crime in Los Angeles County found that an overwhelming majority felt that the criminal justice system had failed them and believed that resources should be diverted from incarceration into crime prevention and community support.[26]

Contrast this to a victim-centric model of repentance—one that focuses on the importance of the perpetrator owning fully the harm they caused, on making amends and an apology that center on the victim and their needs, on enabling the transformation work necessary so that the perpetrator never commits that kind of harm again. Much would need to be changed in the current system to arrive at a process in which consequences are appropriate and proportionate to the harm caused, those consequences do not perpetuate cycles of harm and violence, and the perpetrator is supported in walking the path of repentance not just over the short term but for the rest of their life.

So then what? If we take issue with a punitive model that forces those who cause significant criminal harm (and whose experience of abuse, poverty, systemic racism, violence, and/or isolation may be a driver for that harm) to suffer, perhaps for the rest of their lives, in conditions that are antithetical to their growth in the ability to take responsibility, and that does not meaningfully serve the victims of harm, what options might be available to us? Do other models exist?

Of course they do. They are each imperfect, each limited in some ways, but perhaps by looking more closely at what is, we can begin to think about what can be.

Conversations about repentance and criminal justice often move quickly to conversations about restorative justice, transformative justice, and community accountability, for good reason.

Restorative justice is defined by the criminologist John Braithwaite as "... a process where all stakeholders affected by an injustice have an opportunity to discuss how they have been affected by the injustice and to decide what should be done to repair the harm."[27] It may be used in the context of a criminal trial, with offenders who are already incarcerated (and indeed, facing the harm one has caused has been shown to reduce recidivism),[28] in schools, and in other institutional and noninstitutional community settings.

The goal of transformative justice is to help all those involved in an incident of wrongdoing, including the larger community. The point is not just restoring both parties, perpetrator and victim, to their original, pre-harm state. Rather, transformative justice focuses on how individual justice and collective change are necessarily intertwined. For example, if a person commits a crime in part due to their own situation of poverty and trauma, restoring them to the state they were in shortly before the crime occurred will likely be insufficient; the social conditions contributing to the harm must be addressed as well. Transformative justice is concerned for the overall well-being of the perpetrator, the victim, and the community as a whole.[29]

Community accountability may be part of the work of restorative justice or transformative justice, or it may be distinct from them. Community accountability focuses on addressing harm outside the framework of policing and incarceration. So, for example, since restorative justice work can happen within the structure of the state's criminal justice system or outside of it, noting that a process is happening as part of community accountability signals that this work is taking place outside the system.

Restorative justice was very explicitly crafted based on a number of other models for addressing harm; Howard Zehr, widely considered the pioneer of the modern framework of restorative justice, acknowledges his debt to both Indigenous peoples of what's now the United States and Canada and to Te Tangata Whenua I Aotearoa, often known as the Māori peoples of New Zealand.[30] Utu, a concept found in Māori culture, describes the process of restoring relationships to an equal or harmonious state. Hirini Moko Mead, a Māori leader and educator, describes it as part of a three-stage process that seeks to restore the relationship between a wronged party and an offender.[31]

In Navajo culture, a peacemaking process helps a person who has caused harm to see how they erred. This process helps an offender realize that what they have done is incorrect, and then brings the offender and the victim together to talk to each other. As Honorable Robert Yazzie, chief justice emeritus of the Navajo Nation Supreme Court, puts it, "The first order of business the relatives would do in the peacemaking process is to get to the bottom of a problem . . . What matters here is: Why did this act happen in the first place? There's a reason why the harm has occurred. Let's deal with that. If we can get to the bottom of a problem, all the other stuff will fall into place. The damage can be acknowledged by you, and I can go away happy from the process, knowing that you say that you're not going to do it again."[32]

The Cree approach similarly focuses on holding offenders responsible and healing the victim, offender, and community. As the Cree sociologist John Hansen writes, the elders in his community regard "the harm of one [as] the harm of all" and seek an accountability process that helps the offender better understand what they have done and work toward healing for not only victim and perpetrator, but for the community as well. Notably, consequences are understood not as punishment, but rather reflect "the pain, disharmony or destruction caused by an action . . . So the consequences a wrongdoer has to learn or become aware of is the pain and disharmony [their] actions have caused in others. Only when this is understood can a wrongdoer understand accountability."[33]

Zehr, inspired by models such as these, offers six guiding questions for restorative justice work:

1. Who has been hurt?
2. What are their needs?
3. Whose obligations are these?

4. What are the causes?
5. Who has a stake in the situation?
6. What is the appropriate process to involve stakeholders in an effort to address causes and put things right?[34]

In contrast, he argues, criminal justice asks only three questions, of a very different nature:

1. What laws have been broken?
2. Who did it?
3. What do the offender(s) deserve?[35]

While Maimonides' repentance process is not baked into any of these Indigenous models or those of community accountability, restorative justice, or transformative justice, it resonates strongly with them, in my opinion. The focus in all of these spaces is accountability: making it possible for the offender to face and own the harm they have caused (confession); doing the work to become different in order to not err in the same ways (transformation); making things right to those hurt both concretely (amends) and emotionally (apology); and living out those commitments to transformation in the real world (making different choices). That these approaches have evolved in different cultures and at different times and places speaks, I believe, to their universal necessity and effectiveness.

That said, I would be remiss if I did not acknowledge that Judaism—and Maimonides himself—also recommends punitive consequences for many offenses, following the lead of the Torah. However, the scope of these crimes and trials was both narrower and more rigorous than what is found in the American criminal justice system. Property crimes—such as theft—were regarded "more as a business dispute than a murder," as Rabbi Jill Jacobs puts it, and the focus of this "sentencing system [in Jewish law] is restitution for the injured party, not the removal of the offender from the community."[36] For crimes that impact human safety or life—such as assault, murder, or manslaughter—the conviction demanded rigorous evidence, such as the testimony of two reputable eyewitnesses who had seen the entire crime (rather than circumstantial evidence) and who could even speak to motive.[37] Indeed, removal of the offender from the community—banishment—was very much a last resort, something used only in extreme circumstances. Temporary banishment—incarceration—was a known concept but primarily associated with non-Jewish criminal justice settings. As Rabbi Jacobs puts it, "In Jewish contexts, imprisonment was only used as a last resort, when no other options for maintaining order were available."[38]

In any case, I don't think that we need to be bound by the criminal penalties articulated in Maimonides' writing; rather, we can continue using his repentance framework to help penetrate our own questions about what justice might look like today.

Typically, what happens in restorative justice or transformative justice spaces is something like this: First, there is the harm caused. Perhaps the person or people involved are already inside the criminal justice system—perhaps, for example, the person responsible has already been arrested or even imprisoned. Perhaps people are coming to this process outside the framework of policing and incarceration. In most cases both victim and offender must consent to be part of the process (though sometimes, if the victim of harm declines to be part of the process for their own well-being or some other reason, the offender meets with someone who survived similar harm). A facilitator or several facilitators who are trained in the work of restorative justice or transformative justice will meet with both perpetrator and victim separately. These sessions, and the process involved, could take anywhere from weeks to months to well over a year.

On the harmed party's side, the work is about assessing their needs, both material and emotional; helping them get clear on what kinds of amends they would like to ask of the perpetrator; sorting through what they want out of, and would like to say in, an eventual meeting; and determining who they would like there as support. On the perpetrator's side, there is work invested in making sure they truly understand the harm caused and their obligations to the victim, as well as perhaps unlearning harmful beliefs that contributed to the harmful action. Ideally, surfacing and engaging with the root causes of this harm—the offender's experiences of poverty, violence, abuse, or systemic oppression, for example—is part of this work as well. (This maps onto step two of Maimonides' repentance process—beginning to change.) In transformative justice, the causes and context of the harm are assessed and addressed in whatever ways might be possible. If the offender and victim are working with different guides through the process, those guides are in frequent contact.

Ultimately, a plan is developed to help meet the victim's self-identified needs—to name what amends should look like. As Sered puts it, "For many harmed parties, the opportunity to shape what repair looks like can be the most transformative part of the accountability process. Trauma is fundamentally about powerlessness, so having the power to direct the future that arises out of the past can contribute significantly to a person's healing process."[39]

Decisions are also made about which people, on both offender's and victim's sides, will be present to support, witness, and hold accountable the two parties in an eventual meeting. One thinks of Maimonides' dictum that the offender must bring friends with them to apologize if the first apology didn't land—the hard work is never meant to be done in a vacuum, in isolation.[40]

Eventually, when all involved are ready, they come together to sit in circle, as it's called in the restorative justice world—to meet, face-to-face, with their support people and the restorative justice facilitators.

Perhaps this is a chance for the victim to ask why this happened to them. Perhaps it's a chance for them to understand what was going through the offender's mind when the victim protested or ran away. Perhaps it's a chance for them to say the thing that they have been wanting to say all this time, or to tell their version of the story, to say out loud what they experienced and what the impact has been.

Perhaps the offender is already remorseful, ready to apologize. Perhaps they don't really get it until the victim tells their story. Perhaps sitting in circle provides closure for them both. Perhaps it's just the beginning of a longer process.

For example, Ana was on the subway one evening when she and her friends were brutally attacked by a group of young people; she was punched and kicked, and some of her hair was pulled out. The trauma impacted her significantly—among other things, she stopped taking the train, which, in turn, impacted her life in a myriad of ways.

Eventually one of her assailants, Trish, wound up in a restorative justice program, and the support team worked with them both to outline what might be done to address the harm—things like work, education, apologies, reading assignments, and community service. But for Ana, that still didn't feel like enough, given what she'd been through. Ana said, "Everywhere I go, I think about this girl. When I wake up, I think about her . . . When I get on the bus instead of the train, I think about her. And when I go to sleep and can't fall asleep, I think about her . . . She's everywhere for me. I want to be everywhere for her." After some discussion, she and the teams reached the agreement that Trish would not be able to ride the subway for the next year and had to keep a daily journal for reflecting on how she thinks Ana might be feeling after the attack.

Trish's initial entries were short and not terribly thoughtful: "I think she felt angry." "I think she felt mad." But eventually, over time—deep in the profound inconvenience of being kept off the trains, forced by the process to have Ana everywhere in her life, something happened. She began writing things like, "I bet she felt so tired of waking up angry. I bet she was frustrated that everything changed because of me, because of something she didn't even do, something she didn't even choose, something that wasn't meant for her. I bet she felt so sad because she didn't know if that feeling would ever go away. I bet she hated me for causing her that pain. I bet she hated hating me, too."[41]

Trish kept her word to stay off the trains, stayed in school, and stayed out of trouble. Ana's trauma symptoms began to subside as a result of this process. Finding the right request for amends helped open the door to the transformation that both of them desperately needed.

Indeed, in many cases, this work is very strong medicine.

Sered told the story of a young man who had been in a gang since he was eight years old. He had witnessed, and survived, and committed, many kinds of violence over the years. He was finally arrested for a robbery and assault, and he eventually found his way into Common

Justice, the restorative justice program that Sered founded. This led to three months of work, culminating in sitting in circle with the peer he had robbed and beaten and the victim's mother.

After the circle ended and everyone had gone, the young man asked Sered if he could sit in her office for a few minutes before leaving. She asked him why. She reported that he said, "I just don't want to go back outside until my hands stop shaking." He told her, "You know, for all I've done and all that's been done to me, I don't know if I've ever heard a real apology before. Do you think I did all right?" She told him that she thought he did a great job.

He responded, "Pardon my language, that is the scariest shit I ever did."[42]

Restorative justice and similar processes are, indeed, powerful for many, and they facilitate meaningful repentance in a great many cases. Survivors who take part in restorative justice in the United States report 80 to 90 percent satisfaction rates, as compared to 30 percent satisfaction from more conventional court systems. In one study out of the University of Pennsylvania, survivors participating in restorative justice reported 37 percent fewer symptoms of post-traumatic stress than those who participated in conventional court processes.[43] Significant research across the United States, the United Kingdom, Australia, and Canada also indicates that it reduces recidivism rates by 44 percent and helps break cycles of violence.[44] Its impact is real. However, it's never going to be the right approach for every situation.

The psychologist and attorney Shira Berkovits, who creates and helps implement policy addressing sexual abuse in the Jewish community, believes that restorative justice can be a powerful alternative model for how Jewish communities handle abuse cases, one that promotes healing and accountability and can minimize trauma for all involved. But as powerful as it can be, she cautions, restorative justice cannot and should not be the only answer:

> Many mediators will not mediate if a case involves abuse, and for good
> reason. Abuse cases have, at their core, a power dynamic that is so

deep, so problematic, that mediation can revictimize the victim. Mediation assumes that both parties have approximately equal power, and that's simply not always the case. Restorative justice is not mediation, but it too requires a safe playing field. When done right, restorative justice includes significant planning so that conversations can be held in a manner where the individual harmed feels safe and supported. Sometimes, though, restorative justice is used in faith communities as a way to pressure victims towards forgiveness. In other cases, restorative justice is imposed upon those who have been harmed.[45]

One synagogue that Dr. Berkovits knows of requires individuals to agree to a restorative justice process before filing a complaint, in an attempt to emphasize the importance of compassion and repentance for all. And yet, as she notes,

Individuals who have been harmed should not be asked to think about the impact on the person who caused them harm when filing a complaint. They should be told that the complaint will be taken seriously, and handled immediately, fairly, and as compassionately as possible. They should not be urged to consider the consequences of the offender's actions on the offender's own life. Nor should they be required to commit to a particular way forward.

Restorative justice can be profound and transformative if the person harmed wants this process. And it can be an especially useful tool in healing between organizations and a community—it can be powerful for stakeholders in an organization to hear the pain the organization has caused. But such restorative justice circles must be victim-initiated. Not just victim-centered. If [restorative justice] is pushed on people, it is not victim initiated. When organizations and institutions talk about restorative justice, it must be named clearly as one option—not the only option. And there must be education about what it is, and what it is not (i.e., a mechanism for compelling forgiveness). We must be careful and cautious, and proceed with humility—this is one answer, not *the* answer. We must never prioritize education and reform for the individual who caused harm over the emotional safety of the individual who has been harmed.[46]

Indeed, there are several different kinds of restorative justice circles—in the most well known, the perpetrator meets their victim face-to-face. In another kind, called vicarious restorative justice, the perpetrator meets with a victim of a similar harm, so that the person that they themselves harmed does not risk the trauma of sitting in circle with the perpetrator. Though this second type can sidestep some of the risks already mentioned, Dr. Berkovits reminds organizations that use vicarious restorative justice as part of a larger process of reintegration to always check in with the person harmed and incorporate their voice into the process.[47]

When restorative justice processes happen in the context of conventional criminal justice systems—when participating becomes a means of avoiding prison or getting a reduced sentence, there is the risk, as the law professor Daniel J. H. Greenwood notes, "that mediation will become, or be perceived as, a mere ritualistic ratification of imposed solutions. Ritualized condemnation, apology, forgiveness, and catharsis always threatens to become an empty masquerade."[48] That is, if the choice is between seeming sorry (even if you're really not, or if you haven't yet had the necessary emotional breakthrough) or going to prison, maybe you'll just look sorry in front of whoever needs to sign off on your process. That's not repentance or repair.

And when the work happens outside the system, there are other kinds of challenges.

When Kyra was in college, she was sexually assaulted by Malcolm, a guy she knew from the local activist community. She wanted accountability, but she did not file charges. The contemporary criminal justice system could not be trusted to hold "us or to hold perpetrators accountable," she wrote when she decided to go public about the assault, knowing that only 8 percent of assaults reported to police result in incarceration, and that the process was usually traumatic to survivors along the way.[49] She knew that these systems would not be just or fair either to her, as a sexual assault survivor and a Black woman, or to him, as a Black man. Rather, she wanted to find ways to protect her wider community without involving the police.

Eventually, a local organization helped them set up a transformative justice process through the framework of community accountability—outside the criminal justice system. Both Kyra and Malcolm were connected to support teams to help them begin to reckon with this harm. They spent more than a year doing exercises with their respective teams—trust-building measures, hard conversations, and, for Malcolm, a deep education in topics related to sexual violence and consent, and the work of integrating these ideas, so that they would not just remain theoretical. Though Kyra and Malcolm did not speak during this time, their teams were in ongoing contact. Kyra eventually asked for amends that included a public apology from Malcolm and his stepping back from publicly speaking—given that he was known as a prominent activist for social and racial justice—about violence against Black women and sexual violence.[50]

After fifteen months, they met in circle with their respective support people and trained facilitators—a meeting which, they both reported afterward, was profound. Kyra described it as "healing," and Malcolm wrote,

> I felt overcome with remorse, empathy, and gratefulness after sharing space with Kyra. I am appreciative of her strength to be engaged in this process and being open enough to allow me an opportunity to make amends. Being able to apologize directly to Kyra for sexual assault without needing to contradict myself or try to misname the harm was the first step in my process . . . I am still committed to being led by Kyra in figuring out how we occupy the same organizing spaces in ways that make her feel most safe and confident. I am hopeful that what I've learned this year has made me a more capable person to deal with ways to prevent harm and to make amends for harms I've caused. I cannot apologize to Kyra without equally saying thank you. All the labor that went into this—emotional, physical, and spiritual—all the folks who struggled to this point, I say thank you.[51]

It's a beautiful end to the story—but unfortunately, in this case, it's not the end of the story.

The first signs of trouble began when Malcolm broke his agreement; he began speaking as an authority about sexual violence on social media and trying to get involved with documentaries and community projects around sexual violence. Then other women began to come forward, sharing on social media that he had assaulted them as well,[52] prior to the transformative justice process. Eventually, another woman published a piece stating that Malcom had raped her at least a year after he and Kyra had sat in circle.[53]

Kyra told me that while she was, of course, furious, she remained glad that she had undergone the community accountability process. "It was a net positive, a huge step in my healing process."[54] Elsewhere, she wrote,

> Transformative justice did not fail. Malcolm did. No matter what method of accountability is chosen, at the end of the day the person who caused harm is the only one who can stop themselves from re-offending. To blame me or [our facilitators] or the field of [transformative justice] is further releasing Malcolm from accountability. It perpetuates rape culture and victim blaming. What the process did was give Malcolm the information and tools he needed to stop being a rapist. What he did with those guides was up to him.[55]

Ultimately, systems cannot force repentance. Systems absolutely can hamper the work or foster it. They can offer tools for the cultivation of the process, they can offer guides and supports and direction, but the work of transformation ultimately rests with the perpetrators of harm.

Needless to say, these are not novel problems. Indeed, as the law professor Daniel J. H. Greenwood notes, "Jewish law accounts are plagued by the problem of the powerful person who ignores the mandate" of the Jewish communal court attempting to impose consequences and foster repentance, such as "the person who uses connections in the gentile world to overturn the court's mandate, or the person who simply refuses to agree voluntarily to the restitution the court sees as necessary. At this point the historical system seems to have simply given up: there was nothing to do about the person who ignores social sanctions, but wait for God to send a snake" to bite them—that is, for the person to experience divinely imposed consequences, since those imposed by human beings weren't working out so well. "And sometimes," Greenwood notes wryly, "one must wait a long time indeed for God or snakes."[56]

So what about us? What are our options for unrepentant perpetrators of harm, besides lying in wait for the appropriate reptile to show up? How are we to think about consequence and accountability if the perpetrator is unwilling to do the work? Or if they are willing to do the work but unable to keep from offending again? Or if the best-established systems for repentance work aren't safe for their victims? What can or should consequences look like then?

Some people who are engaged in this conversation suggest that, though restorative justice and similar kinds of work can never fully replace prisons, it could significantly reduce the number of people who are imprisoned, in concert with significant changes in how our society treats mental illness and addiction—that is, if we offered support and treatment for those who need care rather than criminalization and incarceration. They argue that, for people who cause significant harm and are unrepentant, unwilling to move through a deep restorative justice process, or for whom that process is ineffective or inappropriate, removal from society or restriction of movement may be appropriate. Which doesn't necessarily mean an embrace of many of the cruelties of the current American carceral system.

Proponents of this line of thinking often point to other models of incarceration, such as those found in Scandinavia, where it's not uncommon for prisoners to wear their own clothes, cook their own food (yes, even with knives), possibly commute to offsite work or study, have a phone to contact family at any time, and take furloughs for time with family. Officers in the prison system may wear name tags but do not carry guns, handcuffs, batons, or tasers. Each prisoner has a point person on staff who, starting on day one, helps them along the process of rehabilitation and reentry into society. Those who have been incarcerated are sometimes called "returning neighbors," pointing both to an enduring sense of connection and an understanding that the prison sentence is temporary. In Scandinavia, recidivism rates are from one-half to one-third of those in the United States.[57]

The Norwegian criminologist Nils Christie, who had a strong influence on the development of this system, concluded in the early

1990s that the more a person meting out consequences sees themselves as *unlike* a perpetrator of crime, the harsher the punishment
that person is likely to suggest. This observation reveals a lot about
how racism and other forms of bias can riddle criminal justice systems,
even when those systems are not (as they are in the United States)
deeply intertwined with the legacy of slavery and white supremacy.[58]
By contrast, identification with a perpetrator leads to empathy and,
perhaps, to the understanding that repentance is possible. There is
more willingness to put another human being in an environment
where that work might happen.[59] Such an attitude may inform the
calls for leniency made by white members of the media when prominent white people are arrested. But, as Adnan Khan notes, this is part
of the problem, since "we can't think about prisons as detached from
[American] socioeconomic systems or white supremacy. It's hard to
have prisons like there are in Norway when we don't have the social
structures that they have in Norway."[60]

Indeed, some consider a kinder, gentler system of incarceration to
be wildly insufficient and suggest that the whole prison model is at
odds with what repentance, transformation, and safety can and should
look like. They argue that major social transformation is needed in
order to significantly minimize the harm caused in our society. This
transformation would not only find more productive ways to meet
challenges like addiction and mental illness, but would also address
root issues like systemic racism, economic exploitation, and other
sources of social inequality. They assert that a model that focuses
on offenders' humanity, that regards them as moral agents capable of
change, is critical to creating a more whole society.

As the activist and organizer Mariame Kaba puts it,

> Disposing of people by locking them away in jails and prisons does
> nothing significant to prevent, reduce, or transform harm in the ag-
> gregate. It rarely, if ever, encourages people to take accountability
> for their actions. Instead, our adversarial court system discourages
> people from ever acknowledging, let alone taking responsibility for,
> the harm they have caused. At the same time, it allows us to avoid
> our own responsibilities to hold each other accountable, instead

delegating it to a third party—one that has been built to hide away social and political failures.

Some people may ask, "Does this mean that I can never call the cops if my life is in serious danger?" [Advocacy for prison abolition] does not center that question. Instead, abolition challenges us to ask, "Why do we have no other well-resourced options?" and pushes us to creatively consider how we can grow, build, and try other avenues to reduce harm. Repeated attempts to improve the sole option offered by the state, despite how consistently corrupt and injurious it has proven itself, will neither reduce nor address the harm that actually required the call.

Let's begin . . . not with the question "What do we have now and how can we make it better?" Instead, let's ask, "What can we imagine for ourselves and the world?" If we do that, then boundless possibilities of a more just world await us.[61]

It's notable that, as a result of her community accountability process, Kyra now considers herself a prison abolitionist and remains steadfast in her decision to keep Malcolm out of the law enforcement system.

Even now, even after everything.

It's impossible to talk about crime and punishment and consequences and accountability and repentance without talking about the larger systems in which people are embedded. We do not cause harm in isolation, we cannot be held accountable in isolation, and we cannot do the hard, hard work of repentance, transformation, and change in isolation.

Judge Joseph Flies-Away, former chief judge for the Hualapai Tribal Court in Arizona, says that in his community, when a person commits a criminal act, "People say, 'He acts like he has no relatives.'" Flies-Away regards the law as a tool not to punish, but rather to bring people back into their communal context and to help them heal. He notes, "People do the worst things when they have no ties to people. Tribal court systems are a tool to make people connected again."[62]

Sometimes a single statement speaks volumes. "He acts like he has no relatives" so powerfully evokes that sense of not being accountable to others, to not being in caring relationship with people who want the best for you, to not being clear on how your own actions impact others, to not being able to get help when help is needed. To being given a harsher punishment because the person making that determination regards you as unlike them. These are, in many ways, drivers of harm. And their opposite—embeddedness in community—shows the path back to empathy, to concern, to remorse, repentance, and repair. This is, of course, the opposite of a carceral system that tries to remove a perpetrator from society and from the places in which they are rooted.

Donnell, a young man who had been arrested in a violent altercation and eventually found his way into a restorative justice program, described accountability as "answering to the people of the community that surrounded the person I harmed. It was answering the community of people that surrounded me. It was basically being able to answer to all points, and you can't do that when you're locked up."[63]

Yet it's also true, in a way, that the nature of our embeddedness today and the nature of the points to which we are accountable can also be profoundly challenging in the work of repair. As Sarah-Bess Dworin, a restorative justice teacher and facilitator, notes,

> Today's [restorative justice] circles encounter challenges that were likely not present in the past. Today, participants who sit in circle to build community or resolve conflict have different lived experiences and different value systems. Circle participants in the past would have likely shared kinship ties or meaningful trade relationships. That's not the same encounter as a scenario where one person denies the humanity of another, like having a [white adherent of the far-right conspiracy theory] QAnon and a person of color in circle together.
>
> The size at which our [local, national, and global] community has grown—it's grown past our ability to feel deeply connected, and that's when we lose accountability—our sense of belonging to each

other. You simply can't know that many people—there's an empathy
exhaustion that happens.

   The answer to the question "To whom am I responsible?" would
have been so different 200 or 400 years ago.[64]

When harm happens, we must ask, "To whom am I responsible?"[65]
And we must be willing to extend our sense of responsibility beyond
those with whom we have an immediate sense of identification or
kinship. We must remember that we can and should wish to offer
to anyone the same opportunities for a just hearing and appropriate
consequence, the same chance to hear and be heard, that we might
wish a friend or a neighbor's teenager might have. All assailants are
someone's kid, someone's neighbor. So are all victims. We must create
systems and structures that first and foremost serve victims yet do
not cut the bonds that underlie all of our shared responsibility in a
myriad of ways.

   And we also must make sure to ask, "Who is truly responsible?"
For example, the International Criminal Court made the decision to
define Congolese militia leader Thomas Lubanga's recruiting of young
people to join armed conflict as a human rights violation and a crime
against humanity—by coercing or pressuring them to become killers
and rapists. Notably, according to the legal scholar Martha Minow,

> In the international human-rights context, it is the adults who recruit
> the young people into armed conflict who are to blame. It's not the
> young people themselves. And in international criminal law there's
> mostly a decision to not punish young people, even if they did really
> horrible things, and that's a very striking contrast to how the United
> States treats juvenile offenders . . . Young people get caught up in
> the drug trade, or other kinds of crime, often because adults have
> created a world that either recruits them or coerces them, or doesn't
> give them other options. [66]

The larger context matters. The systems in which people are embedded matter, and the choices they may or may not have matter. And

the support given to someone who is struggling in their repentance work matters critically.

After Malcolm was named as committing sexual assault even after he completed his transformative justice process with Kyra, Mariame Kaba, who had overseen Malcolm and Kyra's process, made a public statement, sharing that she was "disappointed and angry" that he had perpetrated again. She called his actions a "double betrayal," given how much time and labor his accountability team had put into trying to help him grow. But then she added this:

> However, and this will be counterintuitive to some, we also need those who are part of Malcolm's current accountability team to lean into this moment to reduce future harm. Because if everyone cuts ties in this moment, community safety will be further compromised. None of us can be bystanders. We all have a role to play in ending sexual violence. This is a collective responsibility.[67]

As we'll see in the next chapter, typically Maimonides demands that a genuinely penitent perpetrator ask their victim for forgiveness multiple times, but that, at a certain point, they are off the hook with regards to continuing to apologize—Jewish law regards them as having done enough. Except for one very strange exception: Maimonides writes, "But [if the victim] happened to be their rabbi—the perpetrator's spiritual teacher—[the penitent] should go and come to them for forgiveness even a thousand times until [the rabbi] forgives."[68]

This line always bothered me, since Maimonides makes it clear that, generally, people should forgive small slights—but a great, holy teacher of Torah is allowed to hold a grudge and demand almost a thousand apologies!? And then I found a commentary that suggested that this line should ultimately be understood as a pedagogical technique—that the rabbi, as the perpetrator's teacher, is able, more than pretty much anyone else in their life, to see how much change has been made, if enough change has been made, and if more needs to be made. The embeddedness in relationship matters, and the context matters. Sometimes a teacher can guide a penitent through the process to ensure that it has been taken to the deepest extent possible. Helping people remain in those relationships when they're struggling matters, matters critically.[69]

What would our society look like if we focused on addressing the root causes of significant harm, including poverty, systemic racism, and other drivers of trauma and violence; if we helped those who are struggling (for whatever reason, in whatever way) before they potentially offend—for a myriad of reasons, including that our values include helping those who are struggling; if we focused on helping the victims of harm get what they need and moving perpetrators toward the work of repentance and repair? And how might these processes upend some existing systems of power—what might *that* do?

If we want to build a world that determines appropriate consequences for harm, that centers the needs and healing of those most impacted, and that helps the perpetrator transform into an agent of healing, repair, and ongoing renewal, we have tremendous cultural and systemic work to do. A great many structures in our society today will need to change. But change is possible, if there is the communal will to demand it. If we are to make space for a way to address harm that does not cause more harm, we must take the repentance process seriously. We must be willing to facilitate hard inner work, connection, listening, and understanding. We must help people stay embedded in community, whenever possible, and get supports of accountability with and from people who see them, care about them, and want what's best for them. We must listen to victims and survivors, to understand that there might not be a one-size-fits-all package, that one approach may not work in all cases, for all power dynamics, for all perpetrators. What is now, is not what must be. We can find ways of addressing harm and seeking justice that are themselves just.

Repentance is so often possible, in the deepest of ways.

Sered tells the story of one young man with whom she worked through a restorative justice process:

> We were walking back from court, where the felony charges against him had just been dismissed, and I asked, "Now that the threat of

prison is no longer hanging over your head, are you just going to go back and do the same stuff you used to do?" He said, "Nah." (He was never much of a talker.) I asked him to be more specific. He looked at me straight in the eye and said, "No. It's just that, you know," and he pointed to his heart, "the judge is in here now." [70]

CHAPTER SEVEN

FORGIVENESS; OR, THE FUNCTION AND LIMITS OF CLEARING DEBTS

In 1943 a group of prisoners from the Janowska concentration camp was sent to a nearby Nazi army hospital to clear medical waste. Among them was a thirty-five-year-old man, an architect by training named Simon, who was chosen somewhat randomly to be pulled out of his regular work duties. A German nurse asked him if he was a Jew, and when he answered in the affirmative, she brought him into a room in the hospital where a Nazi soldier lay dying.

The soldier told Simon that he had joined the SS as a volunteer. He then shared with Simon some of his personal story and eventually confessed to his participation in a horrific crime—an unspeakable mass murder of three hundred Jews, a burning alive of innocents, of children. He expressed great remorse for his actions and his abetting of profound evil. He told Simon that he would be willing to suffer great agonies if he could only find a way to bring back the dead. As Simon later recounted,

> Here was a dying man—a murderer who did not want to be a murderer but who had been made into a murderer by murderous ideology. He was confessing his crime to a man who perhaps tomorrow must die at the hands of these same murderers. In his confession there was true repentance, even though he did not admit it in so many words.[1]

The dying Nazi begged Simon's forgiveness, as a Jew, on behalf of the Jews that he had murdered.

Simon Wiesenthal stood up, considered the question for a few moments.

And then he walked out of the room, without a word.

The word "forgive," in English, comes the Old English *forgyfan*, which translates primarily as "to give, grant, or bestow." One Old English dictionary connects it to the Hebrew word for "gift."[2] It's a present that is offered, something that is granted to someone freely, without, necessarily, a conversation about whether or not they have earned it. It's an offering, of sorts.

And that is, I think, much the way we talk about forgiveness in contemporary America. It's regarded as a universal good, as something we should give, freely, regardless of whether the perpetrator of harm has done the work of repentance, regardless of whether they have fully owned their harm, regardless of whether they have done the work of repair, regardless of whether they have done the work to change. As one Twitter user put it, "In my white, Christian, middle-class culture, not forgiving someone is seen as a bigger sin than the original action. It . . . calls into question whether you're 'godly' enough."[3]

Not long ago, my friend Jason found himself in a difficult situation at work. He was tasked to work with Dan, a colleague who, while not a direct supervisor, had a higher title and position in the organization than he did. Dan threatened and bullied Jason in a number of ways, including warning Jason that if he didn't obey Dan in every way, Dan would make sure that Jason would be blamed for errors in *Dan's* work. Jason brought his concerns to his manager and then HR, and the initial "solution" to the problem was to allow Jason to work on other projects, away from Dan. Jason felt that this was workable, and he made it clear that, in order to feel safe working on another project with Dan, he would need an apology, an acknowledgment of the threatening behavior, and assurances that it would not continue—or, at minimum, explicit assurances from HR that similar behavior from Dan in the future would not be tolerated. However, despite the fact that none of these measures were taken, Jason's boss began pushing him to return to his work with Dan on another project. The boss urged Jason to forgive and forget, to regard Dan's behavior as simply a difference in working styles.

So often, pressure to forgive comes with a minimizing of the harm caused, a refusal to see its full impact.

When Kelly Sundberg left her violently abusive husband, a friend reached out. When Kelly told her why she had left, what he had done, the friend, Sundberg later recounted,

> wrote back a long message that I think she thought was compassionate. She told me to dig deep and examine what my triggers were that caused me to stay when things got bad. I read her message, and I was confused. At that time, I didn't have the lexicon that I have now. I didn't even know the term "victim-blaming." Still, I knew that what she was saying didn't feel right . . . She wrote about the power of forgiveness. She wrote about how she believed that Caleb "could and would" change.[4]

Forced and coerced forgiveness is not only toxic—it can be lethal. In abuse cases, well, more than half of all female homicide victims are killed by an intimate partner, with a strong correlation to past abuse, and those numbers are on the rise.[5] The victim-blaming attitude that Sundberg's friend and so many others espouse can be profoundly damaging. As one Twitter user shared with me, "I read a book on healing from sexual assault that asked the victim to look introspectively into their own heart and ask forgiveness for anything they might have done to encourage the abuse or for the ill will they held against the offender/s. As a recent survivor at the time, it nearly killed me. I literally wound up in a psych hospital for suicidality."

This isn't how it should be. This isn't how it always is.

In Hebrew, two different words, each with its own shade of meaning and weight, are used in the context of forgiveness. The first is *mechila*, which might be better translated as "pardon." It has the connotation of relinquishing a claim against an offender; it's transactional. It's not a warm, fuzzy embrace but rather the victim's acknowledgment that the perpetrator no longer owes them, that they have done the repair work necessary to settle the situation. You stole from me? OK, you acknowledged that you did so in a self-aware way, you're in therapy to work on why you stole, you paid me back, and you apologized in a way that I felt reflected an understanding of the impact your actions had on me—it seems that you're not going to do this to anyone else. Fine. It doesn't mean that we pretend that the theft never happened, and it doesn't (necessarily) mean that our relationship will return to how it was before or even that we return to any kind of ongoing relationship. With *mechila*, whatever else I may feel or not feel about you, I can consider this chapter closed. Those pages are still written upon, but we're done here.

Slicha, on the other hand, may be better translated as "forgiveness"; it includes more emotion. It looks with a compassionate eye at the penitent perpetrator and sees their humanity and vulnerability, recognizes that, even if they have caused great harm, they are worthy of empathy and mercy. Like *mechila*, it does not denote a restored relationship between the perpetrator and the victim (neither does the English word, actually; "reconciliation" carries that meaning), nor does *slicha* include a requirement that the victim act like nothing happened. But it has more of the softness, that letting-go quality associated with "forgiveness" in English.

Notably, the Jewish literature of repentance mostly deals with *mechila*, the former type of forgiveness. (I'll translate *mechila* as it appears in original sources as "pardon" but will talk about forgiveness as a broad concept more generally.) The classical sources primarily focus on this question: What needs to be done to close accounts, here? And the answers are more nuanced than one might guess at first glance.

One of the most oft-quoted parts of the Laws of Repentance is the bit about forgiveness. The broader context of this section is about what a person must do in order to be able to ask God for atonement at Yom Kippur, which we'll discuss in the next chapter. It begins by laying out the making amends and apology stages of repentance; we've seen some of this before, but it's worth sharing most of it again:

Even if they returned the money owed, they must appease [the person harmed] and ask that they pardon them. Even if [the harmdoer] only offended the other person verbally, they must make amends and implore them until they pardon them.[6]

After making amends, the harmdoer must go to the victim to apologize—to appease, and to come back a couple more times to try to get it right if the victim still isn't having it. There are a lot of verbs involved here—appease, ask, make amends, implore. We see an intensification of the action, an understanding that it is on the person who harmed to do more and better with regard to the person they hurt (presuming, I believe, that this direct apology is welcome, as discussed in Chapter Two). As always, we must center the victim and their needs, and it's on the person who did the harm to make things right. You can imagine, as these verbs intensify, that the penitent is having to increasingly set aside their pride, to work even harder to let go of that story in which they are always the hero, to cross that bridge over to the place where the needs of the person who has been hurt matter most.

It's easy and tempting to regard other people in a transactional way, and indeed, many of our interactions with other human beings are transactional by their very nature. When you order food in a restaurant, the focus of that interaction is not on the hopes, hurts, and longings of either you or your server—even if the interaction is warm and friendly, the core of that relationship is about both your interest in getting your food in a timely manner, without that allergen on your plate, and your server's concern about your eating your meal, not causing a fuss, and leaving a decent tip. It's transactional on both sides. But there is a difference between transactional and objectifying—a transactional relationship can nonetheless be respectful, courteous, and kind. And there is certainly a difference between a transactional relationship and one in which the other person is regarded in their full subjecthood as a whole, multilayered human being, full of talents and dreams and selfhood, holy and created in the divine image. In which the work is to encounter the other person in their messiness, their fullness, on their own terms, rather than through the lens of your own interests or needs.[7]

Much harm is caused when we regard others as objects, or in transactional ways, and forget to behold their full humanity—to see them as complete human beings whose concerns and feelings matter as much as our own.

I believe that a true apology must be an interaction that honors the full humanity of the other; it is not transactional. As I've mentioned before, you don't apologize *at* a person. You apologize *to* them. It's not, of course, a petulant "But I *said* I was *sorry!*" It's also not about crafting the perfectly contrite words of regret and remorse. There's a difference between saying you're sorry because you realize that a thing you did had a bad consequence, and doing so because you really understand that you hurt someone—and that person's feelings, experience of the world, safety, and self all matter profoundly.

A true apology is about trying to see the human being in front of you, to connect with them and communicate to them, to make it clear—abundantly, absolutely, profoundly clear—that you get it now, and that their feeling better matters to you. Your apology is a manifestation of genuine remorse. It demands vulnerability, and it is a natural by-product of all the work of repentance and transformation that you've been doing up until this point. (This is, incidentally, why I think apology comes later in the process—the apology that is needed is generally one that reflects all of the understanding, transformation, and accountability work that has already been taking place.)

When Alix Wall was an undergraduate in the late 1980s, she decided to take some time off and work on a kibbutz for a semester. Just before leaving, she went to a concert with some friends and then got a ride back with some people she had met that evening, who just happened to be Israeli. One of them asked her to bring a birthday present, some jewelry, to a friend of his in Israel. He wrote the recipient's name and address on the front of the envelope containing the gift, and his own on the back. When Wall was asked at the airport if anyone had given her anything to bring to Israel, she said yes, and showed security the envelope. When she landed in Tel Aviv, three police brought her to an interrogation room in the airport. The package actually contained psychedelic mushrooms. Five hours of anxiety and complication later, they finally let her go. She was privileged, and she was lucky.

Twenty-three years later, she had cause to remember the story and decided to look up the "gift-giver" on Facebook. His name had been on the back of that envelope—she had never forgotten it.

He was thrilled and relieved to hear from her. He hadn't even known her name, hadn't known how to contact her, had been racked with guilt for years. He had spent significant time in therapy trying to figure out how to move on, given that he didn't know how to contact Wall to make amends. Wall reports that "he hadn't touched drugs since, because drugs turned him into a kind of person he didn't want to be." He owned what he had done. And he was transformed by his desire to never cause harm like that again.

His comments reflected an understanding of the impact he may have had on her, a concern for her wholeness and well-being. Wall wrote, "I told him that, in general, I was a trusting person until people gave me reason not to trust them. He said, 'I hope you are still like that, that I didn't have a hand in changing that about you.'" And then, later on in the conversation he said, "I remembered that you were really nice and didn't deserve that."

And, yes, "he apologized, several times, and thanked me profusely for contacting him."[8]

This is truly an apology. One in which the perpetrator acknowledges a debt to the victim, in which the thing that matters most is how the victim is doing. This man took the harm he caused seriously, and he had changed his life as a result. He understood how his actions may have impacted Wall, and his apology flowed naturally from that place.

Though the point of the apology is to make things as right as can be with the victim, to attend to their needs, apologizing well can also be a critical part of the transformation that repentance can offer a perpetrator. As Wall reported, "It was such a gift, he said. He felt he had been carrying the residue from this for all of these years and now, he felt free."[9]

So, OK. You've made your apology. It's a good one, that honors the full, holy humanity of the other person. But still, the person who was hurt might not be able to forgive, even after the asking and imploring.

There might be a lot of good reasons for this. Maybe you didn't do as good a job as you think you did, maybe they just might not be ready yet, maybe the harm was much more serious than you had understood it to be. Maybe something else. Now we get to the part about bringing backup with you, presumably for accountability, to make sure you are doing this right, as discussed in Chapter Two. Maimonides writes:

> If the other person does not wish to pardon, they should bring a line of three people who are their friends and they will approach and ask for [pardon]. If [the victim] still refuses, [the perpetrator] must bring people a second and third time.[10]

We're now up to four separate apologies—the original one, and the coming back three separate times with friends. (Not, as Rabbi X did to Rabbi Ner-David in Chapter Two, just saying sorry three times—it sure seems as though you are meant to go away, figure out what went wrong, do some postgame analysis with your friends, and initiate another truly well-intentioned, full-humanity attempt at an apology.) Let's assume that the penitent person is making a sincere, good-faith effort—they have already done confession work and have begun to change. We assume that they no longer want to be the person who causes this kind of harm and are actively working to try to repair what they have broken. And let's assume that a publicist did not write these apologies, that the person who missed the mark is making an earnest effort to see and attend to the person who was hurt. They're trying, sincerely! But four apologies later, it's still not landing.

Here's what Maimonides recommends at this point:

> If [the victim] is still not appeased, [the perpetrator] should leave them alone, and that person who did not pardon is now the sinner.[11]

Well, *that* just took a turn, didn't it?

This line gets a disproportionate amount of airplay in the Jewish world, honestly, and it is often misquoted to suggest that the sin *for which the perpetrator is apologizing* is now borne by the unforgiving victim, even though that's not in the text. It simply implies that, first

of all, the penitent perpetrator has done, after this fourth apology—
and all of the steps of repentance up to this point—everything in
their power to repair the harm caused and is now free to ask God for
atonement on Yom Kippur. They are off the hook. They have fulfilled
their obligations.

And yet, in addition to this, Maimonides claims that the victim *has*
committed some kind of sin—presumably the one mentioned in the
section immediately following the one we've been discussing:

> It is forbidden for a person to be cruel and not appeased; instead,
> a person should be satisfied easily and get angry slowly. And at the
> moment when the sinner asks for pardon—pardon with a whole
> heart and a desirous soul. And even if they caused them suffering
> and sinned against them greatly, [the victim] should not take revenge
> or hold a grudge.[12]

So it seems that Maimonides is asserting that a victim who refuses
to forgive after four sincere apologies and all the other meaningful repentance work up until that point would be guilty of the sin of being
cruel and holding a grudge.

I want to pause here. The Maimonides text we're discussing—the
one that makes the victim guilty of a sin if they don't forgive—stitches
together a few sources. One Talmudic source teaches that a repentant
perpetrator is no longer obligated to ask for forgiveness if they have
been rebuffed three times, but the Talmud never says that the victim
sins by withholding forgiveness.[13] Another—from the Mishnah, if you
want to get technical—asserts that if a victim doesn't forgive, they are
cruel.[14] However, the idea that not forgiving (after the fourth sincere
apology) actually constitutes a sin is from a homiletical source[15]—that
is to say, also from a rabbinic text, but one that's much less authoritative for Jewish law than the Talmud is. So it's curious that Maimonides chose to go out of his way to include this homiletical source,
to drive off the main highway in order to rule that not forgiving is a
sin. (In Judaism, we generally don't like to rule that things are in the
technical category of "sin" if we can avoid it, because then you're giving people more opportunities to transgress Jewish law—which, you

know, can only go poorly.) Maimonides could simply have stuck with the Talmud and suggested that a victim should not be cruel without wading into this heavier category. Rabbi Aryeh Sklar suggests that Maimonides "probably struggled with the logic as to why a person would be free from continuing to ask for forgiveness for his entire life. The Talmud says he is free after the third attempt. It must be because he is no longer in the wrong; the other guy is."[16]

There isn't space here to get into all of the ways in which Maimonides' philosophy of Jewish law and mine differ. I will simply say that I disagree with Maimonides' choice here and believe that it has caused significant undue harm to victims (which will be discussed further on in this chapter). I wish that he had chosen not to bring in the homiletical source and that he had instead included the Jerusalem Talmud text we discussed in Chapter Three—the one about how you don't ever have to forgive if you're a victim of slander—that is to say, irreparable harm.[17]

Anyway, to unpack all of this, we need to enter into what I believe was probably Maimonides' intent in including these words; to name the ways in which this text has been used to harm and blame victims; and also to open up a more trauma-informed reading of it. So there are several different layers. (We'll discuss cases of serious abuse later in this chapter; the next few pages focus on less serious types of harm.)

First, on what I believe to be Maimonides' intention: This text does not mean that the victim now "owns" the harm done to them and is now obligated to do the repair *of the harm done to them*. It means that if someone is unforgiving—after a sincerely penitent person has come vulnerably to them, after their confession, after they have truly begun the work of changing, after amends, after asking and begging and imploring, after bringing friends a few times to try to figure out how to make it more right, after sincerely opening themselves—if, after all that, the hurt person can't find a way to close those accounts, maybe they're being unreasonably petty.

We have a vulnerable penitent coming repeatedly to the person that they hurt. The victim is not being asked to give *slicha*—an emotional, empathetic forgiveness, but rather *mechila*, to say, "OK, you know what? You've done enough. You don't owe me anything any-

more. We can consider this a completed situation." It's not about being willing to return the relationship to what it had been before the
harm, and it's not even about returning to any kind of relationship.
Once again, that would be reconciliation, a whole other ball of wax.
This *mechila* is also not about offering absolution, atonement, to the
penitent—only God can do that. But just as we ask the perpetrator
to actually see the hurt person in front of them, we also ask the victim
to try to recognize the hard, sincere repentance work that has been
done, and to allow it to mean enough to settle accounts. To see the full
human being standing there, a sincere penitent.

Maimonides' concern about the victim being unforgiving was
likely at least in part a concern for their own emotional and spiritual
development. I suspect that he thought holding on to grudges was
bad for the *victim* and their wholeness. That is, even if we're hurt,
we must work on our own natural tendencies toward vengefulness,
toward turning our woundedness into a power play that we can lord
over the penitent, or toward wanting to stay forever in the narrative
of our own hurt, for whatever reason. And perhaps he believed that
the granting of *mechila* can be profoundly liberating in ways we don't
always recognize before it happens.

Rev. Nadia Bolz-Weber articulated this, describing the work of
forgiveness in her own Lutheran tradition:

> What if forgiveness . . . is actually a way of wielding bolt cutters and
> snapping the chain that links us? Like, it is saying, what you did
> was so not OK that I refuse to be connected to it anymore . . . Free
> people aren't controlled by the past. Free people laugh more than
> others. Free people see beauty where others do not. Free people are
> not easily offended. Free people are unafraid to speak truth to stupid.
> Free people are not chained to resentment. That's worth fighting for.[18]

Or, to put it another way, someone once told the writer Treva
Draper-Imler that sometimes forgiveness is about "wishing that rot-
ten SOB peace and getting on with your life."[19]

What if Maimonides is saying this: You have to close those books
so that you can move on! For your own good, your own happiness,

your own engagement with the other people in your life! It's time! This person is here, they're doing the work, they're trying sincerely. And if you are still so resolutely attached to the narrative that you were forever wronged, you are harming yourself and putting a kind of harm into the world. Try to respond to those who approach you sincerely—and who are sincerely doing the work—with a whole heart, not with cruelty.

Yet *mechila* is not healing, per se. We do not assume that the granting of *mechila* magically fixes everything for the person who was hurt, though the perpetrator's obligations with regard to them are at an end. Inner or interpersonal work may still need to be done before, after, or both before and after, the apology and the possible granting of *mechila*. And the perpetrator should not be going anywhere near the person they hurt until they've already done a lot of the work of taking responsibility for their actions and their baggage—the work of owning their stuff and working to change is already underway. Repentance is not dependent on receiving forgiveness—the perpetrator can do the work and free themselves of their obligations regardless of their victim's response. Repentance and healing are, by and large, separate processes—and they can take time. People don't change easily, and they don't heal quickly. Perpetrators sometimes need to take some time to work on the ways they've acted out of brokenness, to try not to hurry along a process that needs space, care, and slowness in order to do it properly.

Needless to say, if the repentance work is not sincere, if the amends made are not enough to make up for what has been broken, if the perpetrator seems to be going through the motions, if you don't feel that the person apologizing to you is making an earnest effort to see you or your needs, if someone with power over you ambushes you and drags you into his office where a bunch of his buddies are waiting and mumbles, "*Mechila*," or calls you out of the blue in the middle of the night because that's when it's convenient for *them*, if they don't really get what they did or are not actively working to make sure it doesn't happen again . . . Nobody should be asking you to close those accounts in the first place.

The context of Maimonides' comments presumes that the person coming to apologize has already been doing the deep work of repentance that we have been discussing, lo, these many chapters. The notion that it may be a transgression to be unforgiving comes in the context of a sincere penitent who has come to apologize—to appease, ask, make amends, implore, seek to meet the full human being they have hurt to the best of their ability. And if they didn't do a good enough job, they came back later with their support people to help them figure out how to do better. And after doing that, this person came back two more times, trying, and trying again, to truly see and speak to their victim's pain. If the person asking for forgiveness hasn't done all of this? The victim has no obligation. None. Bupkes. Nada. Zilch.

This is where we often see forgiveness weaponized. In the wider secular culture, in Christian culture, and yes, even in Jewish culture where we use Maimonides and really should know better, there is often pressure on victims to forgive even when the perpetrator hasn't done all of the work, or even any work at all.

It may be interesting to do a little power analysis when this happens: Who is asking who to forgive what? Pressurized focus on forgiveness can be a very convenient way to reinscribe existing power structures. The employee should forgive the donor who sexually harassed her because that would be convenient for the people whose job it is to raise money. The adult child should forgive the sibling who abused them for the sake of keeping the peace over the holidays. The Latino scholar should forgive the white university trustees who publicly dragged out his tenure process because they didn't like his research on for-profit immigration detention centers. And this demand often comes in the form of a guilt trip—as though the perpetrator can't possibly get free until the victim offers them blanket absolution.

But we already know that this isn't the case—the penitent must cross that bridge, must do the humbling, hard work of trying to make things right, and if they are willing to approach the victim enough times in a sincere enough way, they can be discharged of their obligation to continue doing so. None of this depends on the victim—that is to say, the penitent can free themselves of their obligations even if they are never forgiven. And the withholding of forgiveness truly does have the potential to upend a status quo or two, especially in situations where there is reluctance to hold the perpetrator fully accountable for their actions.

Over the course of 2014 and 2015, as the news media began to devote more coverage to the police killings of unarmed Black people, the white historian Sharrona Pearl was struck by how often, immediately following the death of a sibling, a spouse, a parent, or a child, reporters asked family members of the victim if they forgave their loved one's killer.

The question struck her as "grotesque," so she decided to do some tracking.[20] She created a database of 106 of the higher-profile police shootings that occurred from 2013 to 2016, and she found interviews of family members in 74 of those cases. In a whopping 25 percent of them, family members were asked if they forgave their beloved's killer. And these questions were usually asked either immediately after the shooting, on the day that a grand jury chose not to indict the police officer responsible for the death, or immediately following another event that might prove very emotional for the family—times when they were in shock, grieving, taking in loss. And at that moment, the media put them on the spot.

In none of the cases that Pearl tracked did the killer apologize in direct and clear language to the family of the person whose life they took.

The Black writer Chauncey DeVega, looking at this phenomenon, observed that questions like these were not asked of the families of those killed in mass shootings, like those at the Sandy Hook Elementary School and the movie theater in Aurora, Colorado, and they weren't asked of the families of those killed in the Al Qaeda terrorist attacks on September 11, 2001. When the victims are primarily white, the question simply doesn't come up. As DeVega put it, "Forgiveness for racist violence is a given, an unearned expectation of White America."[21] Our white supremacist society has conditioned itself to demand this forgiveness because it depends on it in order to proceed as it always has. According to Pearl, the families of those killed by police are "asked to grant forgiveness to someone who has not asked for it but [are] really being asked to absolve the system—the institution of the police, and maybe the state as a whole—that produced the individual shooter."[22] The request for forgiveness is, functionally, a request to not name an injustice as an injustice; it is a request that the families of victims not demand amends, recourse, or the kind of systemic change that might prevent the same kind of harm in the future.

All too often in our culture, forgiveness granted to an unrepentant perpetrator—or to a partially repentant perpetrator, or to one whose inner work is unclear but who can write a compelling social media post expressing regret—is conflated with absolution. That is, if the person who has been wronged grants the perpetrator forgiveness, it's read as if the victim is closing the books, freeing the perpetrator from any further obligation to do the work of transformation, of change, of making amends, of becoming the kind of person who doesn't do that harmful thing anymore. Of course, this is part of what leads to victim-blaming—the hard emotional labor is foisted upon the victim, and little to nothing is asked of the perpetrator or the systems that produced the harm. This mentality is all too pervasive: "If we can just get the victim to forgive, this unpleasant situation will go away."

But many of the family members whose unarmed, Black loved ones were killed by police were not having it with this line of thinking. Valerie Castile, the mother of Philando Castile, when prodded on CNN, responded that the officer who shot her son during a traffic stop "took my son's life. I can't forget that and I don't forgive him. Bottom line."[23] Esaw Garner, the widow of Eric Garner, in response to the "condolences" offered her family by the officer who choked her husband to death, responded, "The time for remorse would have been when my husband was screaming to breathe. That would have been the time for him to show some type of remorse or some type of care for another human being's life, when he was screaming eleven times that he can't breathe."[24] Katie Wright, the mother of Daunte Wright, who was also shot during a traffic stop, said, "Justice would bring our son home to us. Knocking on the door with his big smile. Coming in the house. Sitting down. Eating dinner with us . . . So 'justice' isn't even a word to me. I do want accountability—one hundred percent accountability. But even then, when that happens, if that even happens, we're still going to bury our son."[25]

There should never be pressure on victims to forgive. Ever.

When people try to force a victim to forgive, they can even cause additional harm, additional trauma. The psychologist Martha Crawford reflects, "I've seen too many survivors of abuse feel pressured into deeper self-negation and self-injury by accepting the pressure of the cultural prescription to forgive. Before they even understand all that they lost—and that alone can take decades sometimes depending on the injury."[26]

A victim-centered approach is, and should always be, concerned with the hurt person's physical, psychological, emotional, and spiritual well-being. This also means that someone who caused harm should consider whether it might negatively impact the victim if they reach out to try to make amends (as discussed in Chapter Two). An apology should never involve demands or coercion, and a true penitent would back way, *way* off at the faintest intimation that their presence might not be welcome. And, needless to say, whether or not a victim has granted their perpetrator *mechila* is not the business of bystanders, third-party witnesses, employers, or anyone else. It is the victim's prerogative and the victim's business.

Sometimes we are neither the perpetrator or the victim, but, rather, invested third parties. It happens. Besides, of course, helping to ensure that the victim's needs are attended to, there are a lot of ways that we can help the harmdoer as they grapple with the work of accountability and change. A person walking the path of repentance should absolutely have a support system! They should be utilizing trusted loved ones, trained professionals, educators, or others to help them do the difficult, sometimes painful work of accountability and transformation. This is, I think, part of why Maimonides instructs the penitent who's having trouble getting that apology to land to bring friends for subsequent attempts—as one commentary suggests, the penitent should bring people that they wouldn't feel embarrassed to have around as they navigate this awkward, vulnerability-inducing situation.[27] It's hard work, and we shouldn't have to do it alone, particularly if there is struggle involved.

And yet, none of this adds up to making the perpetrator's process the victim's problem. As Rabbi Ruti Regan puts it, "We can believe that offenders deserve support without making their victims responsible for providing it."

This, then, leads us to the third dimension of the Maimonides text we discussed earlier in the chapter: the need to apply a trauma-informed lens to any conversation about harm and forgiveness.

In Chapter Three, we talked about how the Jerusalem Talmud taught that "one who commits slander never gains forgiveness"[28] and that this concept became codified in later Jewish law to mean that the injured party in such a case is not ever required to forgive this sin because, it's understood, the damage is irreversible.[29] Similar cases are noted elsewhere—the Talmud notes that one who defrauds with weights and measures can never complete the work of repentance because it's impossible for a merchant to know who they cheated and to track them down in order to make it right.[30] For some reason, Maimonides doesn't throw this principle into the Laws of Repentance; at least one commentator suggests that this likely just seemed so obvious to him that he didn't think he needed to spell it out.[31] Nonetheless, this principle is not obvious to everyone—at least not to a lot of people who have been hurt very, very deeply, and to other people in their lives. Perhaps this is the moment to make the obvious explicit, to extend it in all the ways that I believe live inside Maimonides' original intent: If someone causes harm that is irreparable, there is no obligation to forgive—to offer even *mechila*, that closing of accounts—even if the perpetrator does the work of repentance in a deep and sincere way.

This is important, so I'll say it again: If someone hurts you in a way that causes irreparable damage, you are *never* obligated to forgive.

Does that mean you can't make the choice to forgive, or that forgiveness might not emerge organically at some point? Of course you may forgive, if that feels like the right thing to you. Indeed, it is sometimes exactly the correct next step in the process of healing or letting go. And in these situations, the person doing the forgiving may choose to share with the perpetrator that they have done so, or they may not; forgiveness may lead to reconciliation of some sort, or it may not. Whatever makes sense for each person, each case, each situation is fine. Asserting that someone is not obligated to do something is not the same as saying that they are forbidden from doing so, or that doing so is a terrible idea. Only this: That for deep, indelible harm, forgiveness never needs to be part of the equation if it never feels like the right thing. And that lack of forgiveness does not mean that there has not been healing. Forgiveness and healing are not the same thing.

To be clear, "obligated" here means, "obligated according to Jewish law." If you're not Jewish, you're not obligated to do any of this stuff, from Maimonides' perspective. And I'd add that if you're a Jew who doesn't live in a framework of Jewish law generally, I'd be more than a little suspicious of anyone who suddenly wants to make this the one place where obligation really, really matters.

In fact, trying to put forgiveness ahead of healing has the potential to create more confusion and to prolong a process that requires time and tears, perhaps additional support, and certainly an honest grappling.

Sarah Stewart Holland was a high school junior who was just getting to school—late for the morning prayer meeting she often attended—when a freshman opened fire, killing three students and injuring five. She walked into the building moments after the shooting happened, saw the bodies of her slain classmates. Stewart Holland wrote, years later,

> The fact that the shooting had happened during prayer circle seemed significant to me. I had often attended the early morning prayer meeting, and I felt both blessed I had been late that morning and guilty I hadn't been attending the prayer circle more regularly. My simultaneous feelings of guilt and gratitude manifested in a driving desire to forgive [the shooter] Michael Carneal. I went to the library and spent hours making signs with several of my classmates to display in the school windows.
>
> "We forgive you, Michael," they read. There was also the one I can never forget: "We forgive you because God forgave us."
>
> The signs made an impact. Story after story portrayed our community as a place where forgiveness lived. I was interviewed by ABC News with two of my classmates. I held my Bible in my lap and spoke

of God's love and how it allowed me to forgive the heinous actions of Michael Carneal.

In my mind, forgiving Michael Carneal meant that I could move on. Even at sixteen, I knew forgiveness was the last step in the healing process. I was not injured. I had not witnessed the shooting. I felt no anger or hatred towards the shooter. Surely this meant I was OK.[32]

Setting aside for now the question of whether Stewart Holland and the other students had any right to forgive Carneal, it turns out that saying "We forgive" didn't magically fix things. The next decade of her life was characterized by ongoing anxiety and dread; she became prone to panic attacks. Later, each time she parted from her husband, even for a few minutes, she was convinced that it would be the last time she would see him. Ten years after the shooting, she finally went to counseling and was diagnosed with post-traumatic stress disorder.

Deciding that forgiveness means healing does not automatically make it so. Nor does prematurely declaring forgiveness always mean that the inner work of truly clearing accounts has taken place.

And, in fact, doing so can serve to short-circuit a process that may need to be longer, deeper, and more complex than might feel ideal. Sometimes people rush to forgiveness to get around the hard inner work that must be done. Sometimes people pressure others to forgive in order to avoid facing their own pain and rage. Sometimes healing needs to happen with forgiveness entirely out of the picture. As the psychologist Martha Crawford puts it,

> There are many ways to come to terms with harms and violations perpetrated by others. Forgiveness is only one of them. Holding people accountable is another. Channeling one's energy into rebuilding one's self and supporting others is one more alternative. How people heal from abusive or aggressive actions isn't necessarily dependent upon what they think about their perpetrator but how they come to think about themselves in the aftermath. The idea that the only way one can come to terms with violating or traumatic harm inflicted by another is dependent on how the victim thinks of the perpetrator is a strangely perpetrator-centric idea. There is more than one way to

skin a cat, and there is more than one way to survive, and even possibly sublimate injury and potentially transform that into wisdom or growth—with or without forgiveness.[33]

Healing may look different from situation to situation, and it comes about in a lot of different ways. Forgiveness is only one of them.

But sometimes the two are profoundly connected. A Twitter user who is a survivor of childhood sex trafficking once commented, "I've actually forgiven the people involved in the trafficking ring . . . but it happened very naturally during the course of a twenty year grief process [that involved] giving myself permission to never forgive, and letting go of feeling guilty about [the fact that] my hate was a vital part of surviving and processing." Sometimes healing can come only by allowing oneself to not have to forgive, by understanding that there is no sin in not closing accounts with those who can never, ever repair the harm they have caused. Sometimes forgiveness comes after the permission to never forgive is finally granted. And sometimes forgiveness never comes. And that's OK too.

And in case this needs to be spelled out: The only one who can grant *mechila* is the victim. Not others, on that person's behalf.

Simon Wiesenthal continued to think about the dying Nazi on and off for years. Finally, in the late 1960s, he wrote up the whole episode—the Nazi's request for forgiveness, his own exit, and some of his subsequent struggles with the questions all of it raised. He sent the text to ten wise thinkers—theologians, political and moral leaders—and asked them what they would have done. The resulting volume, his recounting of the story and the widely varying responses to it, was published as *The Sunflower*. By the 1998 edition, the book had expanded to thirty-two contributors from a range of religious, philosophical, racial, ethnic, and geographic perspectives, many of whom had their own experiences of genocide, oppression, and/or exile. It remains a powerful meditation on the nature, and limits, of forgiveness.

The responses are all over the map. Some contributors, certainly, suggested that Wiesenthal should have forgiven the Nazi, arguing that he had a moral responsibility to do so. Some argued that he should have told the Nazi to make his pleas to God, not to another victim of the very system in which he had committed mass murder. Some talked about collective responsibility and collective guilt. Some wondered whether, had he had not been mortally wounded, the soldier would have continued murdering Jews—and how that possibility should be factored into the equation.

Several people noted that the Nazi, in his search for a Jew, any Jew, from whom to request forgiveness, was actually perpetuating Nazi ideology—not honoring Jews as discrete, autonomous individuals but treating them as interchangeable units. He did not yet see Jews as whole human beings; he may have been sorry for his actions, but he hadn't gone deep enough in the work of introspection and transformation to be different. He still objectified Jews. And in his own self-focused desire to feel absolved, he further victimized another victim of the Nazi genocidal regime, burdening Wiesenthal with his guilt and a moral dilemma without his consent. That's not repentance. As the Jewish philosopher Rebecca Goldstein put it, "Had [the Nazi] understood the enormity of his crimes, he never would have dared to ask for forgiveness. Never." Rather, he would have accepted the conclusion that he had "forfeited forever any questionable right to 'die in peace.'"[34]

Some contributors talked about the importance of compassion, even for those who have hurt you, of the spiritual value of endeavoring to see the other as a whole human, even when they treat you brutally.

But it's important to remember that compassion and forgiveness are not the same thing.

Wiesenthal was, in fact, compassionate to the dying Nazi. He held his hand; he swatted away a fly buzzing around his head. A few years later, after the war, still disquieted by the experience at the Lemberg hospital, he went to visit the soldier's mother, hoping to learn something that would cool his ambivalence into something less complex, wondering if "the feeling of sympathy which [he] could not reject could then perhaps disappear."[35] Part of Wiesenthal's struggle lay in the fact that, though he knew at some level that he had no right to forgive, he did indeed feel compassion both for the Nazi who committed—and regretted committing—horrific acts of genocide, as well as for the Nazi's mother. In the end, he did not divulge to her the truth of her son's crimes. He chose not to alter her memory and understanding of her son, to afflict her with the knowledge of what he had done. This is, I think, a profoundly compassionate choice, certainly one that exceeds the boundaries of his obligations.

But as to whether Wiesenthal should have granted his interlocutor *mechila*, whether he had any right to close the accounts of the Nazi's indebtedness to the people he burned alive, *The Sunflower's* Jewish voices were clear.

As Rabbi Abraham Joshua Heschel wrote,

> No one can forgive crimes committed against other people. It is therefore preposterous to assume that anybody alive can extend forgiveness for the suffering of any one of the six million [Jews] who perished. According to the Jewish tradition, even God . . . can only forgive sins committed against [God], not against [human beings].[36]

The work of repentance and the gift of receiving forgiveness are not the same. The work of repentance is demanded of every single one us for the harm we have caused or participated in, even if some accounts can never be closed.

Having to live with that knowledge may, sometimes, just be one of the consequences of our actions.

CHAPTER EIGHT

ATONEMENT; OR, WHAT IS EFFECTED

Every year, on Yom Kippur, which is sometimes called the Day of Atonement, the High Priest of the Temple in ancient Jerusalem would perform an intricate set of duties. There were a lot of steps involved—putting on special clothes, choosing goats, throwing lots, sacrificing bulls, and so forth—but at one special moment in the ritual he moved from the main Temple area into the Holy of Holies. This was the only day all year when he was permitted to enter this space, and he was the only person who was ever permitted to enter it.

It was a pretty big deal.

His main job, back behind this holy curtain that remained closed the rest of the year, was to sprinkle two kinds of blood: the blood of the bull that he had sacrificed as a ritual purgation for him and his household, and the blood of the goat that he had sacrificed as a ritual purgation for the people. "Thus," says the Book of Leviticus, "he shall do ritual purgation of the holy place, because of the everyday states and transgressions of the Israelites, whatever their sins."[1]

I want to note a few things, here. First of all, "everyday states"—often translated as "ritual impurity"—is an ancient concept that's hard to communicate clearly in English. A person acquired this everyday state through things like being near a dead body, menstruating, ejaculating semen, contracting certain diseases, and other things that were generally part of people's normal experience. It wasn't bad, and it wasn't a moral concept, despite what people often infer from translations that use the words "purity" and "impurity." Being in an everyday state was just a thing that happened—but to go to the Temple, one needed to cleanse oneself of contact with death, illness, or loss of potential life, because being at the Temple was a particular, special, sacred thing. As such, if someone came to the Temple and hadn't completed the special purifying process needed to get from the everyday state to the elevated state, they mucked up the holy status of the Temple. So this complex system of sacrifices and ritual was aimed, in the end, at a ritual cleansing of the physical space, purging impurities from the most sacred of sites.[2] The verses describing the High Priest's sacrifices effecting "ritual purgation for himself" (and possibly his fellow priests) and "ritual purgation for the people," involved releasing from culpability anyone who accidentally came to the Temple in this everyday state.[3]

Second, the word that I have translated above as "ritual purgation" comes from the Hebrew root kpr (yep, hence Yom Kippur). In the sixteenth century, William Tyndale did the first translation of the Christian Bible into English directly from Hebrew and Greek texts—including, of course, this passage from Leviticus, since Hebrew Bible texts are also in the Christian Bible. He made the choice to translate all the words with the root kpr as "atonement,"—that is, at-one-ment—implying a reconciliation or unification between human beings and the divine from whom they had been estranged. This language choice may have been informed by his Lutheran-influenced theology and his belief about what Jesus was meant to effect.[4]

But, as I hope you can see, kapparah, in Leviticus, isn't about unification, or reconciliation, or forgiving and letting off the hook. It's a purification. A wiping clean. A sort of spiritual disinfectant.

That said, it's still often translated as "atonement," and I will do so for the rest of this chapter—knowing full well that I'm kind of conflating two concepts that get conflated a lot in our culture. But I want to talk about what happens at that intersection.

Back to Yom Kippur: In addition to purifying the Holy of Holies, the High Priest is instructed to take another goat, put his hands on its head, and confess all the sins of the Israelites—thereby ritually transferring their transgressions onto the animal, which is then sent into the wilderness.[5] (This is the origin of the term "scapegoat," apparently a variation on a practice found throughout the ancient Near East.[6]) So we have two kinds of confessions—one aimed at purifying the space, and one that is a confession of sins of all the people, which helps to effect a different kind of purification—a purification of the Israelites themselves, of the community.

After the Second Temple was destroyed, the rabbis were able to maintain Yom Kippur's status as a day of, well, atonement for our sins, even with no goats to be found anywhere. Prayer replaced sacrifices throughout the rabbinic system; on Yom Kippur, prayer and a formalized confession effect a potent kind of liturgical magic. Indeed, confession becomes part of the work of repentance globally—the articulation of harm, as we've seen throughout this book. As our friend Maimonides put it, "At this time, when the Temple does not stand and [as such] we do not have an altar for atonement, there is nothing else left but repentance."[7] For the rabbis, and then for Maimonides, each person's (and perhaps our collective) repentance work replaces the labors of the High Priest, and the combination of repentance and this particularly sanctified day can lead to purification.

However! Yom Kippur's power as the day that wipes clean the spiritual slate is not infinite; there are things that it cannot do. The Mishnah teaches, "Yom Kippur atones for transgressions between a person and God, but for a transgression against their neighbor, Yom Kippur cannot atone, until they make things right with their neighbor."[8] In other words, the confession and prayer done on the day of Yom Kippur can, if sincere, atone—purify—if you have committed a sin that impacts only your commitments to the divine. This would include, say, negligence or transgression with regard to ritual commandments, the kinds of things that don't harm other people but violate your integrity with regard to your spiritual commitments.

(OK, you may be thinking, what does this have to do with me if I'm not Jewish, or don't believe in God, or both? To which I say: We're getting there. But we can only get there if I explain what atonement is, and what it isn't, and why. Keep reading.)

For interpersonal harm—the subject of this book and all the stories we've seen up until now—you can show up to services on the Day of Atonement and pray and weep and pour out your heart, but it's not going to do a dang thing until you've actually done the work we've been discussing all this time. You must own the harm you have caused, you must do the work to change, you must make amends, apologize, and, if the opportunity arises, you must make different choices next time. If you have walked the path of repentance with earnest willingness to face what you've done, to repair and transform—then, by the time you get to Yom Kippur, there's the potential for something special to happen. The alchemy of the day just might help you hit that spiritual reset button, to be washed clean of everything you did that wasn't OK. "Though your sins are crimson, they can turn white as snow,"⁹ proclaims a verse from the Book of Isaiah used in our liturgy. A fresh start, in every way.

It's attractive. We all want that spiritual reset button. We all want the things we have done, the things that stain our hearts, to be bleached, purified. We want to be washed clean. We want atonement.

Let's face it: It's deeply uncomfortable to confront the fact that we have caused harm. Research has shown that feelings of guilt can impact how we feel in our bodies; it makes us feel literally weighed down, causing even basic tasks to require more effort than usual.¹⁰ And, of course, guilt—the awareness or belief that I have *done* something bad—can easily trigger, or morph into, shame, the belief that I *am* bad. It may be tempting to look for ways to hack the process, to get to that place where we no longer feel burdened by our conscience, where things *feel* better. Crossing that bridge over into reckoning with what we have done seems like the agonizing opposite of removing this heavy awareness. Instead of getting to the white, we have to walk straight into the crimson? That doesn't seem right! It's easy to panic, to try to figure out if there's a way around the system.

But the only way out is through. And trying to skip to the end without all the work in the middle means that, instead of making different choices, we repeat variations on that same crimson harm.

Austin Channing Brown, in her masterful memoir *I'm Still Here: Black Dignity in a World Made for Whiteness*, recounts an experience at church, when she and a white friend spoke about a trip they had taken to the South—about a horrific experience visiting a plantation and a powerful one at a museum teaching the history of lynching, about Brown's experiences of antiblack racism, about their friendship. And then, inevitably, the deluge. As Brown recounts it, "By the time we stepped off the stage, white people were lining up to offer their racist confessions." Story after story of people's bigotry, failures, micro-aggressions, and, frankly, macro-aggressions—past harms caused to coworkers, acquaintances, potential dates—were dropped into her lap by people ostensibly coming to congratulate her on her talk or ask a question. And, she confirmed later, no one was lining up to tell these stories to her white friend—but the Black women who helped lead worship that day were also being similarly burdened. As Brown put it,

> None of these confessions involved me. No one was apologizing for not listening to me, for being mean to me, or judging me unfairly . . . For every confessor, my body had become the stand-in for the actual people who had been harmed in those situations . . . I was expected to offer absolution.
>
> But I am not a priest for the white soul.
>
> [The white people who approach me with these stories] want me to tell them "it's OK" and give them a handy excuse for their behavior. Youth, ignorance, innocence—anything to make them feel better . . . But just as I cannot make myself responsible for the transformation of white people, neither can I offer relief for their souls."

I sincerely hope that you, by this point in the book, are able to see the deeply problematic choices these white people were making. As Brown points out, it's downright racist to make her the proxy for other individuals who were hurt by an audience member's behavior. And, as she has noted elsewhere, it further harmed her to be exposed to the toxic actions, thoughts, and words of various people in the audience. And, of course, you know by now that this is not actual repentance. These confessions cause further harm; they do not show evidence of a nuanced reckoning; there is no crossing of the bridge to face their own choices, no work of repair. These people, as far as we know, have done no work toward transformation, to make concrete amends, to apologize to those to whom apologies are actually owed—though it's possible that some may have done so after their destructive unloading to Brown and before your reading of this book.

They arrived at the place of harm and, instead of making different choices, committed the same harm in a new way—regarding Brown not as a whole, complex, complete human being full of her own hopes, dreams, needs, and experiences but as a generic Black woman. They did not consider her own feelings and agency; they simply assumed that she was available to them to assist as they unburdened their souls. They did not ask her permission or gain her consent. They did not remunerate her financially for her labor. They did not consider how their stories of racist actions might affect her. And it seems they hoped that confessing to Brown might bring them relief from their sense of guilt, rather than the healthy discomfort of reckoning fully with their past choices and the damage it caused to others. Apparently they craved a release from responsibility rather than the opportunity to begin the work of repentance. They wanted to be told "It's OK now," despite what they had done. They wanted to feel purified.

Brown observes that she was being treated as something of a priest, in line with the Catholic approach to confession and absolution: The penitent confesses their sins and the priest absolves them. Needless to say—to, uh, put it mildly—the sacrament of confession within that tradition does not function by ambushing a non-Catholic lay person unawares.

In the framework we've been discussing, atonement works only if you've done the necessary work of owning harm and undergoing transformation—repentance. And if that harm has an interpersonal dimension, atonement is entirely impossible without repair, amends, and, in most cases, apology. Atonement is available, but it's the last step, after everything else is complete.

Brown, it should be noted, knows this, and has taken to trying to push the white people who seek relief from her in the direction of the bridge. She writes,

> I don't accept confessions like these anymore. Nowadays, when someone confesses about their racist uncle or that time they said the n-word, I determine to offer a challenge toward transformation. For most confessions, this is as simple as asking, "So what are you going to do differently?" The question lifts the weight off my shoulders and forces the person to move forward, resisting the easy comfort of having spoken the confession. The person could, of course, dissolve into excuses, but at that point the weight of that decision belongs to them, not to me.[12]

The literature in my tradition has a lot to say about how atonement, this washing-clean, happens. It's definitely not limited to Yom Kippur. A person's wedding day is said to be their own personal Yom Kippur, their own reset button, since it's traditionally considered the beginning of a new life.[13] The rabbis regarded death itself as a process that releases much of what had been clinging to us—if it is accompanied by repentance.

Most critically for the purposes of this book, the Mishnah, and then Maimonides after that, teach that the work of repentance itself can atone for less serious forms of harm.[14] Atonement is the logical conclusion of the repentance process, and in most cases, doing all of the steps with seriousness and care, walking the path of repair and transformation, is enough to purify your own polluted shrine.

The work of repentance can, itself, bring you to that expiation, that wholeness. As Rabbi Aaron Alexander put it, atonement "doesn't even erase the past, and it certainly can't wipe away all our shame. But it does offer a moment to feel free, once again . . . while our past may stay with us, even haunt us, it need not totally define us. And that is something to celebrate."[15]

Luis, who's now twenty, had what he describes as a "typical Chicago" upbringing—that is to say, "exposed to violence, drugs, some kind of abuse." When he was in junior high, his brother was shot and killed. The previously quiet kid became more rebellious, acting out a hurt he didn't understand at the time. He made friends with some kids who were involved in gang violence; he was drawn to them because he felt that they'd have his back. Later, he would understand that he was "searching to replace that brother bond" that he'd lost. He also thought that if he hung out on the streets, he could find out what had happened to his brother.

Eventually his mother, noticing what he was getting involved with, sent him to live in the suburbs with his sister, but even there—despite hoping to start a normal life—his reputation followed him. "People wanted to hang out with me, not to do homework, but to be associated with the streets," he told me. Soon he started stealing, doing drugs, drinking, getting into fights. Numbing out, he said. Eventually, his behavior led to expulsion from school, and he was sent to an alternative school. There, he began developing some other tools for handling conflict, but even so, his struggle with addiction continued, eventually landing him in a forty-day inpatient rehab program.

"Rehab was a whole different scene for me," he said. Eventually, he and these other so-called tough guys began opening up about the traumas they had endured, the harms they had committed, the hurts they carried. Luis began to be something of a leader, a big brother to some of the other guys in the program. The one who would follow someone else into their room after a rough group therapy session and be with them as they cried. He also realized that some of the staff had been through their own stuff and that he too someday might be able to help others in this way.

He came back from rehab feeling good, empowered, telling all of his friends that they should get sober, modeling for them what this could look like. But this pink cloud—this initial euphoric rush—proved to be short-lived. Not long after getting back, he got into a relationship with someone who was dealing, and he started using again. He managed to graduate from high school and start college, but then he dropped out, convinced that he just couldn't succeed. He got back in touch with some old friends from his gang days, and one night, well, as he put it, "We had been doing bad things all night" when the people driving decided to go by the house of the opposing gang. When they got there, one of the guys he was with took out a gun and started shooting. At which point the guys at whom they were shooting shot at the car Luis was in, and a bullet went through the left side of his abdomen.

"This is what it feels like, this is what my brother must have felt," he thought to himself. The driver got him to the hospital in only seven minutes, and during that whole time, he told me, he found himself

rethinking everything. And then I started getting cold, and everything outside started feeling like it was going slow, there was speed thinking in my head, I got walked to the hospital—the people left me, they didn't want the car caught on camera—bleeding out, puking up liquor and then blood, feeling so cold.

Eventually I felt like I was coming in and going out—I felt like death was coming to me, and time went even slower, like, blink and they're moving me, blink and they tell me they're transferring me, blink and they're saying, "He's lost too much blood," blink and they're poking me with needles. The whole time I'm thinking: Don't tell my mom. I'm going to die. There were all these things I wanted to do, and I didn't even try to get there. I let myself stay stuck.

He made it through surgery, and from there, resolved to do things differently. He spent a month in the hospital, had to learn how to walk again. He cut off the old people for good, this time.

But he also, over time, tried to cross the bridge toward healing. He apologized to his ex. He urged some of the people who'd been with him on the streets to go back to school. He made the choice to give up having any sort of beef with the guy who shot him—he told people to drop the cycle of vengeance, to let it go. And, more than that, he forgave the shooter himself. "I know that there was no intent to hurt. It was a bunch of kids acting out of anger or trying to prove something," he told me. "I blamed myself for a while, but then I had to remember that I didn't know any better. I know that I'm not going to be in that situation again."

He recognized that he's been offered the kind of second chance that most people don't get:

> I didn't think [a better future] was possible for me—now I just for-give and move on. I don't hold no grudges anymore. I don't have any resentments against anybody that pulled me in those directions—I wish the best for them, but I don't have resentments. I understand that there's a lot of things going in their lives—that's OK. I get angry, bothered, but I can't take on other people's rage.
>
> Once you're trying—and truly trying in every aspect to try to be and do right, you'll see the difference. You'll see things change. It comes. It'll hit you. But you have to play your part. You have to do your part. Don't worry about anybody else. It feels so much better knowing you're not doing any harm to anybody. It feels so great. I'm not the same person I was almost two and a half years ago. And I'm happy to say that. I'm so happy to say that. Now I'm just a kid trying to finish school, work, take care of my mom.

Atonement—this wiping clean, this purifying of the polluted shrine—doesn't erase the past, but it helps us to not be defined by it. To find the freedom that is possible on the other side of repentance.

I'll admit that it's something of a personal pet peeve that the word atonement is thrown around as a synonym for forgiveness in popu-lar discourse. In my tradition, forgiveness is something that people can grant to other people (whether they are informed of it or not, as we've discussed). But atonement is, in the framework of my tradition, something that happens in connection with the divine. And, as we've seen, if you've hurt someone else, atonement is up for discussion only after you've done all the work that must be done with regard to repair, apology, and amends. It's not the equivalent of being forgiven by the people you harmed or being off the hook with regard to consequences; it's not a way to force people to turn the page. It's a singular theological concept, at least in my world.

And, as one early medieval Jewish allegory shows, the path to atonement isn't infinite, or insurmountable. What it demands of us is that we go as far as we can. That we do what is within our power.

> A ruler had a child who had gone astray on a journey of a hundred days. The child's friends said, "Return to your parent." The child said, "I cannot." Then the ruler sent a message to the child, saying, "Return as far as you can and I will come the rest of the way to you." In a similar way, God says, "Return to me and I will return to you."[16]

We don't have to get all the way there. We just have to start walking.

And whatever your own Jewishness or lack thereof, whatever your own theology, atheism, or agnosticism, I hope, by the time you have reached these pages, you have been able to see the transformative power of setting out on the journey of repentance. Swallowing your pride and facing, again and again, the harm you have caused through carelessness, through ignorance, through problematic beliefs, through acting from places of pain and trauma and brokenness, through thinking it'll be OK, through thinking nobody will find out, through desperation, through opportunism, through all the reasons that cause us to harm one another. Even if we didn't mean to. Even if we didn't know better. Even if we were being lazy, or careless, or afraid, even if we were acting out because we have all this hurt inside, or even if we don't know why we did it. Whatever our intentions. Doing the work to cross that bridge and see, for real, the impact that we had, what it means, and what we need to learn or do, how we need to change and grow, what we need to offer of ourselves, how we can repair, what can be different.

It can be different. We know that it can.

You know that it can.

But the only way out is through.

And on that way through, you know—you have seen, here— profound healing can happen. Individual lives and relationships can be transformed. Communities and cultures can move toward care, accountability, restoration. Institutions can do the work needed to protect the people they serve. Nations can face the truth of what they have done—even if the work is imperfect, messy, or haphazard—and can make the choice to write a new story for tomorrow. Repair is possible. Atonement is not out of reach. What is needed—and this is, of course, a great deal—is the willingness to do the work. What is needed is the bravery to begin.

On the other side of that bridge, on the other side of transformation, is another more whole, more full, more free way of being, one that we can't fully imagine from here. A way that we must simply bring into existence, step by step.

The Talmud teaches, in the name of Rabbi Hama Bar Hanina, "Great is repentance, for it brings healing to the world."[17]

ACKNOWLEDGMENTS

Thank you to Amy Caldwell and the whole team at Beacon Press, once again, for all your work bringing this book into being.

Thank you, forever and ever, to Jill Grinberg for her steadfast, thoughtful partnership, for her friendship, and for always getting what I'm trying to do (whether or not I've actually done it). And thank you to everyone at Jill Grinberg Literary Management—especially Denise Page, Sophia Seidner, and Sam Farkas—for all that you do.

To the many people who have looked at some or all of this book while it was in progress and offered feedback and insights, and checked me, thank you. Missteps are mine, improvements are theirs. Thank you, Kyra Jones, Brooke Obie, Ruth Hopkins, Rebecca Jackson, Katlin Curtice, Dr. Katja Schatte, Dr. Maxine Rubin, Thorsten Wagner, Rabbi Ruti Regan, Nylah Burton, Dr. Shira Berkovits, Dr. Guila Benchimol, Keshet Starr, Miriam Brosseau, Heather Corrina, Jericho Vincent, James Moed, Rabbi Jill Jacobs, Rabbi Shais Rishon, Rabbi Yosef Goldman, Rev. Claire Brown, Sarah Pechan Driver, Rabbi Dr. Aryeh Cohen, Rabbi Aryeh Bernstein, Rabbi Michael Adam Latz. Many thanks to Grace Gerardi for support with those footnotes. Thank you so much to Dr. Bernie Steinberg and Dr. Noam Hoffmann for so much Rambam learning and deep-diving with me. I am grateful that you were my guides and sounding boards. Thank you to Rabbi Elka Abrahamson, Ruthie Warshenbrot, Or Mars, and Dara Katzner for making that and so much more possible.

To Jericho Vincent for asking the right questions all those years ago, and to Mike Madden for allowing me to beta-test some of these ideas in his pages.

To Sheila Katz, for her support, friendship, colleagueship, and visionary leadership; I'm so grateful that I get to dream and scheme and make holy noise with you. And to all my extraordinary colleagues at National Council of Jewish Women, and to each and every one of our 200,000 advocates on the ground, thank you. It is a joy and a privilege, every day, to be in this work together.

To the people in my neighborhood, both literal and proverbial, supports and sources of so many different kinds of gratitude: Laura Jackson, Rabbi Sam Finesmith, Sarah-Bess Dworin, Dr. Michael Slater, Dr. Shoshana Waskow, Kalman Slater, Yoni Slater, Andrea Hoffman, Cissy Lacks, Dr. Hanne Blank, Rabbi Rachel Weiss, Ali Kagan, Rabbi Jill Jacobs, Jaclyn Friedman, Kirsten Cowan, Miriam Brosseau, James Moed, Karissa Sellman, Bear Bergman, Rev. Bromleigh McCleneghan, Janet Leeds, Karen Leeds, Dr. Chavi Karkowsky, Kohenet Shamirah Bechirah aka Sarah Chandler, Eddie Dinel, Colin Oltman, Abe Frolichstein-Appel, Josefina Camacho, Kelly Cloonan, and so many others—thank you.

To everyone who shared stories with me, including those whose names have been changed in these pages: I am so grateful for your generosity.

Thank you to Ben, and to Carla, for some of the most crucial kinds of support, love, and care. To Irit, Itzik, Guy, Efrat, Naama, and Michal—*ahava, tamid.*

To Yonatan, Shir, and Nomi, master teachers in life and love, and for whom the urgency of making right my many errors has never been clearer: I love you.

It is difficult to write a book during normal times. It is a whole other thing to write one while attempting to co-parent three children through a global pandemic, while also starting a new job and also, probably especially, while dealing with some gnarly and wildly inconvenient health issues. The fact that this book exists at all is entirely to the credit of my extraordinary spouse, Nir; my love, my rock. We all know that I don't deserve you, and I'm so grateful that you're here with me through it all nonetheless.

NOTES

INTRODUCTION

1. Orge Castillino, "Spain Is Suddenly Turning Down Many Jews Who Apply for Citizenship. Why?," *Jewish Telegraph Agency*, August 23, 2021, https://www.jta.org/2021/08/23/global/why-spains-jewish-citizenship-laws-acceptance-rate-has-plummeted.

2. Michael Novak, "The First Institution of Democracy: Tocqueville on Religion, What Faith Adds to Reason," *European View* 6, no. 1 (December 2007): 87–101, https://doi.org/10.1007/s12290-007-0012-8.

3. Louis Henkin, *The Age of Rights* (New York: Columbia University Press, 1996), 2. As he put it, in the United States "individual rights have long been thought of as consisting only of 'immunities,' limitations on what government might do to the individual. Human rights . . . also include positive 'resource claims' . . . what society is required to do for the individual."

4. Herbert Hoover, "Principles and Ideals of the United States Government," speech, October 22, 1928, https://millercenter.org/the-presidency/presidential-speeches/october-22-1928-principles-and-ideals-united-states-government.

5. Sara Konrath, "No, Empathy Isn't a Universal Value," *Psychology Today*, July 17, 2017, https://www.psychologytoday.com/us/blog/the-empathy-gap/201707/no-empathy-isn-t-universal-value, referring to W. J. Chopik, E. O'Brien, and S. H. Konrath, "Differences in Empathic Concern and Perspective Taking Across 63 Countries," *Journal of Cross-Cultural Psychology*, October 14, 2016, https://journals.sagepub.com/doi/abs/10.1177/0022022116673910.

6. Christopher Ingraham, "World's Richest Men Added Billions to Their Fortunes Last Year as Others Struggled," *Washington Post*, January 1, 2021, https://www.washingtonpost.com/business/2021/01/01/bezos-musk-wealth-pandemic/.

7. Michael Sainato, "'We Are Not Robots': Amazon Warehouse Employees Push to Unionize," *The Guardian*, January 1, 2019, https://www.theguardian.com/technology/2019/jan/01/amazon-fulfillment-center-warehouse-employees-union-new-york-minnesota.

8. Eric Spitznagel, "Inside the Hellish Workday of an Amazon Warehouse Employee," *New York Post*, July 13, 2019, https://nypost.com/2019/07/13/inside-the-hellish-workday-of-an-amazon-warehouse-employee/.

9. Jaclyn Diaz, "New York Sues Amazon over COVID-19 Workplace Safety," NPR, February 17, 2021, https://www.npr.org/2021/02/17/968568042/new-york-sues-amazon-for-covid-19-workplace-safety-failures; "Amazon Faces Backlash over COVID-19 Safety Measures," *BBC News*, June 17, 2020, https://www.bbc.com/news/technology-53079624; Dave Lee and Taylor Nicole Rogers, "'The Ultimate David and Goliath Story': The Fight to Open a Union at Amazon," *Financial Times*, April 7, 2021, https://www.ft.com/content/a7ee3ec0-f59d-4188-899f-34ceecf7f026.

10. It's the first of his 95 Theses.

11. Dietrich Bonhoeffer, *The Cost of Discipleship*. (New York: Touchstone, 1995). As Rev. Chris McCreight has put it, "Christianity in America all too often embraces an ethic of cheap grace where forgiveness is expected—quickly—for the benefit of easing tension and erasing conflict. We have heard this uttered when clergy and laity reference Christ's response to [his disciple] Peter, who asked, 'Lord, if another member of the church sins against me, how often should I forgive? As many as seven times?' Jesus said to him, 'Not seven times, but, I tell you, seventy-seven times.' Endless grace; infinite forgiveness; and yet, it neglects that just earlier in the text, Jesus offers instruction to the disciples and the community on *how* to forgive: 'If another member of the church sins against you, go and point out the fault when the two of you are alone. If the member listens to you, you have regained that one. But if you are not listened to, take one or two others along with you, so that every word may be confirmed by the evidence of two or three witnesses. If the member refuses to listen to them, tell it to the church; and if the offender refuses to listen even to the church, let such a one be to you as a Gentile and a tax-collector. Truly I tell you, whatever you bind on earth will be bound in heaven, and whatever you loose on earth will be loosed in heaven.'" https://www.facebook.com/the.mccreights/posts/10164314379775304.

12. Personal correspondence, November 14, 2019, based on her own work on theology and privilege.

13. "The North to the South: Henry Ward Beecher on the Duty of the Hour," *New York Times*, April 6, 1865, https://www.nytimes.com/1865/04/06/archives/the-north-to-the-south-henry-ward-beecher-on-the-duty-of-the-hour.html. It is worth noting that many white abolitionists were racist; they wished to end the institution of slavery but would not embrace the concept of racial equality and ultimately preferred a white supremacist society.

14. Edward J. Blum, *Reforging the White Republic: Race, Religion, and American Nationalism, 1865–1898* (Baton Rouge: LSU Press, 2015), 88.

15. Dr. Hanne Blank, personal correspondence, January 23, 2021.

16. Blum, *Reforging the White Republic*, 89.

17. Rev. Henry Ward Beecher, *New York Independent*, January 14, 1866; page 2 in *Lecture Room Talks, Number 36 Love to Enemies*. Thanks to Daniel José Camacho for sharing this with me and helping point me in the right direction in this inquiry.

18. Indeed, as Blum puts it, "In order for northerners to prove that their desire for reconciliation among whites was genuine, northern white Protestants largely abandoned [Black Americans] in the early 1870s . . . Even when Protestants realized that suffrage had not brought racial peace and justice, they pressed for national reconciliation nonetheless." (*Reforging the White Republic*, 90.)

19. Blum, *Reforging the White Republic*, 118.

20. Nick Bromell, *The Powers of Dignity: The Black Political Philosophy of Frederick Douglass* (Durham, NC: Duke University Press, 2021).

21. Frederick Douglass, "Address at the Graves of the Unknown Dead at Arlington, Virginia," speech, May 30, 1871, Library of Congress, https://www.loc.gov /exhibits/civil-war-in-america/ext/cw0211.html.

22. Aja Romano, "These Memes Want Democrats and Republicans to Be Friends: Good Luck!," *Vox*, November 6, 2020, https://www.vox.com/21549994 /political-conversations-trump-bob-and-sally-meme.

23. Charles P. Pierce, "I'm Not Listening to Any Calls for 'Unity' from the People Who Fueled This," *Esquire*, January 11, 2021, https://www.esquire.com/news-politics /politics/a35179244/republicans-call-for-unity-after-capitol-attack/.

24. Marco Rubio (@marcorubio), "Biden has a historic opportunity to unify America behind the sentiment that our political divisions have gone too far," Twitter, January 10, 2020, 8:34 a.m., https://twitter.com/marcorubio/status/1348277056509980676; "'We Love What They Did': Florida Sen. Marco Rubio Supports Pro-Trump Caravan That Swarmed Biden Bus," *CBS Miami*, November 3, 2020, https://miami .cbslocal.com/2020/11/03/florida-senator-marco-rubio-supports-pro-trump -caravan-swarmed-biden-bus-texas/.

25. Pierce, "I'm Not Listening to Any Calls."

26. Mekishana Pierre, "Stop Calling for Unity; I'm Not 'Coming Together' with Domestic Terrorists," *Popsugar*, January 7, 2021, https://www.popsugar.com/news /stop-calling-for-empathy-for-trump-voters-personal-essay-47955988.

27. S. Harsey, E. Zurbriggen, and J. J. Freyd, "Perpetrator Responses to Victim Confrontation: DARVO and Victim Self-Blame," *Journal of Aggression, Maltreatment, and Trauma*, 26, 2017, 644–63, http://www.tandfonline.com/doi/full/10.1080 /10926771.2017.1320777.

CHAPTER ONE. A REPENTANCE OVERVIEW

1. Sefaria.org is a wonderful website that makes finding the sources that a particular text cites easier than should be legal. Click on the footnote of each law of the *Mishneh Torah* and your gemara/Talmud citation is right there, and you can open it with another click. Back when I was a rabbinical student and in the early days of my rabbinate, we had to use, like, reference skills. It was terrible.

2. The First Temple stood from the tenth to sixth century BCE; the Second Temple stood from 530 BCE to 70 CE.

3. Mishnah Yoma 8:9.

4. Maimonides, *Mishneh Torah*, Laws of Repentance 1:1.

5. Maimonides, *Mishneh Torah*, Laws of Repentance 2:5.

6. Maimonides, *Mishneh Torah*, Laws of Repentance 2:5.

7. Kevin Spacey (@KevinSpacey), "I have a lot of respect and admiration for Anthony Rapp as an actor . . . ," Twitter, October 29, 2017, https://twitter.com /KevinSpacey/status/924848412842971136.

8. Neal Justin, "'I Think I Have to Leave This Country,' Garrison Keillor Says After Firing," *Star Tribune*, November 30, 2017, http://www.startribune.com /garrison-keillor-fired-for-improper-behavior/460802703/.

9. Constance Grady, "Matt Lauer's Public Apology Isn't Much of an Apology," *Vox*, November 30, 2017, https://www.vox.com/culture/2017/11/30/16719492 /matt-lauer-public-apology.

10. Jaime Ducharme, "Mario Batali's Misconduct Apology Came with a Cinnamon Rolls Recipe," *Time*, December 16, 2017, https://time.com/5067633/mario -batali-cinnamon-rolls-apology/.

11. Andy Swift, "Charlie Rose Suspended by PBS, CBS, After 8 Women Accuse Him of Sexual Harassment," *TVLine*, November 20, 2017, https://tvline.com/2017 /11/20/charlie-rose-sexual-harassment-allegations-apology-statement/.

12. William Cummings, "Bill O'Reilly Is 'Mad at God' for Sexual Harassment Scandal," *USA Today*, October 24, 2017, https://www.usatoday.com/story/money /business/2017/10/24/bill-oreilly-mad-god-sexual-harassment-report/795331001/.

13. "Louis C.K. Responds to Accusations," *New York Times*, November 10, 2017, https://www.nytimes.com/2017/11/10/arts/television/louis-ck-statement.html.

14. Megan McCluskey, "Dan Harmon Gives 'Full Account' of Sexually Harassing Community Writer Megan Ganz," *Time*, January 11, 2018, https://time.com /5100019/dan-harmon-megan-ganz-sexual-harassment-apology/.

15. Ira Glass, "674: Get a Spine!," *This American Life*, Chicago Public Media, May 10, 2019, https://www.thisamericanlife.org/674/transcript.

16. Glass, "674: Get a Spine!"

17. Jonah Engel Bromwich, "Megan Ganz on Dan Harmon's Apology: 'I Felt Vindicated,'" *New York Times*, January 13, 2018, https://www.nytimes.com/2018/01 /13/arts/dan-harmon-megan-ganz.html.

18. Bromwich, "Megan Ganz on Dan Harmon's Apology."

19. The *mikveh*, a Jewish ritual bath, comprised of at least some amount of "living water" (rainwater, water from a natural spring or groundwater wells, and so on), is used for spiritual purification. It's employed in the central ritual of the Jewish conversion process; to transform new kitchenware to kosher for cooking; after menstruation and childbirth, before resuming sexual relations; before holy time such as Shabbat and the Day of Atonement; and for other purposes.

20. Maimonides, *Mishneh Torah*, Laws of Repentance 2:3.

21. Thank you to Rabbi Michal Fox Smart for her framing of this.

22. Maimonides, *Mishneh Torah*, Laws of Repentance 2:1.

23. Maimonides, *Mishneh Torah*, Laws of Repentance 2:4.

24. Ka'nhehsí:io Deer, "Why It's Difficult to Put a Number on How Many Children Died at Residential Schools," *CBC News*, September 29, 2021, https://www .cbc.ca/news/indigenous/residential-school-children-deaths-numbers-1.6182456.

25. National Centre for Truth and Reconciliation, "Residential Schools Overview," University of Manitoba, 2015, https://web.archive.org/web/20160420012021/http://umanitoba.ca/centres/nctr/overview.html.

26. Government of Canada, "Statement of Apology to Former Students of Indian Residential Schools," Indigenous and Northern Affairs Canada website, June 11, 2008, https://www.aadnc-aandc.gc.ca/eng/1100100015644/1100100015649.

27. Martin Lukacs, "Canadian Government Pushing First Nations to Give Up Land Rights for Oil and Gas Profits," *The Guardian*, March 3, 2015, https://www.theguardian.com/environment/true-north/2015/mar/03/documents-harper-pushing-first-nations-to-shelve-rights-buy-into-resource-rush.

28. Martin Lukacs, "Justin Trudeau's Lofty Rhetoric on First Nations a Cheap Simulation of Justice," *The Guardian*, September 16, 2016, https://www.theguardian.com/environment/true-north/2016/sep/19/justin-trudeaus-lofty-rhetoric-on-first-nations-a-cheap-simulation-of-justice.

29. Khelsilem, "Justin Trudeau Promised to Protect Indigenous Rights: He Lied, Again," *The Guardian*, June 19, 2018, https://www.theguardian.com/world/commentisfree/2018/jun/19/salish-sea-pipeline-indigenous-salish-sea-canada-trans-mountain.

30. Leyland Cecco, "Trudeau Files Last-Ditch Appeal Against Billions for Indigenous Children," *The Guardian*, October 29, 2021, https://www.theguardian.com/global-development/2021/oct/29/trudeau-government-canada-indigenous-children.

31. Lukacs, "Justin Trudeau's Lofty Rhetoric."

32. Steven Loft, "Reconciliation . . . Really? From Macdonald to Harper: A Legacy of Colonial Violence," *Reconcile This! West Coast Line #74* 46, no. 2, (Summer 2012): 40–47.

33. Big thanks to the wonderful Brooke Obie for raising this question.

34. Maimonides, *Mishneh Torah*, Laws of Repentance 2:9.

35. Maimonides, *Mishneh Torah*, Laws of Personal or Property Injury 1:1.

36. "Beyond 94: Truth and Reconciliation in Canada," *CBC News*, March 19, 2018, https://newsinteractives.cbc.ca/longform-single/beyond-94?&cta=87.

37. District of Columbia Court of Appeals, *Bernard Freundel, Appellant, v. United States, Appellee*. No. 15-CO-899. Decided: September 15, 2016, https://caselaw.findlaw.com/dc-court-of-appeals/1748488.html.

38. Maimonides, *Mishneh Torah*, Laws of Repentance 2:9.

39. Jacob Dunne, "Restorative Justice: Jacob's Story," *Positive News*, March 7, 2017, https://www.positive.news/society/restorative-justice-jacobs-story/.

40. Lindy West, "What Happened When I Confronted My Cruellest Troll," *The Guardian*, February 2, 2015, https://www.theguardian.com/society/2015/feb/02/what-happened-confronted-cruellest-troll-lindy-west.

41. "If You Don't Have Anything Nice to Say, Say It in ALL CAPS," *This American Life*, episode 545, https://www.thisamericanlife.org/545/transcript.

42. West, "What Happened When I Confronted."

43. Likutey Moharan II, 112.

CHAPTER TWO. REPENTANCE IN PERSONAL RELATIONSHIPS

1. Jeremy Hobson, "How to Acknowledge Mistakes and Learn from Them," WBUR, April 9, 2019, https://www.wbur.org/hereandnow/2019/04/09/how-to -acknowledge-mistakes.

2. See, for example, *Mishneh Torah*, Laws of Human Dispositions 6:1–2.

3. Conversation with Dr. Noam Hoffman, November 11, 2019.

4. See, for example, Maimonides' Guide for the Perplexed 3:36.

5. Daniel Lavery, "Dear Prudence: I Abused Past Partners. Do I Have to Tell My Current Boyfriend?" *Slate*, June 15, 2019, https://slate.com/human-interest/2019 /06/dear-prudence-abusive-past-disclose-to-partner.html.

6. Amy Poehler, *Yes Please* (New York: Dey Street Books, 2014), 71.

7. Personal correspondence, April 2, 2021.

8. Maimonides, *Mishneh Torah*, Laws of Repentance 2:4.

9. Meiri, Hibur HaTshuvah 1:9, as cited in HaDerech L'Tshuvah on *Mishneh Torah* Laws of Repentance 2:4, https://hebrewbooks.org/rambam.aspx?mfid =19782&rid=396.

10. Maimonides, *Mishneh Torah*, Laws of Repentance 7:3.

11. Maimonides, *Mishneh Torah*, Laws of Repentance 7:3.

12. Danielle Sered, *Until We Reckon: Violence, Mass Incarceration, and a Road to Repair* (New York: The New Press, 2021), 107.

13. Abraham Joshua Heschel, *God in Search of Man: A Philosophy of Judaism* (New York: Farrar, Straus and Giroux, 1976), 401–3.

14. Maimonides, *Mishneh Torah*, Laws of Repentance 2:9.

15. Babylonian Talmud, Yoma 87a.

16. The stated reason is a homiletic reading of Job, but the rabbis were masters at playing with homiletic readings to reach their desired call to action. (And I don't mean that in a bad way! They delighted in language and its possibilities, riffed on the Torah like jazz musicians trying to figure out what else their instruments were capable of.) The classic source on this is the Babylonian Talmud, Yoma 87a: "Rav Ḥisda said: And one must appease the [one he has insulted] with three rows of three people, as it is stated: 'He comes [*yashor*] before men, and says: I have sinned, and perverted that which was right, and it profited me not' (Job 33:27)." Rabbi Adin Steinsaltz gives this explanation: "Rav Ḥisda interprets the word *yashor* as related to the word *shura*, row. The verse mentions sin three times: I have sinned, and perverted, and it profited me not. This implies that one should make three rows before the person from whom he is asking forgiveness." Interestingly, Maimonides tells us that the perpetrator should bring not three witnesses, but three friends—but there's a little bit of ambiguity about whose friends they are, which raises a few questions. Theoretically, if the perpetrator is bringing three of their own friends, it could enable them to feel more supported in being more vulnerable, or push them to make sure that they are coming correct, as they say—there are eyes ensuring that the penitent is doing the work as is needed. Theoretically, if the committee consists of three of the victim's friends, this could enable the victim to feel supported, because there are people present who have their back and will help hold the perpetrator to real accountability.

17. A lot of times in Jewish spaces, where a certain level of Hebrew and relationship to source texts is presumed, we'll use the classical Hebrew words to refer to traditional concepts, rather than dull things down with translation. She knew exactly what he meant.

18. Maimonides, *Mishneh Torah*, Laws of Repentance 2:9.

19. Haviva Ner-David, *Dreaming Against the Current: A Rabbi's Soul Journey* (Fairfield, CA: Bink Books, 2021), 73.

20. This story is a combination of personal conversation, July 15, 2019, and Ner-David, *Dreaming Against the Current*, 72–74.

21. Mishnah Yoma 8:9.

22. Maimonides, *Mishneh Torah*, Laws of Repentance 2:9.

23. The concept is called *onaat devarim*. This principle, that it is better not to apologize to an unaware victim of gossip if it would hurt them, comes from Rav Yisrael Salanter, as quoted in Rabbi Moshe Sternbuch's Moadim U'Zmanim 1:54.

24. Holly Whitaker, "The Patriarchy of Alcoholics Anonymous," *New York Times*, December 27, 2019, https://www.nytimes.com/2019/12/27/opinion/alcoholics -anonymous-women.html; harMONEY samiruhh, "How Alcoholics Anonymous Psychologically Abuses the Marginalized," The Establishment, May 24, 2017, https:// theestablishment.co/how-alcoholics-anonymous-psychologically-abuses-the -marginalized-ad92410fc0d7/index.html; Jo-Anne D. Fleming, "A Critique of Alcoholics Anonymous from an Anti-oppressive Perspective," master's thesis, McMaster University, 2006, https://macsphere.mcmaster.ca/handle/11375/9735.

25. Personal correspondence, February 11, 2020.

26. Anonymous, "I Confronted My Rapist by Text Message," *Vice*, March 25, 2015, https://www.vice.com/en/article/gq893m/i-confronted-my-rapist-by-text -message-771.

27. Personal correspondence, February 11, 2020.

CHAPTER THREE. HARM IN THE PUBLIC SQUARE

1. Mishnah Yoma 8:9.

2. Jerusalem Talmud Bava Kama 8:7.

3. See, for example, the Rema in the Shulchan Aruch, Orech Hyyim 606.

4. See, for example, Joseph Telushkin, *A Code of Jewish Ethics, Volume 1: You Shall Be Holy* (New York: Random House, 2006), 199.

5. Maimonides, *Mishneh Torah*, Laws of Repentance 4:1.

6. Aja Romano, "J. K. Rowling's Latest Tweet Seems Like Transphobic BS: Her Fans Are Heartbroken," *Vox*, December 19, 2019, https://www.vox.com/culture /2019/12/19/21029852/jk-rowling-terf-transphobia-history-timeline.

7. A. J. Perez, "Five Years Later, Setting the Record Straight on the Ray Rice Video," *USA Today*, September 7, 2019, https://www.usatoday.com/story/sports/nfl/2019/09 /07/nfl-how-ray-rice-video-has-changed-our-views-domestic-violence/2206919001/.

8. Fiona Godlee, Jane Smith, and Harvey Marcovitch, "Wakefield's Article Linking MMR Vaccine and Autism Was Fraudulent: Clear Evidence of Falsification of Data Should Now Close the Door on This Damaging Vaccine Scare," *BMJ: British*

Medical Journal 342, no. 7788 (January 8, 2011), 64–66, http://jstor.org/stable /25766651.

9. Ugur Nedim and Zeb Holmes, "The Influence of the Media on Copycat Crimes," *Sydney Criminal Lawyers*, October 31, 2018, https://www.sydneycriminal lawyers.com.au/blog/the-influence-of-the-media-on-copycat-crimes/.

10. Sian Ferguson, "Calling In: A Quick Guide on When and How," *Everyday Feminism*, January 7, 2015, https://everydayfeminism.com/2015/01/guide-to-calling-in/.

11. Katie Herzog, "Cancel Culture: What Exactly Is This Thing?" *The Stranger*, September 17, 2019, https://www.thestranger.com/slog/2019/09/17/41416013/cancel -culture-what-exactly-is-this-thing.

12. Aja Hoggatt, "An Author Canceled Her Own YA Novel over Accusations of Racism: But Is It Really Anti-Black?" *Slate*, January 31, 2019, https://slate.com/culture /2019/01/blood-heir-ya-book-twitter-controversy.html.

13. Herzog, "Cancel Culture."

14. American Friends Service Committee, *Speak Truth to Power, a Quaker Search for an Alternative to Violence: A Study of International Conflict* (Philadelphia: American Friends Service Committee, 1955), https://palmm.digital.flvc.org/islandora /object/ucf%3A5598.

15. Guthrie Graves-Fitzsimmons (@GuthrieGF), "I deleted a book recommendation thread because the authors I highlighted in it are, to my knowledge, all white . . . ," Twitter, March 19, 2020, https://twitter.com/GuthrieGF/status /1240656099109482497.

16. Gwen Snyder (@gwensnyderPHL), "Not sure what happened to the person who was in my mentions all last year calling out my ableist language . . . ," Twitter, March 11, 2020, https://twitter.com/gwensnyderPHL/status/1237841505651314689.

17. Shannon Downey (@badasscrossstitch), "I have consumed so much media the last week that I'm sad to say I cannot, for the life of me, find the audio interview I was listening to . . . ," Instagram, June 3, 2020, https://www.instagram.com/p/CA _NIp9M34D/?igshid=189pdydfuxoto.

18. Ferguson, "Calling In."

19. Ngọc Loan Trần, "Calling IN: A Less Disposable Way of Holding Each Other Accountable," BGD blog, December 18, 2013, http://www.bgdblog.org/2013 /12/calling-less-disposable-way-holding-accountable/.

20. Babylonian Talmud Arachin 16b.

21. Maimonides, *Mishneh Torah*, Laws of Human Dispositions 6:6.

22. Maimonides, *Mishneh Torah*, Laws of Human Dispositions 6:6.

23. Maimonides, *Mishneh Torah*, Laws of Human Dispositions 6:7.

24. Maimonides, *Mishneh Torah*, Laws of Human Dispositions 6:8. For a discussion of the second half of this law, check a couple notes down from this one.

25. Brené Brown, "Listening to Shame," TED video, March 16, 2012, https:// www.youtube.com/watch?v=psN1DORYYV0.

26. Jeremy Hobson, "How to Acknowledge Mistakes and Learn from Them," WBUR, April 9, 2019, https://www.wbur.org/hereandnow/2019/04/09/how-to -acknowledge-mistakes.

27. Midrash Genesis Rabbah 54:1.

28. It is also true that Maimonides might actually condone putting people on blast if the situation warrants it. As he writes in the Laws of Human Dispositions 6:8, the importance of private rebuke "is about interpersonal relationships; but with regards to heavenly matters, if the sinner does not repent after being rebuked privately, they should be shamed publicly; their sin should be proclaimed, harsh words should be used in their presence, they should be shamed and cursed until they repent and take up the good path, even as all of the prophets in Israel did." For the phrase "interpersonal relationships," he uses *ben adam l'havero*, standard traditional language that translates literally as "between a person and their friend." The flip side in the standard formulation is *ben adam l'Makom*, "between a person and God" (*HaMakom*, the Place, is a name of God in Judaism). But here, instead of *ben adam l'Makom*, he uses "heavenly matters," *divrei shamayim*. The surface meaning of this text is that if someone violates interpersonal commandments—say, if they gossip maliciously or act rudely to a guest—one should call them in quietly until they see the harm they've done. But if, for example, they're habitually breaking Shabbat or kosher laws (that is to say, breaking commandments between a person and God) and don't respond to quiet criticism, they should be called out publicly, lest their bad example mislead other people. However, Maimonides is very intentional about language and certainly uses *ben adam l'Makom* elsewhere in the *Mishneh Torah*, whereas *divrei shamayim* appears to be a novel phrase. Something else may be going on here. As he notes in the Laws of Repentance, sins between a person and God should *not* be confessed publicly, and in this section he cites the prophets as models of this public shaming. Most of the time, the prophets did not yell at people for violating Shabbat. While *divrei shamayim* could refer to idolatry, a lot of the time, the prophets weren't focused on ritual matters. They were known best for rebuking the people, loudly and publicly, about harming the poor, exploiting workers, getting complicit with tyrants. As such, I think Maimonides might be hinting that there are appropriate times for calling someone out publicly, which might cohere with a lot of contemporary wisdom about doing so for public acts of oppression.

29. Maimonides, *Mishneh Torah*, Laws of Repentance 2:5

30. See, for example, the commentary of Rabbi Menachem Krakowsky, *Avodat HaMelech*, on this halakha.

31. Melena Ryzik, Cara Buckley, and Jodi Kantor, "Louis C.K. Is Accused by 5 Women of Sexual Misconduct," *New York Times*, November 9, 2017, https://www .nytimes.com/2017/11/09/arts/television/louis-ck-sexual-misconduct.html.

32. Ryzik, Buckley, and Kantor, "Louis C.K. Is Accused."

33. Gwen Snyder (@gwensnyderPHL), "(thread) One of the most useful organizing lessons I was ever taught was the difference between public and personal relationships . . . ," Twitter thread, August 2, 2019, https://twitter.com/gwensnyderphl /status/1157339454257991680?s=11.

34. *Dictionary.com*, s.v. "Cancel Culture," https://www.dictionary.com/e/pop -culture/cancel-culture/.

35. Snyder, "(thread) One of the most useful."

36. Caroline Framke, "The Sexual Harassment Allegations Against Louis C.K., Explained," *Vox*, November 9, 2019, https://www.vox.com/culture/2017/11/9/16629400/louis-ck-allegations-masturbation.

37. Madeleine Aggeler, "What Happened to the Women Louis C.K. Harassed?" *The Cut*, August 30, 2018, https://www.thecut.com/2018/08/what-about-the-careers-of-louis-ck-victims.html.

38. Wynter Mitchell Rohrbaugh (@wyntermitchell), "I know two of the women Louis CK harassed and they scrubbed their entire social history because of threats . . . ," Twitter, August 23, 2018, https://twitter.com/wyntermitchell/status/1034441418717065217.

39. Halle Kiefer, "Louis C.K. Returns to Stand-up for the First Time Since Admitting to Sexual Misconduct," *The Cut*, August 28, 2018, https://www.thecut.com/2018/08/louis-ck-performs-for-first-time-since-misconduct-admission.html.

40. Maya Salam, "Louis C.K., Back on Tour, Looks to Accelerate His Comeback," *New York Times*, November 2, 2019, https://www.nytimes.com/2019/11/02/arts/louis-ck-tour-rules.html.

41. Jordan Moreau, "Louis C.K. Downplays His Sexual Misconduct in Controversial New Special," *Variety*, April 4, 2021, https://variety.com/2020/digital/news/louis-ck-stand-up-special-metoo-1234571387/.

42. Moreau, "Louis C.K. Downplays."

43. Aditya Mani Jha, "Review: 'Sorry' Shows Tantalising Glimpses of Louis CK at His Peak, but Devolves into Awkward, Undirected Rage," DeadAnt, December 23, 2021, https://deadant.co/review-sorry-shows-tantalising-glimpses-of-louis-ck-at-his-peak-but-devolves-into-awkward-rage/.

44. Gwen Snyder (@gwensnyderPHL), "People talk about 'cancel culture,' when actually what's going on is accountability culture . . . ," Twitter, April 20, 2020, https://twitter.com/gwensnyderPHL/status/1252246202495705089.

45. Jonathan Capehart, "How Derek Black Went from Golden Boy of White Nationalism to Outspoken Critic," *Washington Post*, December 4, 2018, https://www.washingtonpost.com/opinions/2018/12/04/how-derek-black-went-golden-boy-white-nationalism-outspoken-critic/.

46. Larry Getlen, "How I Freed Myself from the KKK," *New York Post*, October 6, 2018, https://nypost.com/2018/10/06/how-david-dukes-godson-freed-himself-from-the-kkk/.

47. Eli Saslow, "The White Flight of Derek Black," *Washington Post*, October 15, 2016, https://www.washingtonpost.com/national/the-white-flight-of-derek-black/2016/10/15/ed5f906a-8f3b-11e6-a6a3-d50061aa9fae_story.html.

48. Derek Black and Matthew Stevenson, interview by Krista Tippett, "Befriending Radical Disagreement," *On Being with Krista Tippett*, podcast, May 17, 2018, https://onbeing.org/programs/derek-black-and-matthew-stevenson-befriending-radical-disagreement/.

49. Derek Black and Eli Saslow, interview by Terry Gross, "How a Rising Star of White Nationalism Broke Free from the Movement," *Fresh Air*, NPR, https://www.npr.org/transcripts/651052970.

50. Black and Stevenson, "Befriending Radical Disagreement." Black acknowledged, "I think I didn't realize how much it hurt my friends at school to be inviting me to their Shabbat dinners and to be arguing with me and to be reading about and thinking about the white nationalist world that hurt them and trying to be my friend and trying to help me. But then I would leave the room, and they would say, This is making our lives worse; why are we doing this, and having to come to the conclusion that it's because we're Derek's friends and we have to do this." (Black and Saslow, "How a Rising Star.")

51. Molly Conger (@socialistdogmom), "If there is someone in your life who you've lost to a hate movement . . ." Twitter, September 6, 2021, https://twitter.com /socialistdogmom/status/1434922962730242050.

52. Derek Black, email to Mark Potok of the Southern Poverty Law Center, July 15, 2013, https://www.splcenter.org/sites/default/files/derek-black-letter-to-mark -potok-hatewtach.pdf.

53. Black and Saslow, "How a Rising Star."

54. Personal correspondence, February 20, 2020.

55. Maimonides, *Mishneh Torah*, Laws of Repentance 2:4.

56. Getlen, "How I Freed Myself."

57. Ron Wagner, "Former White Nationalist Derek Black to Speak at Straighttalk Series," *Furman News*, September 3, 2019, https://news.furman.edu/2019/09/03 /straighttalk-series-concludes-talk-former-white-nationalist-derek-black/.

58. Black and Saslow, "How a Rising Star."

59. Black and Stevenson, "Befriending Radical Disagreement."

60. Black and Saslow, "How a Rising Star."

CHAPTER FOUR. INSTITUTIONAL OBLIGATIONS

1. Rabbi Yitz Greenberg, "SAR's 50th Anniversary Dinner: Rabbi Yitz Greenberg's Speech," SAR Academy, January 16, 2019, video, 14:42, https://www.youtube .com/watch?v=yBnAXaZrH8c.

2. *Jane Doe v. Salanter Akiba Riverdale Academy*, filed to the Bronx County Clerk, October 3, 2019.

3. Ari Feldman, "Prestigious Jewish School Knew About Predator's Abuse but Rehired Him Anyway," *Forward*, October 7, 2018, https://forward.com/news /national/411583/prestigious-jewish-school-knew-about-predators-abuse-but -rehired-him/.

4. *Robert Eckmann v. Salanter Akiba Riverdale Academy*, filed to the Bronx County Clerk, February 6, 2020.

5. Feldman, "Prestigious Jewish School Knew."

6. Ben Sales, "NY Jewish School Officials Knew of Abuse by Administrator Who Molested 12 Students," *Jewish Telegraphic Agency*, October 5, 2018, https:// www.jta.org/2018/10/05/united-states/ny-jewish-school-officials-knew-abuse -administrator-molested-12-students.

7. Private conversation with Rabbi Irving "Yitz" Greenberg, May 18, 2020.

8. Private conversation with Rabbi Irving "Yitz" Greenberg, May 18, 2020.

9. Heather J. Smith, "New Law Lets Old Students Sue SAR Decades After Alleged Abuse," *Riverdale Press*, September 22, 2019, https://riverdalepress.com/stories/new-law-lets-old-students-sue-sar-decades-after-alleged-abuse,70035. The SAR fiftieth-anniversary gala was on January 12, 2019, and the New York Child Victims Act was passed on January 28, a mere sixteen days later.

10. Private conversation with Rabbi Irving "Yitz" Greenberg, May 18, 2020.

11. Kirstyn Brendelen, "SAR Academy Starts Rebuild Days After Admin's Arrest," *Riverdale Press*, September 20, 2019, https://riverdalepress.com/stories/sar-academy-rebuild-administrator-arrest-pornography-bronx-nyc,70046.

12. Heather J. Smith and Kirstyn Brendelen, "This Time Around, SAR Is Much Quicker to Act," *Riverdale Press*, September 29, 2019, https://riverdalepress.com/stories/striving-to-rebuild-trust,70102.

13. See, for example, Ari Feldman, "Is SAR Reckoning with a Sex Abuse Scandal—or Looking for a Scapegoat?" *The Forward*, October 5, 2018, https://forward.com/news/national/411493/is-sar-reckoning-with-a-sex-abuse-scandal-or-looking-for-a-scapegoat/.

14. Personal conversation, June 25, 2020.

15. Maimonides, *Mishneh Torah*, Laws of Repentance 2:9.

16. Personal conversation, June 25, 2020.

17. He learned, about a year and a half after approaching SAR, about the passage of the New York Child Victims Act and decided to file a lawsuit against the school.

18. Dr. Shira Berkovits, personal conversation, May 6, 2020. I strongly recommend that organizations look at the work of Sacred Spaces and spend time with this organizational *cheshbon hanefesh,* guide to taking stock: https://www.aleinu campaign.org/wp-content/uploads/2020/09/Cheshbon-Hanefesh-Organizational-Reflection.pdf. The three factors that Dr. Berkovits has noticed tend to be in play when institutions get things right are humility, a champion within the institution, and a preexisting relationship with anti-abuse work, an anti-abuse organization, or an expert consultant. This, of course, does not mean that an organization without such a preexisting relationship cannot succeed in the work of repentance and transformation, and it most definitely does not mean that they should not try to!

19. Maimonides, *Mishneh Torah*, One Who Injures a Person or Property 1:1, based on the Mishnah Bava Kamma 8:1.

20. Personal conversation, July 7, 2020.

21. Yosef Blau, "The Role of Rabbis in Combating Abuse in the Orthodox Community," *Jerusalem Post*, November 16, 2014, https://www.jpost.com/Opinion/The-role-of-rabbis-in-combating-abuse-in-the-Orthodox-community-381976; "Rabbi Yosef Blau Speaks Up for Child Sex Abuse Survivors," Survivors for Justice website, April 5, 2017, https://www.survivorsforjustice.org/index.php?option=com_content&view=article&id=2955:rabbi-yosef-blau-yu-speaks-up-for-child-sex-abuse-survivors&catid=2:news&Itemid=57.

22. Kelly Clark, "The Troublemakers," *Gospel of Bill (W)* (blog), September 25, 2013, https://12stepspirituality.wordpress.com/.

23. "Kelly was unique among lawyers in that he had a spiritual way of approaching his cases," said Paul Mones, a friend and Portland attorney who worked as co-counsel on one of his cases. "If it meant a client wasn't going to become whole again or better from the legal process, he wasn't interested in the case. He'd tell clients, 'You've got a good case, but you need to take care of yourself first.'" In his letter of disclosure to clients, he wrote, "I don't go a day without remembering where I have been, what were my mistakes and who I hurt." Aimee Green, "Portland Attorney Kelly Clark Dies, Was Nationally Recognized as Defender of Sex-Abuse Victims," *Oregon Live*, December 17, 2013, https://www.oregonlive.com/portland/2013/12/portland_attorney_kelly_clark.html.

24. Dr. Shira Berkovits, personal correspondence, July 9, 2021. Dr. Berkovits has consulted with synagogues and other community organizations on issues related to the reintegration of sex offenders. Consultations cover numerous practical considerations, including the organization's willingness and ability to implement safeguards, the offender's openness to a limited access agreement, the community's interest in having direct conversations about complex and painful topics, and the impact such reintegration might have on victim-survivors of this offender or the community at large. Safe reintegration, she says, is possible some of the time, but it must be trauma-informed, must prioritize safety, and must ensure respect for the dignity of all parties. Reintegration is not always possible or recommended, but it can, in the right instance and done the right way, result in greater safety and healing for all involved. If your organization requires a consultation on this or other abuse-related concerns, visit www.jewishsacredspaces.org/programs/case-consults.

25. Kelly Clark, "Institutional Child Sexual Abuse—Not Just a Catholic Thing," *William Mitchell Law Review* 36, no. 1 (2009), https://open.mitchellhamline.edu/cgi/viewcontent.cgi?article=1328&context=wmlr.

26. Clark, "Institutional Child Sexual Abuse."

27. Carly Parnitzke Smith and Jennifer J. Freyd, "Dangerous Safe Havens: Institutional Betrayal Exacerbates Sexual Trauma," *Journal of Traumatic Stress* 26, no. 1 (2013), https://doi.org/10.1002/jts.21778; Carly P. Smith and Jennifer J. Freyd, "Insult, Then Injury: Interpersonal and Institutional Betrayal Linked to Health and Dissociation," *Journal of Aggression, Maltreatment, and Trauma* 26, no. 10 (2017), https://doi.org/10.1080/10926771.2017.1322654; Lindsey L. Monteith et al., "Perceptions of Institutional Betrayal Predict Suicidal Self-Directed Violence Among Veterans Exposed to Military Sexual Trauma," *Journal of Clinical Psychology* 72, no. 7 (2016), https://doi.org/10.1002/jclp.22292.

28. Monteith et al., "Perceptions of Institutional Betrayal."

29. Paul G. Mattiuzzi, "Pouring Salt on the Wound: Psychologists Identify the Effects of 'Institutional Betrayal,'" *Huffington Post*, October 3, 2014, https://www.huffpost.com/entry/pouring-salt-on-the-wound_b_5924048.

30. Personal conversation, July 7, 2020.

31. Clark, "Institutional Child Sexual Abuse."

32. Sandra G. Boodman, "Should Hospitals—and Doctors—Apologize for Medical Mistakes?," *Washington Post*, March 12, 2017, https://www.washingtonpost

.com/national/health-science/should-hospitals--and-doctors--apologize-for
-medical-mistakes/2017/03/10/1cad035a-fd20–11e6–8f41-ea6ed597e4ca_story.html.

33. Boodman, "Should Hospitals—and Doctors—Apologize?"

34. Boodman, "Should Hospitals—and Doctors—Apologize?"

35. Bonnie G. Ackerman, "You Had Me at 'I'm Sorry': The Impact of Physicians' Apologies on Medical Malpractice Litigation," *National Law Review* 8, no. 310 (2018), https://www.natlawreview.com/article/you-had-me-i-m-sorry-impact-physicians -apologies-medical-malpractice-litigation.

36. Boodman, "Should Hospitals—and Doctors—Apologize?"

37. "Our Founder," Institutional Courage, https://www.institutionalcourage.org /our-founder. This may also be a good place to note the work of Amy Edmondson and her book *The Fearless Organization: Creating Psychological Safety in the Workplace for Learning, Innovation, and Growth* (Hoboken, NJ: Wiley, 2018), which in part looks at systems that organizations can create to receive negative feedback from employees about mistakes that higher-ups may be making.

38. "Our Founder," Institutional Courage.

39. The phrase "women and minorities," as Citigroup used, does a disservice to Black women, Indigenous women, and other women of color, who, of course, fit into both of Citigroup's categories ("women" and "minorities") yet are often erased in these conversations. However, I am leaving the formulation as is because it would be difficult to evaluate Citigroup's data outside of this formulation. It is a pity that the company did not also share how much women of color make compared to white women or men of color, since, given national trends, the gap between women of color's pay and that of white men's is likely to be the largest of all—and behind what white women and men of color make. Equity demands that we name these things explicitly and that repairs are handled transparently. I also look forward to the day when large corporations release data about their nonbinary, intersex, and gender-nonconforming employees.

40. See, for example, "Women of Color and the Wage Gap," Center for American Progress, November 17, 2021, https://www.americanprogress.org/article /women-of-color-and-the-wage-gap/; "Black Women and the Pay Gap," American Association of University Women, https://www.aauw.org/resources/article /black-women-and-the-pay-gap/; "Quantifying America's Gender Wage Gap by Race/Ethnicity," Fact Sheet, National Partnership for Women and Families, January 2022; Chris Morris, "Mind the Wage Gap: Women, Especially Women of Color, Still Earn Less than Men," Nasdaq, March 30, 2021, https://www.nasdaq.com /articles/mind-the-wage-gap%3A-women-especially-women-of-color-still-earn -less-than-men-2021-03-30; "Quantifying America's Gender Wage Gap by Race/ Ethnicity," National Partnership for Women and Families, January 2022, https:// www.nationalpartnership.org/our-work/resources/economic-justice/fair-pay /quantifying-americas-gender-wage-gap.pdf.

41. Thank you to Dr. Guila Benchimol for alerting me to this case. Kyle O'Brien, "Citi Commits to Closing the Gender Pay Gap on International Day of the Girl,"

The Drum, October 11, 2019, https://www.thedrum.com/news/2019/10/11/citi
-commits-closing-the-gender-pay-gap-international-day-the-girl.

42. Michael Corbat, "Gender Pay Gap Is 'a Challenge We Need to Tackle Together,'" Citigroup, September 25, 2019, https://www.citigroup.com/citi/news
/executive/190926Ea.htm.

43. Hugh Son, "Citigroup CEO Corbat Defends Bank's Pay Gap: 'I Started in
1983 at $17,000' Salary," CNBC, May 2, 2019, https://www.cnbc.com/2019/05/02
/citigroup-ceo-corbat-defends-pay-gap-i-started-in-1983-at-17000.html.

44. See, for example, *Mishneh Torah,* Damages to Property 12:22, based on
Talmud Arachin 7a and Bava Batra 175b.

45. For example, Mishnah Ketubot 10:2 and Talmud Ketubot 90b, 91a.

46. "The Lemon Project," William and Mary, https://www.wm.edu/sites
/lemonproject/.

47. Adam Clark, "Rutgers Confronts Ties to Slavery by Renaming Buildings,
Walkway," *NJ.com,* February 8, 2017, https://www.nj.com/education/2017/02
/rutgers_renames_campus_spaces_after_former_slaves.html.

48. "Memorial to Enslaved Laborers," University of Virginia, 2019, https://
slavery.virginia.edu/memorial-for-enslaved-laborers/.

49. Lawrence "Larry" Bacow, "Initiative on Harvard and the Legacy of Slavery,"
Harvard University, November 21, 2019, https://www.harvard.edu/president/news
/2019/initiative-on-harvard-and-the-legacy-of-slavery.

50. Bacow, "Initiative on Harvard."

51. Bacow, "Initiative on Harvard."

52. "Universities Studying Slavery," University of Virginia, https://slavery.virginia
.edu/universities-studying-slavery/.

53. Angelique M. Davis, "Racial Reconciliation or Retreat? How Legislative
Resolutions Apologizing for Slavery Promulgate White Supremacy," *Black Scholar*
42, no. 1, Integration (Spring 2012), 37–48.

54. Meagan Flynn, "Slaves Helped Build Virginia Theological Seminary: The
School Will Spend $1.7 Million in Reparations," *Washington Post,* September 10,
2019, https://www.washingtonpost.com/nation/2019/09/10/virginia-theological
-seminary-reparations-slavery/.

55. "Princeton Theological Seminary Announces Plan to Repent for Ties to
Slavery," *Gather: Princeton Theological Seminary Magazine,* October 18, 2019, https://
gather.ptsem.edu/princeton-theological-seminary-announces-plan-to-repent-for
-ties-to-slavery/.

56. Rachel L. Swarns, "Is Georgetown's $400,000-a-Year Plan to Aid Slave
Descendants Enough?," *New York Times,* October 30, 2019, https://www.nytimes
.com/2019/10/30/us/georgetown-slavery-reparations.html/.

57. Gillian Brockell, "In 1850, a Racist Harvard Scientist Took Photos of Enslaved People: A Purported Descendant Is Suing," *Washington Post,* November 5,
2021, https://www.washingtonpost.com/history/2021/11/05/harvard-agassiz
-racist-enslaved-photos/.

58. Ed Shanahan, "$27 Million for Reparations over Slave Ties Pledged by Seminary," *New York Times*, October 21, 2019, https://www.nytimes.com/2019/10/21/nyregion/princeton-seminary-slavery-reparations.html.

59. Kelly Brown Douglas, "A Christian Call for Reparations," *Sojourners*, July 2020, https://sojo.net/magazine/july-2020/christian-call-case-slavery-reparations-kelly-brown-douglas.

60. Douglas, "A Christian Call for Reparations."

CHAPTER FIVE. ON NATIONAL REPENTANCE

1. Maimonides, *Mishneh Torah*, Laws of Repentance 7:5.

2. That is to say, the TRC's mandate began in 1996, but the enabling legislation, the Promotion of Truth and National Reconciliation Amendment Act (known as the TRC Act), was passed in 1995.

3. As the white international relations scholar Maxine Rubin notes, "The blueprint for apartheid in many respects began under the colonial regimes (especially the British, which actually introduced land segregation). Some argue that we cannot separate racism in South Africa from capitalism—the extractive economy that was developed here under colonialism [and that] needed cheap labour." (Personal correspondence 11/22/20.) See also Mahmood Mamdani, "Amnesty or Impunity? A Preliminary Critique of the Report of the Truth and Reconciliation Commission of South Africa (TRC)," *Diacritics* 32, no. 3/4 (2002): 33–59, https://www.jstor.org/stable/1566444?seq=1.

4. Notably, the African National Congress (ANC) and Pan Africanist Congress (PAC) were not considered political parties during the time of apartheid; they were regarded more as political organizations and liberation movements.

5. Mamdani, "Amnesty or Impunity?"

6. Michelle Sieff, "Parliament Debates Truth Commission Report," *Inter Press Service*, February 28, 1999, http://www.ipsnews.net/1999/02/politics-south-africa-parliament-debates-truth-commission-report/.

7. "Brain-Damaged Biko Was Made to Stand for a Day, TRC Told," *South African Press Association*, September 10, 1997, https://www.justice.gov.za/trc/media/1997/9709/s970910k.htm.

8. See, for example, Martina Schwikowski, "South Africa Is More Unequal Than Ever, Twenty Years After the Post-Apartheid TRC," *Deutsche Welle*, October 29, 2018, https://www.dw.com/en/south-africa-is-more-unequal-than-ever-20-years-after-the-post-apartheid-trc/a-46059235; Gilbert A. Lewthwaite, "Airing Apartheid's Filthy Linen Honesty: All the Terrible Misdeeds of South African Apartheid Are Being Publicly Exposed by Archbishop Desmond Tutu's Truth Commission in Hopes of Achieving a National Reconciliation," *Baltimore Sun*, December 17, 1996, https://www.baltimoresun.com/news/bs-xpm-1996-12-17-1996352009-story.html; and Bonny Ibhawoh, "Do Truth and Reconciliation Commissions Heal Divided Nations?" *The Conversation*, January 23, 2019, https://theconversation.com/do-truth-and-reconciliation-commissions-heal-divided-nations-109925.

9. Martha Minow, *Between Vengeance and Forgiveness: Facing History After Genocide and Mass Violence* (Boston: Beacon Press, 1998), 56.

10. Minow, *Between Vengeance and Forgiveness*, 61.

11. Lewthwaite, "Airing Apartheid's Filthy Linen."

12. Lewthwaite, "Airing Apartheid's Filthy Linen."

13. Lewthwaite, "Airing Apartheid's Filthy Linen."

14. *Wex*, s.v. "South African Truth Commission," Legal Information Institute, https://www.law.cornell.edu/wex/south_african_truth_commission.

15. Ereshnee Naidu-Silverman, "What South Africa Can Teach the U.S. About Reparations," *Washington Post*, June 25, 2019, https://www.washingtonpost.com /outlook/2019/06/25/what-south-africa-can-teach-us-about-reparations/. The TRC also recommended symbolic reparations, in the form of memorials, the renaming of streets, a day of remembrance, and so forth. This too is a complex topic. See, for example, Ereshnee Naidu, "Symbolic Reparations: A Fractured Opportunity," the Centre for the Study of Violence and Reconciliation, 2004, http://www.csvr.org.za /docs/livingmemory/symbolicreparations.pdf.

16. Jina Moore, "Truth Commissions: Can Countries Heal After Atrocities?" *CQ Researcher Online* 4, no. 1 (January 2010), http://library.cqpress.com/cqresearcher /document.php?id=cqrglobal2010010000.

17. As the white international relations scholar Maxine Rubin put it, "The TRC's definition of 'gross human rights violations' was extremely limiting and reduced the apartheid crimes that it would consider to those that involved political and physical violence. This had the benefit of 'impartiality' in that anyone who was the victim of such violations could be recognised, [but] it did not consider violence perpetrated on the basis of race alone as a criterion for its investigations—apartheid was recognised as a crime against humanity and that was it. The TRC focused on politically motivated crimes." (Personal correspondence, November 22, 2020.) See also Mamdani, "Amnesty or Impunity?"

18. Mamdani, "Amnesty or Impunity?"

19. Schwikowski, "South Africa Is More Unequal Than Ever."

20. Mary Kay Magistad, "South Africa's Imperfect Progress, 20 Years after the Truth & Reconciliation Commission," *The World*, April 6, 2017, https://www.pri .org/stories/2017-04-06/south-africas-imperfect-progress-20-years-after-truth -reconciliation-commission.

21. Eugene Baron, "Remorse and Repentance Stripped of Its Validity: Amnesty Granted by the Truth and Reconciliation Commission of South Africa," *Studia Historiae Ecclesiasticae* 41, no. 1 (2015): 169–84, http://dx.doi.org/10.17159/2412-4265 /2015/v41n1a12.

22. Baron, "Remorse and Repentance."

23. "Tutu: 'Unfinished Business' of the TRC's Healing," *Mail and Guardian*, April 4, 2014, https://mg.co.za/article/2014-04-24-unfinished-business-of-the -trc-healing/.

24. "Tutu: 'Unfinished Business' of the TRC's Healing."

25. Maimonides, *Mishneh Torah*, Laws of Repentance 2:11.

26. Maimonides, *Mishneh Torah*, Laws of Repentance 2:5.

27. Christian Pross, *Paying for the Past: The Struggle over Reparation for Surviving Victims of the Nazi Terror* (Baltimore: John Hopkins University Press, 1998), 22.

28. Paragraphs 4ff. of the Federal [Compensation] Law of September 18, 1953.

29. Stephanie Wolfe, *The Politics of Reparations and Apologies* (New York: Springer-Verlag, 2014), 113. "The March 12, 1951 Note [by the Israeli government] indicated a deep bitterness and hostility towards Germany. It estimated 6 million Jewish dead, an estimated value of $6 billion in property seized, including fines, levies, and taxes applied to Jewish persons by the Third Reich. It also repeatedly stressed the idea that Germany could never atone for the genocide, nor would material compensation equate to atonement; what could be done, however, was secure compensation for the heirs of the victims and rehabilitate those who remained alive."

30. Germany's reparations and other forms of repentance work for harm caused to other populations—disabled people, LGBTQIA+ individuals, Romani survivors and the Romani community, and so forth—have been much less robust. Notably, the initial decriminalization of homosexuality did not begin until 1969 in West Germany, and the relevant provision of the German criminal code was not removed in its entirety until 1994. Systemic discrimination against Romani people continues to this day. For more on this, see Wolfe, *The Politics of Reparations and Apologies*, 87–152.

31. For example, Hans Globke, who rose in the ranks of the German government in the 1930s for his exemplary work drafting antisemitic legislation. He served as chief legal advisor to the Office for Jewish Affairs under Adolf Eichmann and became one of the most important people in Adenauer's government, serving as his chief of staff.

32. Jeffrey Herf, "Amnesty and Amnesia," review of *Adenauer's Germany and the Nazi Past: The Politics of Amnesty and Integration*, by Norbert Frei, trans. Joel Golb, *New Republic*, March 9, 2003, https://newrepublic.com/article/66780/amnesty-and-amnesia.

33. Tony Judt, *Postwar: A History of Europe Since 1945* (New York: Penguin Press, 2005), 271.

34. Lorraine Adams, "The Reckoning," *Washington Post*, April 20, 1997, https://www.washingtonpost.com/archive/lifestyle/magazine/1997/04/20/the-reckoning/7c82f131-20c7-40c1-accd-3c035b4fc2d0/.

35. Melissa Eddy, "For 60th Year, Germany Honors Duty to Pay Holocaust Victims," *New York Times*, November 17, 2012, https://www.nytimes.com/2012/11/18/world/europe/for-60th-year-germany-honors-duty-to-pay-holocaust-victims.html.

36. Adams, "The Reckoning."

37. Michael Leonard Graham Balfour, *Withstanding Hitler in Germany, 1933–45* (Abingdon-on-Thames, UK: Routledge, 1988), 263. The historian Katja Schatte suggests that these Allied efforts included "lots of performative measures, such as trips to concentration camp sites, without concerted interest in getting to the root of the problem. Just to name two examples: So-called 'Persilscheine,' that is, documents

certifying that one had not been involved in any significant way with the Nazi regime, were increasingly easy to come by for most. And the West German criminal police was founded by taking over entire training cohorts from Nazi leadership institutions, most notoriously the so-called Charlottenburger, a group of trainees from an SS leadership academy in Berlin-Charlottenburg. All this happened under the 'watchful' eyes of the Allies. German police tried to ignore that history until historians finally dug up so much material in the early 2000s that they no longer could." (Personal correspondence, September 5, 2020.)

38. Conversation with historian Thorsten Wagner, executive director of Fellowships at Auschwitz for the Study of Professional Ethics, August 24, 2020.

39. Richard J. Evans, "From Nazism to Never Again: How Germany Came to Terms with Its Past," *Foreign Affairs*, January/February 2018, https://www.foreign affairs.com/articles/western-europe/2017-12-12/nazism-never-again.

40. The Central Office of the State Justice Administrations for the Investigation of National Socialist Crimes, or Zentrale Stelle der Landesjustizverwaltungen zur Aufklärung nationalsozialistischer Verbrechen, was founded in 1958, after the trial of the Einsatzkommando, with the understanding that many crimes committed by German troops outside German borders had gone uninvestigated.

41. Evans, "From Nazism to Never Again." As Hannah Arendt wrote in 1963, "There is little hope that things will change now, even though the Adenauer administration has been forced to weed out of the judiciary a hundred and forty-odd judges and prosecutors, along with many police officers, with a more than ordinarily compromising past, . . . and to dismiss the chief prosecutor of the Federal Supreme Court, Wolfgang Immerwahr Fränkel . . . It has been estimated that of the eleven thousand five hundred judges in the Bundesrepublik, five thousand were active in the courts under the Hitler regime." Hannah Arendt, "Eichmann in Jerusalem—I," *The New Yorker*, February 8, 1963, https://www.newyorker.com/magazine/1963/02/16/eichmann-in-jerusalem-i.

42. Personal correspondence, November 25, 2021. As she put it, "Who really wanted to know that their parents had a hand in killing millions of human beings at worst, or had turned" away, while knowing full well what was going on, at best? Harald Welzer and Sabine Möller's book *Opa war kein Nazi* (*Grandpa Was No Nazi*) is a key text on this.

43. Damien McGuinness, "Holocaust: How a US TV Series Changed Germany," *BBC News*, January 30, 2019, https://www.bbc.com/news/world-europe-47042244.

44. Conversation with historian Thorsten Wagner, Executive Director of Fellowships at Auschwitz for the Study of Professional Ethics, August 24, 2020.

45. Speech by Federal President Richard von Weizsäcker during the ceremony commemorating the 40th anniversary of the end of war in Europe and of National-Socialist tyranny, May 8, 1985, at the Bundestag, Bonn, https://www.bundespraesident.de/SharedDocs/Downloads/DE/Reden/2015/02/150202-RvW-Rede-8-Mai-1985-englisch.pdf?__blob=publicationFile.

46. "Germany Officially Recognises Colonial-Era Namibia Genocide," *BBC News*, May 28, 2021, https://www.bbc.com/news/world-europe-57279008. According to the *UN Whitaker Report on Genocide, 1985*, roughly sixty-five thousand people were murdered. Jeremy Sarkin-Hughes argues, in *Colonial Genocide and Reparations Claims in the Twenty-First Century: The Socio-Legal Context of Claims Under International Law by the Herero Against Germany for Genocide in Namibia* (Westport, CT: Praeger, 2009), that a hundred thousand victims is likely a more accurate number.

47. Evans, "From Nazism to Never Again." In 2015, a study found that former West Germans were less xenophobic than their former East German counterparts in every generation, and that, immediately following World War II, the likelihood that successive generations of West Germans would harbor anti-foreigner sentiments dropped by 25 percent. The same was not true for East Germans. Even for people born after the war, being raised in a culture that was doing more thoughtful and intentional reckoning with a genocidal past had an impact. As of 2014, only 17 percent of the German population lived in the east, but a whopping 47 percent of xenophobic hate crimes took place there. See, for example, Dagmar Breitenbach, "Where Racism and Xenophobia Are Manifest in Germany," *Deutsche Welle*, August 18, 2015, https://www.dw.com/en/where-racism-and-xenophobia -are-manifest-in-germany/a-18656139. The note on the denazification process is from personal correspondence with the historian Katja Schatte, September 15, 2020.

48. Yet a certain kind of cognitive dissonance remains; many Germans still tend to minimize their own family's culpability in the crimes of the Nazi era. See, for example, Harald Welzer, "Grandpa Wasn't a Nazi: The Holocaust in German Family Remembrance," *International Perspectives* 54 (New York: American Jewish Committee, 2005).

49. William Cook, "Europeans No Longer Fear Germany: But Do the Germans Still Fear Themselves?" *The Spectator*, December 13, 2014, https://www.spectator. co.uk/article/europeans-no-longer-fear-germany-but-do-the-germans-still-fear -themselves-.

50. Griff Witt and Luisa Beck, "Angela Merkel Welcomed Refugees to Germany: They're Starting to Help the Economy," *Washington Post*, May 5, 2019, https://www .washingtonpost.com/world/europe/angela-merkel-welcomed-refugees-to-germany -theyre-starting-to-help-the-economy/2019/05/03/4bafa36e-6b60-11e9-bbe7 -1c798fb80536_story.html.

51. Emily Schultheis, "Teaching the Holocaust in Germany as a Resurgent Far Right Questions It," *The Atlantic*, April 10, 2019, https://www.theatlantic.com /international/archive/2019/04/germany-far-right-holocaust-education-survivors /586357/; Erbil Basay, "Islamophobia on the Rise in Germany," Anadolu Agency, July 1, 2021, https://www.aa.com.tr/en/europe/-islamophobia-on-the-rise-in-germany -/2291727; Matthew Barakat, "Germany Says Antisemitic Crimes up 15 Percent in 2020, Far-Right Attacks on the Rise," *Times of Israel*, May 4, 2021, https://www

.timesofisrael.com/germany-says-far-right-attacks-on-the-rise-antisemitic-crimes
-up-15-in-2020/.

52. Valeriya Safronova, "In Germany, a Jewish Millennial Argues That the Past
Isn't Past," *New York Times*, January 16, 2020, https://www.nytimes.com/2020/01
/16/books/max-czollek-germany-desintegriert-euch.html.

53. Conversation with historian Thorsten Wagner, Executive Director of Fellowships at Auschwitz for the Study of Professional Ethics, August 24, 2020.

54. Talmud Yoma 87b and Maimonides, *Mishneh Torah*, Order of the Prayer
4:2. In most of Jewish liturgy, we pray in the first person plural—not I, but we. Because it's about all of us—our awe, our gratitude, the things we ask for, even the way
we take responsibility. It's almost never just about me.

55. *Orchot Tzadikim*. Thank you to the wonderful Rabbi Jill Jacobs for gen-
erously sharing the source sheet with all of the sources in this brief section; her
teaching on this was connected to work that her organization, T'ruah: The Rabbinic
Call for Human Rights, had done related to racial justice.

56. Waziyatawin, *What Does Justice Look Like? The Struggle for Liberation in
Dakota Homeland* (St. Paul, MN: Living Justice Press, 2008), 30–35.

57. Waziyatawin, *What Does Justice Look Like?*, 39.

58. Mary Lethert Wingerd, *North Country: The Making of Minnesota*, annotated
by Kirsten Delegard (Minneapolis: University of Minnesota Press, 2010), cccxlviii.

59. Vincent Schilling, "The Traumatic True History and Name List of the Dakota 38," *Indian Country Today*, December 26, 2020, https://indiancountrytoday
.com/news/traumatic-true-history-full-list-dakota-38. Execution, here, as the issuing
of capital punishment—distinct from participation in a massacre, such as the slaughter of nearly three hundred Lakota people by U.S. Army soldiers in 1890, or when the
Philadelphia Police Department dropped a C-4 bomb on the MOVE organization,
killing eleven people, including five children, and wiping out 61 homes in two city
blocks, in 1985. And it is certainly distinct from massacres such as those that took
place in Rosewood, FL or Tulsa, OK that were primarily perpetrated by civilians.

60. Waziyatawin, *What Does Justice Look Like?*, 51–52.

61. Waziyatawin, *What Does Justice Look Like?*, 61. Of course, genocide and
forced assimilation have also been disastrous for the Indigenous peoples of Central
and South America, but those stories are outside the scope of this book.

62. Waziyatawin, *What Does Justice Look Like?*, 71.

63. Waziyatawin, *What Does Justice Look Like?*, 91–93.

64. Waziyatawin, *What Does Justice Look Like?*, 94.

65. Waziyatawin, *What Does Justice Look Like?*, 74–76.

66. Waziyatawin, *What Does Justice Look Like?*, 174.

67. Lewthwaite, "Airing Apartheid's Filthy Linen."

68. Thadeus Greenson, "Eureka Schedules Ceremony for Return of Duluwat
Island to the Wiyot Tribe," *North Coast Journal*, October 12, 2019, https://www
.northcoastjournal.com/NewsBlog/archives/2019/10/12/eureka-schedules-ceremony
-for-return-of-duluwat-island-to-the-wiyot-tribe.

69. Mario Koran, "Northern California Esselen Tribe Regains Ancestral Land After 250 Years," *The Guardian*, July 28, 2020, https://www.theguardian.com/us-news/2020/jul/28/northern-california-esselen-tribe-regains-land-250-years.

70. *McGirt v. Oklahoma*, 591 U.S. __ (2020), https://www.supremecourt.gov/opinions/19pdf/18-9526_9okb.pdf; Kaylee Douglas, "Cherokee Nation Files Brief with U.S. Supreme Court as Oklahoma Continues to Fight McGirt Ruling," *Oklahoma's News 4*, October 29, 2021, https://kfor.com/news/oklahoma-media-center/cherokee-nation-files-brief-with-u-s-supreme-court-as-oklahoma-continues-to-fight-mcgirt-ruling/.

71. Shawn Goggins, "Tribes in Okanogan County Celebrating After Being Given 9,200 Acres of Land That Was Taken from Them in 1892," *iFiberOne*, October 20, 2021, https://www.ifiberone.com/columbia_basin/tribes-in-okanogan-county-celebrating-after-being-given-9-200-acres-of-land-that-was/article_a49c0f46-3208-11ec-b9d8-a778f93d3344.html.

72. Waziyatawin, *What Does Justice Look Like?*, 131.

73. Waziyatawin, *What Does Justice Look Like?*, 150–51; Sid Tafler, "A Gift Meant to Correct a Dark Moment in History," *Globe and Mail*, March 27, 2007, https://www.theglobeandmail.com/news/national/a-gift-meant-to-correct-a-dark-moment-in-history/article681740/.

74. Dalton Walker, "Leech Lake Homelands Returned," *Indian Country Today*, December 23, 2020, https://indiancountrytoday.com/news/leech-lake-homelands-returned; "Now on the President's Desk: A Bill to Transfer Land Back to the Ojibwe in Minnesota," KNSI Radio, December 4, 2020, https://knsiradio.com/2020/12/04/now-on-the-presidents-desk-a-bill-to-transfer-land-back-to-the-ojibwe-in-minnesota/.

75. Hannah Yang, "'Steps Toward Healing': Dakota Tribe Reclaims Its Land—and Its Story," *MPR News*, March 3, 2021, https://www.mprnews.org/story/2021/03/03/tribe-reclaims-its-land-and-its-story.

76. Frost, "ChangeMakers."

77. Waziyatawin, *What Does Justice Look Like?*, 158.

78. Personal correspondence, September 14, 2020.

79. Maneesh Arora, "The Promise of Black Lives Matter," *Public Seminar*, January 18, 2022, https://publicseminar.org/essays/the-promise-of-black-lives-matter/; "The Real-Life Changes Won by the Protests," *Axios*, https://www.axios.com/black-lives-matter-protest-police-reform-64c6efb2-31a5-463a-bc1d-2db7b24360d5.html.

80. Keeanga-Yamahtta Taylor, "Did Last Summer's Black Lives Matter Protests Change Anything?" *The New Yorker*, August 6, 2021, https://www.newyorker.com/news/our-columnists/did-last-summers-protests-change-anything.

81. "Accomplices Not Allies: Abolishing the Ally Industrial Complex, an Indigenous Perspective," Indigenous Action Media, May 2, 2014, https://www.indigenousaction.org/wp-content/uploads/simple-file-list/accomplices-not-allies-print-friendly.pdf.

82. Ta-Nehesi Coates, "The Case for Reparations," *The Atlantic*, June 2014, https://www.theatlantic.com/magazine/archive/2014/06/the-case-for-reparations/361631/.

83. Michelle Alexander, *The New Jim Crow: Mass Incarceration in the Age of Colorblindness* (New York: The New Press, 2012); Nikole Hannah-Jones, *The 1619 Project: A New Origin Story* (New York: One World, 2021). By early 2022, at least thirty-six states had introduced or adopted laws or policies that restrict teaching about race or racism.

84. Dana White (@ItsDanaWhite), "The truth is this country . . . ," Twitter, June 23, 2020, https://twitter.com/ItsDanaWhite/status/1275634089287131138.

85. The Kairos Document 3.1, https://kairossouthernafrica.wordpress.com/2011 /05/08/the-south-africa-kairos-document-1985/.

CHAPTER SIX. JUSTICE SYSTEMS

1. Wendy Sawyer and Peter Wagner, "Mass Incarceration: The Whole Pie 2020," Prison Policy Initiative, March 24, 2020, https://www.prisonpolicy.org/reports/pie 2020.html; "Criminal Justice Fact Sheet," NAACP, https://www.naacp.org/criminal -justice-fact-sheet/.

2. Overcrowding and Overuse of Imprisonment in the United States," report, ACLU, 2020, https://www.ohchr.org/sites/default/files/Documents/Issues/Rule OfLaw/Overincarceration/ACLU.pdf.

3. "Criminal Justice Fact Sheet," NAACP.

4. Sawyer and Wagner, "Mass Incarceration."

5. Lorna Collier, "Incarceration Nation," *Monitor on Psychology* 45, no. 9 (October 2014): 56, https://www.apa.org/monitor/2014/10/incarceration.

6. Mariame Kaba, "So You're Thinking About Becoming an Abolitionist," *Medium*, October 30, 2020, https://level.medium.com/so-youre-thinking-about -becoming-an-abolitionist-a436f8e31894.

7. Adam Looney and Nicholas Turner, "Work and Opportunity Before and After Incarceration," Brookings Institution, March 2018, https://www.brookings.edu /wp-content/uploads/2018/03/es_20180314_looneyincarceration_final.pdf.

8. Mariame Kaba and Kelly Hayes, "A Jailbreak of the Imagination: Seeing Prisons for What They Are and Demanding Transformation," *Truthout*, May 3, 2018, https://truthout.org/articles/a-jailbreak-of-the-imagination-seeing-prisons-for -what-they-are-and-demanding-transformation/.

9. "Data Snapshot: School Discipline," *2011–12 CRDC Data Reports*, no. 1 (March 2014), https://www2.ed.gov/about/offices/list/ocr/docs/crdc-discipline -snapshot.pdf; Libby Nelson and Dara Lind, "The School-to-Prison Pipeline, Explained," *Vox*, October 27, 2015, https://www.vox.com/2015/2/24/8101289 /school-discipline-race.

10. Adnan Khan (@akhan), "Holding someone accountable isn't built into our carceral system . . . ," Twitter, February 21, 2021, https://twitter.com/akhan1437 /status/1363662239148900354?s=11.

11. Adureh Onyekwere, "How Cash Bail Works," Brennan Center for Justice, December 10, 2019, https://www.brennancenter.org/our-work/research-reports /how-cash-bail-works.

12. Alex Emslie, "Kamala Harris and Rand Paul Introduce National Bail Reform Bill," KQED, July 20, 2017, https://www.kqed.org/news/11577944/kamala-harris -and-rand-paul-introduce-national-bail-reform-bill; Wendy Sawyer, "How Race Impacts Who Is Detained Pretrial," Prison Policy Initiative, October 9, 2019, https:// www.prisonpolicy.org/blog/2019/10/09/pretrial_race/.

13. Private conversation, December 15, 2020.

14. Private conversation, December 15, 2020.

15. Greg Lorentzen, "Discrimination Against Formerly Incarcerated People," San Francisco Living Wage Coalition, https://www.livingwage-sf.org/mass-incarceration /discrimination-against-formerly-incarcerated-people/.

16. Chris Uggen, Ryan Larson, Sarah Shannon, and Arleth Pulido-Nava, "Locked Out 2020: Estimates of People Denied Voting Rights Due to a Felony Conviction," The Sentencing Project, October 30, 2020, https://www.sentencing project.org/publications/locked-out-2020-estimates-of-people-denied-voting -rights-due-to-a-felony-conviction/.

17. Lorentzen, "Discrimination Against Formerly Incarcerated People."

18. Danielle Sered, *Until We Reckon: Violence, Mass Incarceration, and a Road to Repair* (New York: The New Press, 2021), 3–4.

19. Sered, *Until We Reckon*, 3–4 and 66.

20. Rabbi Jill Jacobs, *There Shall Be No Needy: Pursuing Social Justice Through Jewish Law and Tradition* (Woodstock: Jewish Lights Publishing, 2010), 211.

21. Private conversation, December 15, 2020.

22. Sered, *Until We Reckon*, 23–30.

23. Clark Neily, "Prisons Are Packed Because Prosecutors Are Coercing Plea Deals. And, Yes, It's Totally Legal," *NBC News*, August 8, 2019, https://www.nbc news.com/think/opinion/prisons-are-packed-because-prosecutors-are-coercing -plea-deals-yes-ncna1034201.

24. Negar Katirai, "Retraumatized in Court," *Arizona Law Review* 62, no. 1 (2020), https://arizonalawreview.org/pdf/62-1/62arizlrev81.pdf.

25. Rabbi Dr. Aryeh Cohen, *Justice in the City: An Argument from the Sources of Rabbinic Judaism* (Boston: Academic Studies Press, 2011), 151.

26. "Victims of Violent Crime in Los Angeles County Favor Investments in Crime Prevention over Incarceration, New Survey Finds," Californians for Safety and Justice, March 4, 2021, https://safeandjust.org/news/victims-of-violent-crime-in-los -angeles-county-favor-investments-in-crime-prevention-over-incarceration-new -polling-finds/.

27. John Braithwaite, "Restorative Justice and De-Professionalization," *Good Society* 13, no. 1 (2004).

28. Lorenn Walker and Janet Davidson, "Restorative Justice Reentry Planning for the Imprisoned: An Evidence-Based Approach to Recidivism Reduction," in *Routledge International Handbook of Restorative Justice*, ed. Theo Gavrielides (London: Routledge, 2018).

29. Candace Smith, "Restorative Justice and Transformative Justice: Definitions and Debates," Center for Justice and Reconciliation, March 25, 2013, http://

restorativejustice.org/rj-library/restorative-justice-and-transformative-justice
-definitions-and-debates/; "Transformative Justice," TransformHarm.org, https://
transformharm.org/transformative-justice/.

30. Howard Zehr, afterword, *Changing Lenses: A New Focus for Crime and Justice* (Harrisonburg, VA: Herald Press, 2005): 268–69. "Te Tangata Whenua I Aotearoa" is the correct name for both the peoples and their land; thank you to Te Tangaroa Turnbull for their help on this.

31. Tai Ahu, Rachael Hoare, and Māmari Stephens, "Utu: Finding a Balance for the Legal Māori Dictionary," *Victoria University of Wellington Law Review* 42, no. 2 (2011), https://ndhadeliver.natlib.govt.nz/delivery/DeliveryManagerServlet?dps _pid=FL7375936.

32. Laura Mirsky, "Restorative Justice Practices of Native American, First Nation, and Other Indigenous People of North America: Part One," International Institute for Restorative Practices Graduate School, April 27, 2004, https://www.iirp .edu/news/restorative-justice-practices-of-native-american-first-nation-and-other -indigenous-people-of-north-america-part-one.

33. John G. Hansen, "Countering Imperial Justice: The Implication of a Cree Response to Crime," *Indigenous Policy Journal* 23, no. 1 (2012), https://1library.net/document /z3onn89z-countering-imperial-justice-implications-cree-response-crime.html.

34. Zehr, afterword, *Changing Lenses*, 271.

35. Howard Zehr, *The Little Book of Restorative Justice* (Intercourse, PA: Good Books), 2002.

36. Jacobs, *There Shall Be No Needy*, 195–96.

37. Talmud Sanhedrin 37b. But as Rabbi Aryeh Bernstein puts it, "By the time the named sages teach those laws [demanding a high bar for conviction in capital cases], Jewish courts had long ceased to operate . . . as Beth Berkowitz puts it, 'The rabbinic ritual of execution is particularly difficult to use as any kind of model for today, since it was likely never implemented: The Rabbis may have been willing to embrace the death penalty precisely because they did not have the chance to actually impose it' (*Execution and Invention*, p. 20). The [Babylonian Talmud] already shows amoraim [that is, the rabbis of that era] struggling with the purpose of discussing death penalty laws, since they are not operable . . . Abbaye concludes that their purpose is 'to be studied for the sake of metaphysical reward, regardless of practical application' in Talmud Sanhedrin 51b."

38. Jacobs, *There Shall Be No Needy*, 206. See also Rabbi Chaim David Halevi Responsa *Aseh lechah rav* III: 57, "Incarceration in Jewish Law," trans. Rabbi Dr. Aryeh Cohen, *Journal of Jewish Ethics* 6, no. 1 (2020), 118–32, https://www.jstor.org /stable/10.5325/jjewiethi.6.1.0118.

39. Sered, *Until We Reckon*, 114.

40. Maimonides, *Mishneh Torah*, Laws of Repentance 2:9.

41. Sered, *Until We Reckon*, 116–17.

42. Sered, *Until We Reckon*, 102–3.

43. Sered, *Until We Reckon*, 143.

44. Sered, *Until We Reckon*, 133.

45. Personal correspondence, July 9, 2021.

46. Personal correspondence, July 9, 2021.

47. Personal conversation, September 23, 2020.

48. Daniel J. H. Greenwood, "Restorative Justice and the Jewish Question," *Utah Law Review* (2003): 558, https://scholarlycommons.law.hofstra.edu/faculty _scholarship/318.

49. Sarah Youssef, "Trigger Warning: Sexual Assault. Please share widely, but do not tag the survivor," Facebook, November 27, 2015, https://www.facebook.com /sarah.daoud.7/posts/10153327554957972. Statistics from RAINN, https://www .rainn.org/statistics/criminal-justice-system.

50. Personal conversation, July 26, 2020.

51. Transforming Harm, "Summary Statement Re: Community Accountability Process," Tumblr, March 8, 2017, https://transformharm.tumblr.com/post /158171267676/summary-statement-re-community-accountability.

52. Julia Hale, "Time's Up: 'Surviving R. Kelly' Spurs Sexual Assault Survivors to Speak Out," *The DePaulia*, January 14, 2019, https://depauliaonline.com/38266 /focus/times-up-surviving-r-kelly-spurs-sexual-assault-survivors-to-speak-out/.

53. Juju Bae, "Do You Want to Be Well?" Patreon, August 20, 2020, https://www .patreon.com/posts/do-you-want-to-40666536.

54. Personal conversation, July 26, 2020.

55. Transforming Harm, "Statement by Kyra," Tumblr, August 19, 2020, https:// transformharm.tumblr.com/post/626904983470735360/statement-by-kyra-81920.

56. Greenwood, "Restorative Justice and the Jewish Question," 557–58. The snake story to which Greenwood refers appears in the Babylonian Talmud, Sanhedrin 37b.

57. Doran Larson, "Why Scandinavian Prisons Are Superior," *The Atlantic*, September 24, 2013, https://www.theatlantic.com/international/archive/2013/09 /why-scandinavian-prisons-are-superior/279949/; Keramet Reiter, Lori Sexton, and Jennifer Sumner, "Denmark Doesn't Treat Its Prisoners like Prisoners—and It's Good for Everyone," *Washington Post*, February 2, 2016, https://www.washington post.com/posteverything/wp/2016/02/02/denmark-doesnt-treat-its-prisoners-like -prisoners-and-its-good-for-everyone/; Liane Jackson, "Behind Bars in Scandinavia, and What We Can Learn," *ABA Journal*, February 1, 2020, https://www.abajournal .com/magazine/article/behind-bars-in-scandinavia-and-what-we-can-learn. No- tably, in the United States, the Missouri Model approach to juvenile detention has adopted some of these features—detainees sleep in dorm-style quarters and wear their own clothes, and the staff-to-inmate ratios are higher than in typical juvenile detention centers in our country. Yet reports of troubling practices, such as youth being held down for more than two hours, have also surfaced. Vincent Carroll, "Is the Missouri Model Really a Panacea for Youth Corrections?," *Denver Post*, March 18, 2017, https://www.denverpost.com/2017/03/18/is-the-missouri-model-really -a-panacea-for-youth-corrections/.

58. Please watch Ava DuVernay's documentary *13th*, read Michelle Alexander's *The New Jim Crow* and read Jill Lepore's "The Invention of the Police" in the July 13,

2020, issue of *The New Yorker* (https://www.newyorker.com/magazine/2020/07/20/the-invention-of-the-police) if you have any questions about this.

59. Larson, "Why Scandinavian Prisons Are Superior."

60. Personal conversation, March 5, 2021.

61. Kaba, "So You're Thinking About Becoming an Abolitionist."

62. Mirsky, "Restorative Justice Practices."

63. Sered, *Until We Reckon*, 146.

64. Personal conversation, July 2, 2021.

65. Shoutout to Rabbi Josh Feigelson, a mutual friend of Dworin and me, who has really driven home the importance of this question in a healthy society.

66. Isaac Chotiner, "The Laws of Forgiveness," *The New Yorker*, November 18, 2019, https://www.newyorker.com/news/q-and-a/the-laws-of-forgiveness.

67. Transforming Harm, "Statement by Mariame," Tumblr, August 19, 2020, https://transformharm.tumblr.com/post/626907682811576320/statement-by-mariame.

68. Maimonides, *Mishneh Torah*, Laws of Repentance 2:9.

69. Haderech L'Tshuvah on *Mishneh Torah*, Laws of Repentance 2:9, compare Talmud Bavli Yoma 87b, the story with Rav and Rav Huna.

70. Sered, *Until We Reckon*, 107.

CHAPTER SEVEN. FORGIVENESS

1. Simon Wiesenthal, *The Sunflower: On the Possibilities and Limits of Forgiveness* (New York: Schocken Books, 1998), 53.

2. From the Dictionary of Old English, University of Toronto. With many thanks to Dr. Adrienne Williams Boyarin for her assistance on this.

3. Michael (@JustMeMichaelP), "I am so thankful everytime this thread comes up. In my white, Christian, middle-class culture, not forgiving someone is seen as a bigger sin . . . ," Twitter, November 10, 2017, https://twitter.com/justmemichaelp/status/1303895368082624512?s=11.

4. Kelly Sundberg, "This One Is Not About Abusive Men; This One Is About the Women Who Enable Them," https://kellysundberg.com/this-one-is-not-about-abusive-men-this-one-is-about-the-women-who-enable-them/.

5. "Prevalence," Office for the Prevention of Domestic Violence, https://opdv.ny.gov/system/files/documents/2021/07/nys-domestic-violence-fatality-review_0.pdf.

6. Maimonides, *Mishneh Torah*, Laws of Repentance 2:9.

7. Indeed, this is not far off from Martin Buber's I-Thou, but Rabbi Ruti Regan's excellent critique of Buber as having conflated respect with (sometimes unnecessary, sometimes problematic) intimacy certainly merits more attention than can be given here. We can behold one another's humanity and still have good boundaries! And getting into the ways in which Buber has been used by abusers—and, perhaps, some of the challenges that may be baked into Buber's work itself—are beyond the scope of this chapter.

8. Alix Wall, "He Made Me His Drug Mule," *Salon*, May 1, 2013, https://www.salon.com/2013/05/01/he_made_me_his_drug_mule/.

9. Wall, "He Made Me His Drug Mule."

10. Maimonides, *Mishneh Torah*, Laws of Repentance, 2:9.

11. Maimonides, *Mishneh Torah*, Laws of Repentance, 2:9.

12. Maimonides, *Mishneh Torah*, Laws of Repentance 2:10, presumably based on Mishnah Bava Kama 8:7.

13. Talmud Yoma 87a.

14. Mishnah Bava Kama 8:7.

15. By "homiletical source" I mean midrash—Numbers Rabba 19:23.

16. Conversation in a private Torah discussion Facebook group, December 2, 2020.

17. Jerusalem Talmud Bava Kama 8:7.

18. Rev. Nadia Bolz-Weber, "Forgive Assholes," May 30, 2018, https://www.youtube.com/watch?v=VhmRkUtPra8.

19. Treva Draper-Imler, "Survivor Stories, Guest Post: Fitting In and Forgiveness," https://kellysundberg.com/survivor-stories-guest-post-fitting-in-and-forgiveness.

20. Sharrona Pearl, "Staying Angry: Black Women's Resistance to Coerced Forgiveness in Police Shootings," Scholar Strike, September 8, 2020, video, https://www.youtube.com/watch?v=AUsqMU4Qr_E.

21. Chauncey DeVega, "Black America Owes No Forgiveness: How Christianity Hinders Racial Justice," *Salon*, August 23, 2015, https://www.salon.com/2015/08/23/the_hypocrisy_of_Black_forgiveness_partner/.

22. Sharrona Pearl, "Staying Angry: Black Women's Resistance to Racialized Forgiveness in U.S. Police Shootings," *Women's Studies in Communication* 43, no. 3 (2020), https://doi.org/10.1080/07491409.2020.1744208.

23. "Latest on Dallas Police Shooting: Which Candidate Will Keep Americans Safer? Discussion of Police Shootings of Black Men," *CNN Tonight*, July 8, 2016, http://www.cnn.com/TRANSCRIPTS/1607/08/cnnt.02.html.

24. "Eric Garner's Widow on Accepting Officer's Condolences: 'Hell No,'" *CBS News*, December 3, 2014, https://www.cbsnews.com/news/eric-garners-widow-on-accepting-officers-apology-hell-no/.

25. Dylan Stableford, "Daunte Wright's Mother: 'There's Never Going to Be Justice for Us,'" *Yahoo!News*, April 15, 2021, https://news.yahoo.com/daunte-wright-mother-no-justice-for-us-191359930.html.

26. Martha Crawford (@shrinkthinks), "Some victims may have a felt need to participate in 'forgiveness' process—but certainly not all . . . ," Twitter, June 17, 2019, https://twitter.com/shrinkthinks/status/1140652956980785152.

27. HaDerech L'Tshuvah on Maimonides, *Mishneh Torah*, Laws of Repentance 2:9.

28. Jerusalem Talmud Bava Kama 8:7.

29. See the Rema in the Shulchan Aruch, Orech Hyyim 606, for example. And then go to, for example, Joseph Telushkin, *A Code of Jewish Ethics: Volume 1, You Shall Be Holy* (New York: Random House, 2006), 199. Note also that the ethical treatise *Orhot Tzaddikim, Shaar HaTshuvah* suggests that other sins for which it is basically impossible to do proper restitution include stealing an object of unknown

ownership (since you don't know to whom you must offer amends), and the siring of a child through adultery (since their status can never be rectified).

30. Talmud Bava Batra 88b.

31. HaDerech L'Tshuvah on Maimonides, *Mishneh Torah*, Laws of Repentance 2:9.

32. Sarah Stewart Holland, "Memories of a School Shooting: Paducah, Kentucky, 1997," *The Atlantic*, December 17, 2012, https://www.theatlantic.com/national /archive/2012/12/memories-of-a-school-shooting-paducah-kentucky-1997/266358/.

33. Martha Crawford (@shrinkthinks), "Some victims . . . ," https://twitter.com /shrinkthinks/status/1140652956980785152.

34. Wiesenthal, *The Sunflower*, 151–52.

35. Wiesenthal, *The Sunflower*, 87.

36. Wiesenthal, *The Sunflower*, 171.

CHAPTER EIGHT. ATONEMENT

1. Leviticus 16:16.

2. Thanks to Lisa Berman for showing me "everyday states/elevated states" as an excellent and significantly less loaded and misleading way of translating *tumah /taharah*.

3. See, for example, Rashi on Leviticus 16:11.

4. Many thanks to Rev. Dr. Dan Joslyn-Siemiatkoski for his help with this. As he puts it, "Luther emphasizes that Scripture reveals human inability to attain the righteousness that God desires. This results in sin which leads to separation from God. Jesus Christ as the God-Man (channeling Anselm's theology here) accomplishes both what God requires and what humans cannot achieve. The effect is a complete conquest of sin so that those who come to saving faith are thus made righteous in God's eyes by virtue of what Christ did on the behalf of others (thus Jesus as High Priest). This leads to the elimination of the state of sin as a human condition and hence nothing can separate the believer in Christ from God. That is what the concept of atonement is attempting to express, I believe." (Personal correspondence, March 15, 2021.)

5. Leviticus 16:21.

6. Dr. Noga Ayali-Darshan, "The Scapegoat Ritual and Its Ancient Near Eastern Parallels," TheTorah.com, 2020, https://www.thetorah.com/article/the-scapegoat -ritual-and-its-ancient-near-eastern-parallels.

7. Maimonides, *Mishneh Torah*, Laws of Repentance 1:3.

8. Mishnah Yoma 8:9.

9. Isaiah 1:18.

10. Michael Hotchkiss, "Weighed Down by Guilt: Research Shows It's More Than a Metaphor," *Princeton University News*, October 8, 2013, https://www.princeton.edu /news/2013/10/08/weighed-down-guilt-research-shows-its-more-metaphor.

11. Austin Channing Brown, *I'm Still Here* (New York: Convergent Books, 2018), 108–9.

12. Brown, *I'm Still Here*, 110–11.

13. And, indeed, a lot of practices of the Jewish wedding ritual are aimed at pointing us toward the ways in which Yom Kippur, the wedding, and even death are linked. It's customary to wear a kittel, a white ceremonial robe, on both Yom Kippur and one's wedding day, which is a nod to the white shrouds in which we are eventually buried. It's customary to fast on one's wedding day, as one does on Yom Kippur, as one close to death often refuses food and drink, and to recite a confession—as one does on Yom Kippur and on one's deathbed—as part of the regular prayer service on one's own wedding day. Yes, a confession, like the one we do as part of the repentance process. Because we are doing the work of repentance and approaching that wiping-clean of atonement. I, for one, think this is really cool.

14. Mishnah Yoma 8:8, Talmud Yoma 86a and, for example, Maimonides, *Mishneh Torah*, One Who Injures a Person or Property 5:9.

15. Rabbi Aaron Alexander, "Yom Kippur Sermon 5780," speech, Washington, DC, October 9, 2019, https://images.shulcloud.com/1039/uploads/docs/YKSermon 5780-Alexander.pdf.

16. Pesikta Rabbati, 184b–85a.

17. Talmud Yoma 86a.

INDEX